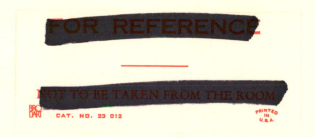

DICTIONARY OF LITERARY-RHETORICAL CONVENTIONS OF THE ENGLISH RENAISSANCE

DICTIONARY OF LITERARY-RHETORICAL CONVENTIONS OF THE ENGLISH RENAISSANCE

MARJORIE DONKER
AND
GEORGE M. MULDROW

Greenwood Press
Westport, Connecticut • London, England

Library of Congress Cataloging in Publication Data

Donker, Marjorie.
   Dictionary of literary-rhetorical conventions of the
English Renaissance.

   Bibliography: p.
   Includes index.
   1. English poetry—Early modern, 1500-1700—Terminology. 2. English language—Rhetoric—Terminology.
3. Poetics—Terminology. 4. Rhetoric—1500-1800—Terminology. I. Muldrow, George M. II. Title.
PR531.D6   821'.3'09   81-4266
ISBN 0-313-23000-5 (lib. bdg.)   AACR2

Library of Congress Catalog Card Number: 81-4266
ISBN: 0-313-23000-5

First published in 1982

Greenwood Press
A division of Congressional Information Service, Inc.
88 Post Road West, Westport, Connecticut 06881

Printed in the United States of America

10 9 8 7 6 5 4 3 2 1

Contents

CONTENTS

CONTENTS

Preface

This dictionary is a collection of essays describing the literary norms and rhetorical controls that inform English poetry of the later sixteenth and earlier seventeenth centuries. It reflects our conviction that responses to the fictions of the English Renaissance are enhanced by a knowledge of their linguistic and critical contexts. Its emphasis is, therefore, upon Elizabethan and Jacobean definitions and descriptions. Each essay begins with a Renaissance term and a Renaissance definition of that term.

Because the study of rhetoric conditioned Renaissance poetics, many of the terms included here come from English rhetoric books or their Latin precursors. The vocabulary of rhetoric is inextricably the vocabulary of poetics. But this book is not a literary history; important matters of politics and religion, of philosophy and biography, receive no attention here. We are concerned with genres, verse forms, metrics, and other formal properties of a text and with those contemporary verbal and linguistic practices that contributed to those formal properties. Although each essay depends upon the labors of many modern scholars to whom our debt cannot be overstressed, we have returned whenever possible to Renaissance texts in order to let the writers of that literary period identify their own perspectives and assumptions.

Arrangement

Discussions of literary conventions and norms are arranged alphabetically. Thus the rubric *anagram* follows *allegory,* and *strong lines* follows *staff.* Cross references are marked by q.v.

Appendixes

Appendix A lists modern literary terms familiar to students of English Renaissance literature, and then locates relevant essays on those topics. Appendix B groups most of the rubrics of this dictionary in appropriate general categories.

Style

The modernized short title of works is used unless the full title is pertinent. For most quotations from Renaissance writers we have retained the original orthography except to substitute *v, u,* and *j* for *u,v,* and *i* respectively; and we have substituted the modern *s* for the old *f, W* for *VV,* and have expanded all contractions of *n* or *m* represented by a tilde above the preceding vowel (e.g., *from* for *frō*). Exceptions are quotations from the works of Shakespeare, which are from *The Works,* edited by G. B. Harrison (1948), and from the works of Milton, from *The Complete Poems and Major Prose,* edited by Merritt Y. Hughes (1957). Unless otherwise noted, all quotations from Italian writers are from Bernard Weinberg, *A History of Literary Criticism in the Italian Renaissance,* 2 vols. (1961). Dates following quotations refer to the date of the edition quoted. Dates of works referred to, other than plays, are those of first publication and are taken from *The New Cambridge Bibliography of English Literature,* edited by George Watson (1974). Dates for plays are those given by Alfred Harbage, *Annals of English Drama 975–1700,* revised by S. Schoenbaum (1964).

Bibliography

The bibliography for each entry is arranged chronologically. All bibliographic citations include the author's name, title of the work, and the date of publication. Works in collections or journals are so identified. Each bibliography is highly selective, but still is designed to suggest the main direction of modern scholarship on the topic in question through 1979. We have not included works in a foreign language, dissertations, bibliographies, or, usually, works written before 1900. We have avoided citing critical readings of particular authors. Neither have we included in individual bibliographies many large works of scholarship that are basic references for any student of English Renaissance literature. Among those works, our special debts are owed to: E. K Chambers, *The Elizabethan Stage,* 4 vols. (1923); C. S. Lewis, *English Literature in the Sixteenth Century* (1954); Bernard Weinberg, *A History of Literary Criticism in the Italian Renaissance,* 2 vols. (1961); Douglas Bush, *English Literature in the Earlier Seventeenth Century 1600–1660* (2nd ed., 1962); David Klein, *The Elizabethan Dramatists as Critics* (1963); F. P. Wilson, *The English Drama 1485–1585* (1969); and Ursula Kuhn, *English Literary Terms in Poetological Texts of the Sixteenth Century,* 3 vols. (1974).

Acknowledgments

For their aid in the preparation of our manuscript we are indebted to Gloria M. Taylor and to the Bureau for Faculty Research, Western Washington University, particularly to Florence E. Preder. Robert Stothart and Cathy Johnson were generous with their time and help. The late Professor Edwin Clapp was our patient critic.

Copyright Acknowledgments

The authors are grateful to the following for permission to quote: Cambridge University Press for excerpts from *The Arte of English Poesie* by George Puttenham, edited by Gladys Doidge Willcock and Alice Walker, 1936, reprint ed., 1970; Harcourt Brace Jovanovich, Inc., for excerpts from *Shakespeare: The Complete Works,* edited by G. B. Harrison, 1948; and Bobbs-Merrill/The Odyssey Press for excerpts from *John Milton: Complete Poems and Major Prose,* edited by Merritt Y. Hughes, © 1957.

Abbreviations: General

c.	*circa,* "about"
ch., chs.	chapter, chapters
d.	died
ed.	editor; edited by; edition
e.g.	*exempli gratia,* "for example"
et al.	*et alii,* "and others"
i.e.	*id est,* "that is"
l., ll.	line, lines
n.d.	no date
no.	number
n.s.	new series
p., pp.	page, pages
q.v.	*quod vide,* "which see"
qq.v.	*quae vide,* "both which see," or "all which see"
rev.	revised
trans.	translator; translated by
vol., vols.	volume, volumes

Abbreviations of Journals Cited in the Bibliographies

BJRL	Bulletin of the John Rylands University Library	JMRS	Journal of Medieval and Renaissance Studies
CE	College English	JPC	Journal of Popular Culture
CL	Comparative Literature	JWCI	Journal of the Warburg and Courtauld Institutes
CLS	Comparative Literature Studies		
CompD	Comparative Drama	MiltonS	Milton Studies
E&S	Essays and Studies	MLN	Modern Language Notes
EIC	Essays in Criticism	MLQ	Modern Language Quarterly
ELH	English Literary History		
ELR	English Literary Renaissance	MLR	Modern Language Review
		N&Q	Notes and Queries
ELWIU	Essays in Literature, Western Illinois University	Neophil	Neophilologus
		PCP	Pacific Coast Philology
		PLL	Papers on Language and Literature
EM	English Miscellany		
ES	English Studies	PMLA	Publications of the Modern Language Association
HLQ	Huntington Library Quarterly		
HUSL	Hebrew University Studies in Literature	PQ	Philological Quarterly
		QJS	Quarterly Journal of Speech
JAAC	Journal of Aesthetics & Art Criticism		
		QQ	Queen's Quarterly
JEGP	Journal of English and Germanic Philology	Ren&R	Renaissance and Reformation
JES	Journal of European Studies	RenD	Renaissance Drama
		RES	Review of English Studies
JHI	The Journal of the History of Ideas	SAB	The Shakespeare Association Bulletin

ABBREVIATIONS OF JOURNALS

SEL	*Studies in English Literature, 1500-1900*	*SP*	*Studies in Philology*
ShakS	*Shakespeare Studies*	*YES*	*The Yearbook of English Studies*
ShS	*Shakespeare Survey*	*YFS*	*Yale French Studies*
SLitI	*Studies in the Literary Imagination*	*YR*	*Yale Review*

DICTIONARY OF LITERARY-RHETORICAL CONVENTIONS OF THE ENGLISH RENAISSANCE

Acrostic:

"Verses whereof the first letter contains some name or sentence" (gloss for the Latin word *Acrostichis* in *Rider's Dictionary,* 1640, an English-Latin dictionary "corrected and much augmented by Francis Holy-Oke"). And Ralph Johnson in *The Scholar's Guide from the Accidence to the University* (1665) says that "An *Acrostich* is a Poem wherein the Initiall Letters of the Lines, make up the Name or Title of a Person, or some other pleasant Device."

Johnson also recognizes other kinds of acrostics common in English Renaissance poetic practice. He says that one that contains a sequence of the letters of the alphabet in the initial letter of each line is called an "Alphabetical Acrostich" and continues, "Sometimes the Name, Motto, or Device goeth crossways from Angle to Angle, writ in a larger Character." Ordinarily a typographical feature ("in a larger Character") calls a reader's attention to the way in which an acrostic patterns certain letters (sometimes words) of each line to spell a word, phrase, or sentence.

William Camden in *Remains Concerning Britain* (1605) calls acrostics one of the "knackes" of "Our Poets," and Johnson thinks of them as one of the "poeticall exercises" suited to the abilities of young students. But English poets of the late sixteenth and early seventeenth centuries found acrostics appropriate even in their most serious endeavors. In the argument (q.v.) at the beginning of his comedy *The Alchemist* (1610), for example, Ben Jonson uses the first letter of each line of a twelve-line acrostic to spell out the two words of the title. Here he follows the practice of Greek authors of the Alexandrian period and of Latin authors, such as Plautus, who often put the titles of their plays in acrostic verses of the arguments. One of the poems in George Herbert's *The Temple* (1633) is a variety of the cross acrostic. The poem, *Coloss. 3. 3. Our life is hid with Christ in God,* spreads across its ten lines the italicized words that form the sentence *"My Life Is Hid In Him That Is My Treasure."*

English writers had a wealth of authority for their acrostics, since acrostics had appeared in both Greek and Latin literature and in devotional and instructional works of the medieval period.

3

Allegory:

"An allegorie is none other thyng, but a Metaphore used throughout a whole sentence, or Oration" (Thomas Wilson, *The Art of Rhetoric,* 1553). George Puttenham praises *allegoria* as "the Courtly figure" in which "we speake one thing and thinke another, and that our wordes and our meanings meete not." It is "the chief ringleader and captaine of all other figures, either in the Poeticall or oratorie science" (*The Art of English Poesy,* 1589).

Allegoria is often contrasted with metaphor in Renaissance rhetoric books. "In Metaphore there is a translation of one word onely; in an Allegorie of many, and for that cause an Allegorie is called a continued Metaphore" (Henry Peacham, *The Garden of Eloquence,* 1593). Metaphor is a single "star," but allegory is "a figure compounded of many stars . . . which we may call a constillation" (Peacham).

The constellation is itself polysemous, that is, not one, but a multiplicity of interpretations can be evoked by a single text. Although sixteenth- and seventeenth-century writers often assume conventional relations between images and ideas (e.g., *the rose* suggests *the Virgin*), the common allegorical language is seldom entirely closed. Both writers and readers felt free to condition the meaning of a verbal image or set of images by its context in a verbal structure.

No single interpretation of a text is necessarily definitive. Sir John Harington notes that "manie times also under the *selfesame words* [italics added] they [poets] comprehend some true understanding of naturall Philosophie, or . . . politike governement, and now and then of divinitie" (*A Brief Apology,* 1591). "Now let any man judge if it be a matter of meane art or wit to containe in one historicall narration either true or fained so many, so diverse, and so deepe conceits," says Harington, praising the writings of ancient poets. He demonstrates the nature of "deepe conceits" with the story of the hero Perseus who slew the Gorgon and then ascended to heaven. In one reading, the Gorgon signifies "a tyrant"; in another, "sinne and vice"; in still another, the "earthlinesse" of our human nature; and in one more, all "bodily substance." Writers were so aware of the multiplicity of response to a text that Edmund Spenser in his *Letter to Raleigh* (1589) about *The Faerie Queene* feels he must describe some of his intentions because he knows how "doubtfully" (i.e., variously) his work may be understood.

Renaissance conceptions of the function of poetry underlie contemporary claims for allegory. One strain of literary theory in the sixteenth and seventeenth centuries puts a heavy emphasis upon "the movement to conception" (Tuve) or "the instantially viewed universal" (Nuttall). For the educated Englishman, it was an accepted formula that the intangible idea requires the "helpe of earthly images." The poet in particular is one who "coupleth the general notion with the particular example" (Sir Philip Sidney, *An Apology for Poetry,* 1595). The concrete and sensory image bodies forth the universal. The apprehension of the intangible "idea" was a recurrent theme, not only of poetics, but of epistemology and mnemonics. Contemporary descriptions of the parallels between painting and poetry were based on their common ability to suggest concepts to the mind (*see* Ut pictura poesis).

Both readers and writers inherited an allegorical habit of mind as the result of a long tradition in which both Christian and classical works were read as allegories. For generations the Bible had been read not only for its literal meaning, but also with a strong sense that beyond the letter was the spirit, an underlying meaning accessible through interpretation and study. St. Augustine (354–430 A.D.), for example, expresses an attitude about the function of language that emphasizes its mystical properties. He praises the figurative and obscure passages of the Bible as a stylistic virtue, which excites a desire to know more and to prevent boredom. And whether the text is obscure or not, wise readers will move through words to Christian realities, from discourse to vision; the words of Scripture act as signs of invisible and inaudible truths (*De doctrina Christiana*).

In an effort to exhaust the truths of their sacred text, biblical exegetes could distinguish four levels of meaning. The first was the literal level; the second was itself called the "allegorical" level, applying the biblical passage to Christ and the Church Militant; the third, the "moral" or "tropological" level, applying the biblical passage to the soul and its virtues; and the fourth, the "anagogical" level, applying the passage to the heavenly realities and the Church Triumphant (*see also* Type and antitype).

Christian exegesis itself is not unlike that applied to the *Iliad* and the *Odyssey* by classical commentators and to Greco-Roman myths by Stoic philosophers. Christian readers also began to "moralize" secular material, so that by the beginning of the sixth century the allegorical nature of stories of the pagan gods was the subject of a huge work, the *Mythologiae* by

5

Fabius Planciades Fulgentius. In this work a series of Roman fables is philosophically explained in their relation either to the natural order or to man's moral life. By the twelfth century, when allegory had become a dominant vehicle for pious expression, mythological exegesis of classical works had grown to mighty proportions. Ovid's *Metamorphoses,* for example, was treated as a mine of sacred wisdom, an attitude that culminated in the encyclopedic *De genealogia deorum gentilium (The Genealogy of the Pagan Gods)*, compiled by Giovanni Boccaccio (1313-75). Ostensibly Boccaccio's work is a digest of classical mythology, but virtually every god and goddess mentioned receives an allegorical interpretation. And early in the seventeenth century Francis Bacon confesses to the opinion "that under some of the ancient fictions lay couched certaine mysteries and Allegories even from their first invention" (*The Wisdom of the Ancients,* 1619 trans. of *De sapientia veterum,* 1609).

Given such traditions, poets could assume readers assiduous in interpretation, although they also assumed a hierarchy of ability to inflect the idea from the image. In his allegorical commentary on his own heroic poem, the Italian poet Torquato Tasso maintains that allegory which "respecteth the passions, the opinions, and customes ... principally in their being hidden & inward" is expressed "with notes ... misticall, such as onely the understanders of the nature of things can fully comprehend" (*The Allegory of the Poem* prefacing *Jerusalem Delivered,* trans. Edward Fairfax, 1600). Those of a "meane conceit," says Abraham Fraunce, will feed their "rurall humor" with the famous exploits of renowned heroes as such. Those who can "reach somewhat further then the external discourse and history" will "finde a morall sence included therein, extolling vertue" and "condemning vice." The rest that are "better borne and of a more noble spirit" shall find "hidden mysteries of naturall, astrologicall, or divine and metaphisicall philosophie, to entertaine their heavenly speculation" (*The Third Part of the Countess of Pembroke's Yvychurch,* 1592).

Bibliography

C. S. Lewis, *The Allegory of Love* (1936); Joshua McClennen, "On the Meaning and Function of Allegory in the English Renaissance," *University of Michigan Contributions in Modern Philology,* 6 (1947), 1–38; Jean Seznec, *The Survival of the Pagan Gods,* trans. Barbara F. Sessions (1953); Edgar Wind, *Pagan Mysteries in the Renaissance* (1958); Erich Auerbach, "Figura," *Scenes from the Drama of European Literature* (1959), pp. 11–76; Edwin Honig, *Dark Conceit: The Making of Allegory* (1959); Don Cameron Allen, *Image and Meaning: Metaphoric Traditions in Renaissance Poetry* (rev. ed., 1968); Graham Hough, "Allegory in *The Faerie Queene*," *A Preface to "The Faerie Queene"* (1962), pp. 82–99; Angus Fletcher, *Alle-*

gory: The Theory of a Symbolic Mode (1964); Robert L. Montgomery, Jr., "Allegory and the Incredible Fable: The Italian View from Dante to Tasso," *PMLA,* 81 (1966), 45–55; Rosemond Tuve, *Allegorical Imagery: Some Mediaeval Books and Their Posterity* (1966); Rhodes Dunlap, "The Allegorical Interpretation of Renaissance Literature," *PMLA,* 82 (1967), 39–43; A. D. Nuttall, *Two Concepts of Allegory* (1967); Michael Murrin, *The Veil of Allegory* (1969); Don Cameron Allen, *Mysteriously Meant: The Rediscovery of Pagan Symbolism and Allegorical Interpretation in the Renaissance* (1970); John MacQueen, *Allegory* (1970); John Erskine Hankins, *Source and Meaning in Spenser's Allegory* (1971); Forrest G. Robinson, *The Shape of Things Known: Sidney's "Apology" in Its Philosophical Tradition* (1972); Gay Clifford, *The Transformations of Allegory* (1974); John M. Steadman, *The Lamb and the Elephant: Ideal Imitation and the Context of Renaissance Allegory* (1974); Isabel MacCaffrey, *Spenser's Allegory* (1976); James Nohrnberg, *The Analogy of "The Faerie Queene"* (1976); Mark L. Caldwell, "Allegory: The Renaissance Mode," *ELH,* 44 (1977), 580–600; Maureen Quilligan, *The Language of Allegory* (1979).

Anagram:

"The *posie* [verse or motto] *transposed,* or in one word *a transpose*" (George Puttenham, *The Art of English Poesy,* 1589). To construct an anagram—to rearrange the letters of one word or phrase to form another word or phrase—is, Puttenham says, "to breed one word out of another." Even the letters of a sentence may be rearranged to create another sentence.

Puttenham admits that the making of anagrams brings neither "any great gayne nor any great losse, unless it be of idle time" and he calls them "trifles," but at the same time he warns his readers against a dour attitude towards life that demands only grave literature. Anagrams are after all, he claims, "convenient solaces and recreations of mans wit." Out of the words *Elissabet Anglorum Regina* he constructs two anagrams: *Multa regnabis ense gloria* ("By thy sword shalt thou raigne in great renowne") and *Multa regnabis sene gloria* ("Aged and in much glorie shall ye raigne").

Along with the pleasure they gave as a kind of playful exercise, anagrams were useful to Renaissance writers as pseudonyms. According to E. K.'s gloss on the "January" eclogue of Edmund Spenser's *The Shepherd's Calendar* (1579), the name of Colin Clout's beloved is an anagram. E. K. tells us that "Rosalinde" is a "feigned name, which being wel ordered, wil bewray the very name" of Colin's mistress.

Although the anagram is of limited value as a poetic tool, George Herbert considered it an appropriate form in religious poetry. Among his collected poems is one entitled *Ana-*$\frac{MARY}{ARMY}$*-gram,* reading: "How well her name an *Army* doth present, / In whom the *Lord of Hosts* did pitch his tent!" Herbert's unembarrassed use of what Puttenham called a "trifle" reflects a general characteristic of his poetry and of much seventeenth-century poetry—a quality of play and wit in the treatment of a serious subject.

Anatomy:

In the literary vocabulary of English writers of the late sixteenth and early seventeenth centuries, the systematic analysis of a large topic. The word literally means *dissection;* and John Bullokar in *An English Expositor* (1616) repeats the common medical meaning when he defines the noun "Anato-mie" as "An incision or cutting. The art of knowing the situation, office, and nature of all the parts of man's body" and the verb "Anatomize" as "To cut and search every part." This attempt to know "every part" of a subject is what English writers meant when they used the word *anatomy* in the titles of their works to indicate their intention and approach. Robert Burton, for example, in *The Anatomy of Melancholy* (1621) says that "It is a disease of the soul [melancholy] on which I am to treat, and as much appertaining to a divine as to a physician"; and he announces his intention to anatomize when he says that he will analyze "What it [melancholy] is, with all the kinds, causes, symptomes, prognostickes & severall cures of it: In three Partitions, with their severall Sections, members & subsections. Philosophically, Medicinally, Historically opened & cut-up."

The term *anatomy* appears in the titles of dozens of contemporary prose works on a variety of subjects. Philip Stubbes, for example, claims that his work *The Anatomy of Abuses* (1583) contains "A Discoverie, or Briefe Summarie of such Notable vices and Imperfections, as now raigne in many Christian Countreyes of the Worlde." Thomas Robinson, in a polemical attack on Roman Catholicism entitled *The Anatomy of the English Nunnery at Lisbon in Portugal* (1622), boasts that his treatise "hath truly anatomized this handmayd of the Whore of Babylon; laying open her principall veines and sinewes in such sort that hee is bold to challenge the proudest Doctor of her acquaintance to traduce his worke."

An anatomy is not a literary genre, but the result of a rhetorical process; it is the breaking down of a large subject into its various parts for close examination. Renaissance rhetoric books call this process *distributio*. As a systematic analysis, anatomizing was a method appropriate for many kinds of writing. For example, the many attributes of ideal courtly behavior are detailed at length in such courtesy books as Sir Thomas Hoby's translation (*The Courtier,* 1561) of Baldassare Castiglione's *Il cortegiano* (1528). Fashionable topics like love and friendship are anatomized in courtly prose romances (*see* Romance) such as John Lyly's *Euphues: The Anatomy of Wit* (1578); and "yong Gentlemen, Marchants, Apprentices, Farmers, and plain Countreymen" are warned about the different kinds of roguery being practiced in London in Robert Greene's *A Notable Discovery of Cozenage* (1591), a realistic prose fiction in which the narrator lists and describes the skills necessary for each kind of trickery. Traits of a human type are enumerated in the literary genre known as the character (q.v.); and the Petrarchan poet-lover is anatomizing when he catalogues the beauties of his beloved in a sonnet (q.v.). In all these instances the writer "dissects" his subject into its logical "every part" in order to clarify and amplify his topic.

The anatomy operates as the opposite of analogy. Renaissance analogies assumed a great network of correspondences among the various levels of existence: the mineral, the vegetable, the animal, and the human; the individual, the society, and the cosmos. Such a habit of mind provided writers with many of their metaphors, such as the analogy that identifies the lion with the king with the sun. The process of anatomizing is the inverse of that of analogizing. An anatomy severs a topic into its component parts; an analogy builds by linking one term with another.

Apology:

"A defence" (Henry Cockeram, *The English Dictionary,* 1623); a prose work in justification of literature or of a particular literary practice.

Apologies occupied a central position in Renaissance literary criticism, especially in Italy, where the defense of poetry began with Books XIV and XV of *De genealogia deorum gentilium* (*The Genealogy of the Pagan Gods*) by Giovanni Boccaccio (1313–75); these books constitute a formal essay justifying poetry against its many opponents. The first of the Elizabethan defenses of poetry is John Rainolds's Latin *Oratio in laudem artis poeticae* (delivered c. 1572), an apology that relies heavily on Cicero's *Pro Archia poeta.* Although English apologies were never so numerous as those in Italy, they represent (along with apologetic comments in rhetoric books) an important contribution to the slowly evolving enterprise of literary criticism.

There are two general kinds of English apologies. In one, writers share a belief in the value of poetry (that is, any imaginative fiction), but disagree among themselves on particular questions. In other defenses, poets and theorists marshal their arguments against detractors of literature, who fortified their attack with objections from both classical and Christian sources. The tone of the attacks on literature is succinctly contained in the subtitle of Stephen Gosson's *The School of Abuse* (1579); it reads, "Con-teining a plesaunt invective against Poets, Pipers, Plaiers, Jesters and such like Catterpillers of a Commonwelth." An apology defines itself in the words of Thomas Lodge, who says, "I speake for Poetes, I answeare your abuse" (*Defense of Poetry,* 1579).

In debates among themselves the friends of literature were all guided by their goal to create a poetry for England that would be worthy of comparison with the achievement of other contemporary nations and that of the classical past. The desire was "to reforme our English verse and to beautify the same with brave devises" (William Webbe, *A Discourse of English Poetry,* 1586); the question was how to do so. Should Latin, rather

11

than the vernacular (*see* Vulgar language) be the language for serious poetry? To what extent should words derived from foreign and classical languages be imported to enrich the native language? To equal the greatness of the ancients, should English versification (*see* Versifying) abandon its native rhyme in favor of unrhymed quantitative forms of classical poetry? Webbe makes his own position clear when he says, "I am fully and certainlie perswaded that if the true kind of versifying in immitation of Greekes and Latines had beene practised in the English tongue, and put in use from time to tyme by our Poets, who might have continually beene mending and pollyshing the same, every one according to their severall giftes: it would long ere this have aspyred to as full perfection, as in anie other tongue whatsoever." Apologists who supported rhyme, the vernacular, and the judicious inclusion of new words carried the day. Other questions concerned the nature of certain genres and the theory of imitation (q.v.). The legitimacy of tragicomedy (q.v.), the extent to which Aristotelian rules for tragedy (q.v.) and epic (*see* Heroic poem) were to be strictly followed or to be modified, the imitation of recent literary works instead of classical models—questions such as these and their various answers further divided theorists.

In defending poetry against its avowed enemies, the apologists vigorously asserted the worth of poetry. In England the denunciation of fictions came from many quarters, but none was more vehement than Puritan attacks, particularly upon the drama. To substantiate their charges against literature, detractors drew upon classical writers, such as Plato in the *Republic,* as well as upon the church fathers. Moral and religious grounds of attacks were aided by a pragmatic attitude discouraging any activity that deterred men from their obligation to work. In all of this controversy three main charges against literature recur. They are "(1) that poetry is a tissue of lies; (2) that poetry encourages immorality; and (3) that even when unobjectionable, it is an imitation of an imitation and hence inherently trivial" (Hardison). Sir John Harington reports that "the summe of . . . reproofe" against poetry is "that it is a nurse of lies, a pleaser of fooles, a breeder of dangerous errors, and an inticer to wantonnes" (*A Brief Apology of Poetry,* 1591).

Apologists had to admit, of course, that abuses of poetry did exist. They called them the misdoings of bad writers who created only "lascivious shewes, scurrelous jeasts, or scandalous invectives" (Thomas Heywood, *An Apology for Actors,* 1612), not an inherent part of the nature of "ever-praise-worthy Poesie . . . full of vertue-breeding delightfulness, and voyde of no gyfte that ought to be in the noble name of learning" (Sir Philip Sidney, *An Apology for Poetry,* 1595). After all, apologists reminded detractors, did not the poet in his role as "maker" resemble the divine Creator of the universe. George Puttenham, for example, writes, "A POET is as much to say as a maker. . . . Such as (by the way of resemblance and reverently) we may say of God; who without any travell to his divine imagination made all the world of nought. . . . Even so the very Poet makes and contrives out of his owne braine both the verse and matter of his poeme" (*The Art of English Poesy,* 1589) Moreover, the first priests, prophets, and legislators had been poets; and poetry had been the force responsible for leading men from barbarity to civility. Sidney's claim is typical: "In the noblest nations and languages that are knowne" poetry "hath been the first light-giver to ignorance, and first Nurse, whose milk by little and little enabled them to feed afterwards of tougher knowledges."

Refutations of the three main charges against poetry tend to follow general patterns. Apologists were particularly sensitive to the charge that poets were liars, for Scriptural injunctions against falsehood were not to be taken lightly. One answer to this charge was to remind critics that certain genres were "true" since their subject matter was based on historical fact or on theology; this applied to genres such as tragedy, the heroic poem, the hymn and the ode (qq.v.). One of the marks of tragedy, for example, is its "truth of Argument" (Ben Jonson, preface to *Sejanus,* 1605); and it is in "historicall poesie" that the "famous acts of princes and the vertuous and worthy lives of our forefathers" are recorded (Puttenham). Another defense was to insist that poets did not claim truth for their fictions: "Now for the poet he nothing affirms," says Sidney, "and therefore never lieth." The poet is unlike other writers and especially historians who, because of incomplete knowledge, "hardly escape from many lies." Paradoxically, the defense that poets do not "affirm" became a claim for the most imaginative fictions in contrast to more "realistic" fictions, because the more fantastic the fiction, the less apparently "affirming" the poet's work would be. "Onely the Poet . . . lifted up with the vigor of his owne invention, dooth growe in effect another nature, in making things either better then Nature bringeth forth, or, quite a newe, formes such as never were in Nature" (Sidney). Still one more defense was an attempt by poets to stake out an area for fictions that was concerned neither with the demonstrably true nor the demonstrably false: tales of long ago and places far away about which historians and geographers had little reliable information.

In defense against the charge of immorality, most apologists repeated the Horatian claim that the function of poetry is to teach and to delight. Webbe, for example, says "I thinke best to confirme [the purpose of English poetry] by the testimony of *Horace,*" who in "his treatise *de arte Poetica,* thus . . . sayth: *Aut prodesse volunt aut delectare poetae, / Aut simul et iucunda et idonea dicere vitae.* As much to saie: All Poets desire either by their works to profitt or delight men, or els to joyne both profitable & pleasant lessons together for the instruction of life." And Sidney incorporates the Horatian formula in his definition of poetry when he writes,

"Poesie therefore is an arte of imitation . . . a representing, counterfetting, or figuring foorth: to speake metaphorically, a speaking picture: with this end, to teach and delight." Other disciplines, such as history and moral philosophy, might show men the way to knowledge and virtue but, in the words of Sidney, only the poet "giveth so sweete a prospect into the way, as will intice any man to enter into it." Poetry taught through its idealized examples. Epic poetry, it was claimed, offered models of virtue for admiration and emulation, and lyric poetry praised virtuous behavior and taught moral precepts. Comedy and satire presented images of vice to be reproved, and in a tragedy spectators learned of the fate of tyrants and of the instability and transience of the phenomenal world. Hence, rather than encourage immorality, poetry best fulfilled "the ending end of all earthly learning . . . virtuous action" (Sidney).

Against the charge that poetry was trivial, a waste of time as only a pale imitation of the fleeting things of this world, apologists argued that, properly written and interpreted, poetry was actually "truer" than history. The good poet rose above the imperfect world of experience to imitate divine ideas; it was the universal, not the ephemeral, that was the proper object of imitation. With an allegorical reading of poetry the careful reader would discover truths so sacred that they must be hidden under a veil of fiction (see Allegory). Thomas Nashe, for example, says, "Poets . . . to the intent they might allure men with a greater longing to learning, have followed two things, sweetnes of verse, and variety of invention, knowing that delight doth prick men forward to the attaining of knowledge, and that true things are rather admirde if they be included in some wittie fiction, like to Pearles that delight more if they be deeper sette in golde. . . . For even as in Vine, the Grapes that are fayrest and sweetest, are couched under the branches that are broadest and biggest, even so in Poems, the thinges that are most profitable, are shrouded under the Fables that are most obscure" (*The Anatomy of Absurdity,* 1589).

With such arguments as these, apologists believed that poetry defended itself from "those slaunders that either the malice of those that love it not, or the folly of those that understand it not, hath devised against it" (Harington).

Bibliography

E. N. S. Thompson, *The Controversy Between the Puritans and the Stage* (1903); C. Gregory Smith, "The Puritan Attack" and "The Defence," *Elizabethan Critical Essays,* vol. 1 (1904), pp. xiv–xxxi; J. E. Spingarn, "The Evolution of English Criticism from Ascham to Milton" and "The General Theory of Poetry in the Elizabethan Age," *A History of Literary Criticism in the Renaissance* (2nd ed., 1908,), pp. 253–81; Phoebe Sheavyn,

"Authors and Readers," *The Literary Profession in the Elizabethan Age* (1909; revised by J. W. Saunders, 1967), pp. 144–206; J. Dover Wilson, "The Puritan Attack upon the Stage," *The Cambridge History of English Literature,* vol. 6, pt. 2 (1910), pp. 421–61; Charles Sears Baldwin, "Sixteenth-Century Poetics," *Renaissance Literary Theory and Practice: Classicism in the Rhetoric* and *Poetic of Italy, France, and England 1400–1600* (1939), pp. 155–89; Vernon Hall, Jr., "England, The Poet and His Purpose," *Renaissance Literary Criticism: A Study of Its Social Content* (1945), pp. 215–28; Robert J. Clements, "Condemnation of the Poetic Profession in Renaissance Emblem Literature," *SP,* 43 (1946), 213–32; Marvin T. Herrick, "The Function of Poetry," *The Fusion of Horatian and Aristotelian Literary Criticism, 1531–1555* (1946), pp. 39-47; J. W. H. Atkins, "The Defence of Poetry" and "The Art of Poetry," *English Literary Criticism: The Renascence* (2nd ed., 1951), pp. 102–78; William K. Wimsatt, Jr., and Cleanth Brooks, "The Sixteenth Century," *Literary Criticism: A Short History* (1957), pp. 155–73; Bernard Weinberg, "Platonism: I. The Defence of Poetry," *A History of Literary Criticism in the Italian Renaissance,* vol. 1 (1961), pp. 250–96; K. G. Hamilton, *The Two Harmonies: Poetry and Prose in the Seventeenth Century* (1963); O. B. Hardison, Jr., ed., "Introduction," *English Literary Criticism: The Renaissance* (1963), pp. 1–14; Joseph Anthony Mazzeo, "St. Augustine's Rhetoric of Silence: Truth vs. Eloquence and Things vs. Signs," *Renaissance and Seventeenth-Century Studies* (1964), pp. 1–28; Baxter Hathaway, *Marvels and Commonplaces: Renaissance Literary Criticism* (1968); Russell Fraser, *The War Against Poetry* (1970); Forrest G. Robinson, *The Shape of Things Known: Sidney's "Apology" in Its Philosophical Tradition* (1972); Howard C. Cole, "The Elizabethan Poet and His Options," *A Quest of Inquirie: Some Contexts of Tudor Literature* (1973), pp. 261–309; William Nelson, *Fact or Fiction: The Dilemma of the Renaissance Storyteller* (1973); S. K. Heninger, Jr., "Poet as Maker" and "Poetics," *Touches of Sweet Harmony: Pythagorean Cosmology and Renaissance Poetics* (1974), pp. 287–397; S. K. Heninger, Jr., "Sidney and Milton: The Poet as Maker," *Milton and the Line of Vision,* ed. Joseph Anthony Wittreich, Jr. (1975), pp. 57–95; Thora Burnley Jones and Bernard de Bear Nicol, "From Robortello to Ben Jonson," *Neo-Classical Dramatic Criticism 1560–1770* (1976), pp. 18–48; A. C. Hamilton, "Sidney's poetics," *Sir Philip Sidney: A Study of His Life and Works* (1977), pp. 107–22; Richard Helgerson, "The New Poet Presents Himself: Spenser and the Idea of a Literary Career," *PMLA,* 93 (1978), 893–911; Andrew D. Weiner, "Moving and Teaching: Sidney's *Defence of Poesie* as a Protestant Poetic," *Sir Philip Sidney and the Poetics of Protestantism* (1978), pp. 28–50.

Argument:

"The summe of a written matter; the summarie, or substance of a Booke, or Chapter" (Randle Cotgrave, *A Dictionary of the French and English Tongues,* 1611); as a Renaissance literary convention, a prose or verse statement placed at the beginning of a literary work, or before sections of it, to summarize the plot and, sometimes, to announce its general meaning.

Like classical Latin writers, English rhetoricians also thought of an argument as a kind of rhetorical proof necessary in an oration, but the Latin word *argumentum* carried the additional meaning of the narration or subject matter of a poem. Quintilian, for example, says that "the subjects of plays, composed for acting on the stage, are called *arguments*" (*Institutio oratoria,* V. 10. 9). Following the tradition of this literary usage, Francis Holyoke glosses one of the meanings of *argumentum* as "the Summe or substance of writing" and another as "a Theame to speake or write of" (*Dictionarium etymologicum Latinum,* 1640).

English writers used the argument in much the same way that orators used the structural division of a speech known as the *narratio.* The second of the five-part arrangement of an orator's material, the *narratio* is that place within the speech where he explains the facts or circumstances of the subject of his discourse. The plot summary in the arguments of literary works is a similar explanation.

In the late sixteenth and early seventeenth centuries English writers often placed arguments before long narrative works, especially heroic poems (q.v.), and less often before printed versions of plays. Sir John Harington, for example, in his *An Advertisement to the Reader* prefacing his 1591 translation of Lodovico Ariosto's *Orlando furioso,* explains his inclusion of arguments by saying, "Also (according to the Italian maner) I have in a staffe of eight verses [*ottava rima*] comprehended the contents of every Book or Canto in the beginning thereof, which hath two good uses, one to understand the picture [pictures accompanying the translation] the perfecter, the other to remember the storie the better."

16

In the stage performance of plays either the prologue or dumb show may act as arguments to summarize the action. Shakespeare's prologue to the first act of *Romeo and Juliet* (c. 1595), for example, announces the general tragic movement of his story of a "pair of star-crossed lovers"; and the dumb show of the play-within-the-play in *Hamlet* (c. 1601) summarizes the action of the play that Hamlet has arranged to "catch the conscience of the King." A clear example of an argument in the printed version of a play is the acrostic (q.v.) labeled *THE ARGUMENT* of Ben Jonson's *Volpone* (c. 1606). It reads:

V OLPONE, childlesse, rich, faines sick, despaires,
O ffers his state to hopes of severall heyres,
L ies languishing; His *Parasite* receaves
P resents of all, assures, deludes: Then weaves
O ther crosse-plots, which ope'themselves, are told.
N ew tricks for safety, are sought; They thrive: When, bold,
E ach tempt's th'other againe, and all are sold.

Aubade:

"Such musicke as minstrels doe play at ones window at the breaking of the day" (Claudius Hollyband, *A Dictionary French and English,* 1593). As a literary form, morning songs belonged to a tradition which extends back to Latin writers and which English poets began to use as early as Chaucer. This tradition also embraces the medieval French *aubade,* usually a joyous praise, and the *alba* ("dawn") of Provençal troubadours, a lament over the parting of lovers at the break of day. Both lament and praise shape the morning lyrics of English poets of the late sixteenth and early seventeenth centuries. In Shakespeare's *Cymbeline* (c. 1609), for example, Cloten attempts to awaken his beloved with the singing of an *aubade* praising the beauties of the morning; and in John Donne's lyric poem *Break of Day* (1633), a woman complains about her lover's hasty departure with the dawn. When this poem was set to music by a contemporary composer, it literally became "morning musicke."

Bibliography

Arthur T. Hatto, ed., *Eos: An Enquiry into the Theme of Lovers' Meetings and Partings at Dawn in Poetry* (1965).

Blank verse:

"English Heroic Verse without Rime" (John Milton, prefatory comments, *The Verse,* to *Paradise Lost,* 1674).

Unrhymed iambic pentameter first appeared in England in the middle of the sixteenth century. An innovation in English prosody, it developed from being a "straunge metre" to one of the most characteristic and distinguished metrical forms of the English Renaissance. After its initial use by Henry Howard, Earl of Surrey, in his translations of Books II and IV of Virgil's *Aeneid,* a handful of Elizabethan writers experimented with blank verse in narrative poems of an epic nature and in philosophical and satiric poetry. Until John Milton chose blank verse for *Paradise Lost* (1667), however, its most significant use was on the public stage, especially for tragedies (*see* Tragedy) and history plays.

The origins of English blank verse, as well as the intentions of poets first writing blank verse, remain somewhat vague. English poets probably found suggestions for their blank verse in Italian *versi sciolti,* unrhymed hende-casyllabic (eleven-syllable) lines with principal accent on the tenth syllable. Surrey must have known, for example, several Italian translations of the *Aeneid* appearing in the 1530s that used *versi sciolti.* Italian critics claimed that blank verse was the most appropriate form for the expression of heroic grandeur in both epic poems and tragedies and that this unrhymed verse was "most capable of all gravity and grandeur." The Italian argument ran that since the form imposed no restraint on the poet through rhyme, *versi sciolti* "must reject anything which is not great in itself or which art cannot make great by virtue of ornamentation and beauty" (Carlo Lenzoini, *In difesa della lingua fiorentina e di Dante,* 1556; quoted in Prince).

Early experimenters in English blank verse also must have derived a general encouragement from the model of classical unrhymed poetry. But there is no indication that blank verse developed as a direct response to the call of purists who attacked the native rhyme and urged a return to the classical tradition of unrhymed poetry. Sixteenth-century poets do not seem

19

to have regarded their blank verse as the specific equivalent of the classical hexameter, the traditional unrhymed form of the Latin epic; and the poetic principle to which they were fervently dedicated, a deliberate counting of syllables, was clearly contrary to the nature of quantitative verse of classical prosody.

Although the immediate Italian model of hendecasyllabics probably did raise the question of an unrhymed or "blank" poetic line, English blank verse was not simply an imitation. The iambic pentameter line itself was a part of the strong native prosodic tradition of rhymed accentual-syllabic verse. Chaucer had enthusiastic admirers, even though English Renaissance poets imperfectly understood his rhymed iambic pentameter verse and considered the meter in his couplets "rough." Closer in time were the rhymed decasyllabics of such early sixteenth-century Scottish poets as William Dunbar and Gavin Douglas; and Surrey clearly had at hand Douglas's complete rendering of the *Aeneid* in iambic pentameter couplets when he undertook his own translations sometime around 1540. Thus, as they worked toward metrical refinements in their own language, Tudor poets were probably influenced as much, if not more, by Scottish models as they were by Italian. Blank verse may well be, then, mainly the result of Tudor experiments in writing an unrhymed line that adhered to the native tradition of accentual-syllabic poetry.

Surrey's translation of Book IV of the *Aeneid* was first published in 1554, with the title page directing attention to the poem's "straunge metre." Three years later both Books II and IV were published by Richard Tottel, who in the same year, 1557, also issued his famous *Miscellany,* which included two epic fragments in blank verse by Nicholas Grimald. Once alerted to the possibilities offered by this metrical form, a number of poets began to experiment. Among the better-known, nondramatic works using blank verse are George Turberville's translations of six verse epistles (*see* Epistle) from Ovid's *Heroides* (1567) and George Gascoigne's *The Steel Glass* (1576). In a prefatory poem to his satire, Gascoigne tells of his hope for fame as a poet, but he says that "ladders made of ryme" are too frail for his ambitious satiric attack on contemporary society. Instead only "rymelesse verse, which thundreth mighty threates" can serve his purpose. Gascoigne here seems to be emulating the Roman practice of adapting a verse form associated with tragedy and the heroic poem to satires of particular force.

Gascoigne's designation of blank verse as the appropriate medium to "thundreth mighty threates" points to the way blank verse contributed to the declamatory quality of much late sixteenth-century drama. Blank verse found its way into drama when, in the Christmas season of 1561, members of the Inner Temple acted *Gorboduc* before Queen Elizabeth. Here for the first time blank verse replaced the rhymed poetry of earlier vernacular drama. Written by Thomas Sackville and Thomas Norton, this Senecan tragedy capitalizes on favorite Renaissance motifs, the horror of civil war and of a kingdom without a ruler. Better plays were to come, and the dramatists who inaugurated the reign of blank verse on the popular stage were Thomas Kyd and Christopher Marlowe. It was Marlowe's blank verse that displaced once and for all the "jigging veins of riming mother wits" with his own "high astounding terms," as the Prologue proudly claims in *I Tamburlaine the Great* (c. 1587). The success of *Tamburlaine* firmly set the fashion for a drama of oratorical splendor in the late sixteenth century, so much so in fact that other dramatists complained. Thomas Nashe, for example, in the preface to Robert Greene's *Menaphon* (1589), criticizes contemporary dramatists, especially "vaine glorious Tragedians" as those "who (mounted on the stage of arrogance) thinke to out-brave better pennes with the swelling bumbast of a bragging blanke verse." He sneers at their "kil-cow" conceits and "the spacious volubilitie of a drumming decasillabon." Within a short time, however, Nashe and Greene were themselves writing plays in blank verse; and Greene was to chide a newcomer on the scene, Shakespeare, as an "upstart Crow," who "with his *Tygers heart wrapt in a Players hyde,* supposes he is as well able to bombast out a blanke verse" as the best of them (preface to *The Groat's Worth of Wit,* 1592).

Until the closing of the theaters in 1642, blank verse remained a medium of expression in all kinds of drama, although it had a special association with tragedy. Advocating unrhymed poetry for drama, Samuel Daniel says that "a Tragedie . . . indeede best comport[s] with a blank verse . . . saving in the Chorus and where a sentence [*sententia*] shall require a couplet" (*A Defense of Rhyme,* 1603).

It was the high quality of blank verse in English tragedy that Milton compliments when he defends his choice of a metrical line for his heroic poem. In a prefatory letter to *Paradise Lost,* Milton explains, "The Measure is *English* Heroic Verse without Rime, as that of *Homer* in *Greek*, and of *Virgil* in *Latin;* Rime being no necessary Adjunct or true Ornament of Poem or good Verse, in longer Works especially, but the Invention of a barbarous Age, to set off wretched matter and lame Meter." Although Milton goes on to say that his measure (metrical arrangement of a line) is that of "our best *English* Tragedies," he marks blank verse with his own distinctive characteristics.

For dramatic and nondramatic works alike, English poets found in blank verse a controlled but supple verse form. Its iambic rhythms are remarkably close to the natural rhythms of modern English speech; but, as a verse form, blank verse is more defined than prose because of the heightened effect of the metrical pattern of the five feet. Isolated, a single line of blank verse might hardly call attention to itself, might even be indistinguishable from prose; but as a kind of building block for a poem or play, it achieves its effects through repetition. When hearing a passage in blank verse, a listener registers the iambic pentameter line without being conscious of it, unless the poet handles each line with metronomic regularity and closes the thought at the fifth stress of each line. Though still the result of design, blank verse frees the poet from the restrictions inherent in patterns based on recurring rhyme schemes. As a means of expression, blank verse allows a poet to extend his discourse until it reaches a natural conclusion. An individual blank verse line, for example, may be broken between two speakers according to the ideas expressed by each. Or the sense of a passage may be "variously drawn out from one Verse to another" (Milton) for as long as needed to complete the thought. Thus Milton constructed his "verse-paragraphs" in *Paradise Lost,* and the dramatists the speeches of their characters.

Bibliography

John Addington Symonds, *Blank Verse* (1895); George Saintsbury, *A History of English Prosody,* vol. 2 (1908), pp. 3–86, 302–20; Jakob Schipper, "Blank Verse," *A History of English Versification* (1910), pp. 219–41; Paull Franklin Baum, "Blank Verse," *The Principles of English Versification* (1922), pp. 133–50; Tucker Brooke, "Marlowe's Versification and Style," *SP,* 19 (1922), 186–205; J. M. Robertson, "The Evolution of English Blank Verse," *The Criterion,* 2 (1924), 171–87; G. K. Smart, "English Non-dramatic Blank Verse in the Sixteenth Century," *Anglia,* 61 (1937), 370–97; C. S. Lewis, "The Fifteenth-century Heroic Line," *E&S,* 24 (1938), 28–41; Howard Baker, "The Formation of the Heroic Medium," *Induction to Tragedy* (1939), pp. 48–105; F. T. Prince, "Milton's Blank Verse," *The Italian Element in Milton's Verse* (1954), pp. 108–44; Ants Oras, *Pause Patterns in Elizabethan and Jacobean Drama: An Experiment in Prosody* (1960); T. R. Barnes, "Blank Verse," *English Verse: Voice and Movement from Wyatt to Yeats* (1967), pp. 25–57; John D. Allen, "II. Elements of English Blank Verse: Shakespeare to Frost," *Quantitative Studies in Prosody* (1968), pp. 1–85; Barbara Herrnstein Smith, "Blank Verse," *Poetic Closure: A Study of How Poems End* (1968), pp. 78–84; Morris Halle and Samuel Jay Keyser, "English III. The Iambic Pentameter," *Versification: Major Language Types,* ed. W. K. Wimsatt (1972), pp. 217–37.

Broadside ballad:

"An Alehouse song of five or six score verses" (William Webbe, *A Discourse of English Poetry,* 1586); a song (q.v.) set to a popular tune, printed on a single sheet of paper (the broadside), and hawked on the streets by professional singers. Besides giving the words of the ballad, the broadside announced the tune for the song, but seldom included the musical notation. Broadside ballads made up a body of popular poetry just beginning to receive some recognition from serious poets in the sixteenth century.

Writers of broadside ballads were often classified in their day as "pot poets." In his prose character (q.v.), John Earle calls the "Pot-Poet . . . the dreggs of wit" (*Micro-cosmography,* 1628). The verses of such poets, Earle says, "run like the tap, and his invention as the Barrell, ebs and flowes at the mercy of the spiggot." "Thin drinke" prompts his ballad, and "the death of a great man, or the fiering of a house furnish him with an Argument." He is "a man now much imploy'd in commendations of our navy, and a bitter inveigher against the Spaniard." His ballads "goe out in single sheets, and are chanted from market to market, to a vile tune, and a worse throat, whilst the poore Country wench melts like her butter to heare them."

Some of the ballads printed on broadsides were versions of older songs, known today as "traditional" ballads; many others, however, were newly composed. Almost anything could, and did, furnish subject matter for broadside ballads. The far-off and legendary appeared along with the scandals and gossip of the moment. Although broadside ballads were most frequently narrative in mode, the lyrical was not out of place. Hence the broadside ballad might be a sentimental love ditty, an exhortation to repentance, a retelling of the adventures of Robin Hood, an account of a strange occurrence, or the news of a murder or execution. While the death of Queen Elizabeth furnished Thomas Churchyard with his subject for a broadside ballad, something quite different served for the "month old" song of Shakespeare's Autolycus (*The Winter's Tale,* c. 1610). Autolycus tells Mopsa that his ballad recounts "how a userer's wife was brought to bed of twenty money bags at a burden, and how she longed to eat adders' heads and toads carbonadoed." Many broadside ballads were scurrilous propaganda for one cause or another; and the zeal with which issues were fought even provoked a Parliamentary ban on ballad printing and ballad singing in 1649.

When topical matters were related in broadside ballads, reportorial accuracy was hardly a consideration. Thomas Nashe, for example, complains of the distortion of facts common in the practice of ballad writers. He says: "What leasings will not make-shyfts invent for money? What wyl they not faine for gaine? Hence come our babling Ballets . . . which every rednose Fidler hath at his fingers end, and every ignorant Ale knight will breath foorth over the potte, as soone as his braine waxeth hote. Be it a truth which they would tune, they enterlace it with a lye or two to make meeter, not regarding veritie, so they may make uppe the verse. . . . But as the straightest things beeing put into water, seeme crooked, so the crediblest trothes, if once they come with in compasse of these mens wits, seeme tales" (*The Anatomy of Absurdity,* 1589). Falstaff catches the tone of such ballads when he threatens Prince Hal that he will have "ballads made on you all and sung to filthy tunes" (*1 Henry IV,* c. 1597).

Although writers of critical treatises tended to associate certain stanzaic and metrical patterns with the ballad, the actual practice of ballad writers was as varied as the subject matter they chose. Speaking of a few verse forms available to English poets, George Gascoigne (*Certain Notes of Instruction,* 1575) thinks of the ballad stanza as primarily a six-line form (*see* Sixain): "There is also another kinde, called Ballade, and thereof are sundrie sortes: For a man may write ballade in a staffe of six lines, every line conteyning eighte or six sillables, whereof the firste and third, second and fourth do rime acrosse, and the fifth and sixth do rime togither in conclusion. You may write also your ballad of tenne sillables, rimyng as before is declared; but these two were wont to be most commonly used in ballade, which propre name was (I thinke) derived of this worde in Italian *Ballare,* which signifieth to daunce. And in deed those kinds of rimes serve beste for daunces or light matters." In practice the "light matters" of the broadside ballads were shaped in many other forms than those Gascoigne says were "most commonly used." Some took the stanzaic pattern known today as the "ballad stanza," a quatrain (q.v.) rhyming *abcb* with the first and third lines containing four accented syllables and the second and fourth lines three accented syllables. Others were in poulter's measure (q.v.). And still many more ballads were in other simple rhyme schemes.

Occasionally ballads found a home in more permanent form than that of easily disposable broadsides. Several of the Elizabethan poetical miscellanies include ballads. One miscellany, *A Handful of Pleasant Delights*

(c. 1584), is devoted entirely to popular songs. According to its title page, this is a book of ballads "newly devised to the newest tunes that are now in use, to be sung: every Sonet orderly pointed to his proper Tune." (*Sonnet* is used here to mean "song," rather than the more precise literary definition discussed under *sonnet*.)

If they bothered to look at the broadside ballads at all, theorists generally treated this popular poetry with scorn. Webbe, for example, in *A Discourse of English Poetry,* mentions broadside ballads only to dismiss them derisively. He writes: "If I let passe the uncountable rabble of ryming Ballet makers . . . who be most busy to stuffe every stall full of grosse devises and unlearned Pamphlets, I trust I shall with the best sort be held excused. For though many such can frame an Alehouse song of five or six score verses, hobbling uppon some tune of a Northern Jygge, or Robyn hoode, or La lubber etc., and perhappes observe just number of sillables, eyght in one line, sixe in an other, and there withall an A to make a jercke in the ende: yet if these might be accounted Poets . . . surely we shall shortly have whole swarmes of Poets." Such "Ballet makers," Webbe claims, should have their "potticall" heads crowned not with the "Garlande due to Poets" but "with fayre greene Barley, in token of their good affection to our Englishe Malt."

In contrast to this typical dismissal of popular poetry Sir Philip Sidney's half-apologetic admiration for the traditional ballad of Chevy Chase is an exception. As part of his defense of the lyric poet as one who "giveth praise, the reward of vertue, to vertuous acts," Sidney writes, "Certainly I must confesse my own barbarousnes: I never heard the old song of *Percy* and *Duglas* that I found not my heart mooved more then with a Trumpet; and yet is it sung by some blinde Crouder, with no rougher voyce then rude stile; which being so evill apparelled in the dust and Cobwebbes of that uncivill age, what would it worke trymmed in the gorgious eloquence of Pindar?" (*An Apology for Poetry,* 1595). The heroic subject matter of the ballad has Sidney's approval; its rough style and its association with a lowly social context do not.

Within a decade matters changed slightly. Although it remained for later times to develop fully the literary ballad (that is, a poem, not a song; a conscious imitation by a poet of the traditional ballad for inclusion among his printed works), at least one Renaissance poem may be considered a forerunner. It is Michael Drayton's patriotic encomium, *To the Cambro-Britains and Their Harp, His Ballad of Agincourt,* published in his *Odes* (c. 1606). Drayton says this ode (q.v.) he "honored in the title of a ballad."

Bibliography

Hyder E. Rollins, "The Black-Letter Broadside Ballad," *PMLA,* 34 (1919), 258–339; C. V. Wedgwood, *Poetry and Politics Under the Stuarts* (1960); Albert B. Friedman, "The Broadside Ballad," *The Ballad Revival: Studies in the Influence of Popular on Sophisticated Poetry* (1961), pp. 35–63; M. J. C. Hodgart, "Introduction," *The Ballads* (2nd ed., 1962), pp. 9–26; Leslie Shepard, *The Broadside Ballad: A Study in Origins and Meaning* (1962); Claude M. Simpson, *The British Broadside Ballad and Its Music* (1966); Edward Lee, "Tudors, Stuarts and Commonwealth," *Music of the People* (1970), pp. 35–51; G. Malcolm Laws, Jr., "Literary Ballad Styles," *The British Literary Ballad* (1972), pp. 1–22; Frederick O. Waage, "Social Themes in Urban Broadsides of Renaissance England," *JPC*, 11 (1977), 730–42.

Canzone:

"A song . . . a dittie" (John Florio, *A World of Words, or Dictionary in Italian and English,* 1598); an Italian lyric poem, composed of intricately structured rhymed stanzas, frequently set to music for singing (*see* Song).

Although probably of Provençal origin, the canzone developed in Italy during the thirteenth century. Francis Petrarch (1304–74) was much admired for his canzoni, as were the later poets Torquato Tasso and Peter Bembo. Reflecting the English interest in canzoni, George Puttenham notes that Petrarch's kind of rhymes "serve . . . to declare high and passionate or grave matter" (*The Art of English Poesy,* 1589).

Early in the fourteenth century Dante, in *De vulgari eloquentia,* outlined elaborate rules for the composition of canzoni. Later Italian poets relaxed his prescriptions, and the canzone became a lyric form of great flexibility. In general, the canzone may be thought of as a poem of medium length with a varying number of stanzas, each alike in structure, and concluding with a short envoy. Each poet determined the number of stanzas for his canzone as well as the number, length, and rhyme patterns of its lines. Frequently each stanza was built of two sections of unequal length, linked by a key rhyme line. The juxtaposition of alternating line lengths created much of the rhythmic harmony. Some unrhymed lines were permitted, although in early Italian canzoni these appeared in fixed positions within the stanzas. Commenting on the freedom that the canzone form allowed for the arrangement of end rhyme sounds within a stanza so that rhyme sounds were widely separated, Puttenham writes, "And all that can be objected against this wide distance is to say that the eare by loosing his concord is not satisfied. So is in deede the rude and popular eare, but not the learned; and therefore the Poet must know to whose eare he maketh his rime, and accomodate himselfe thereto, and not give such musicke to the rude and barbarous, as he would to the learned and delicate eare."

Like the sonnet, the canzone was thought especially appropriate for the praise of love and beauty. It was this theme of praise, usually in Petrarch's canzoni, that first attracted English poets, and not a particular canzone form. This lack of imitation (q.v.) of the canzone form stands in marked contrast to the heavy borrowing by English poets of the form of the Italian sonnet.

The first Tudor poet attracted to Petrarch's canzoni was Sir Thomas Wyatt, who translated Petrarch's words but devised his own rhyme schemes for them or chose available native forms such as rhyme royal (q.v.). The elaborate rhymed stanzas of Spenser's *Epithalamion* (1595) and Milton's *Lycidas* (1638) owe much to the sensitive understanding by those poets of the canzone tradition. Spenser's publication of the *Epithalamion* with his sonnet cycle, the *Amoretti,* also follows a literary convention established by Petrarch when he interspersed canzoni in his sonnet cycle in praise of Laura (*see* Sonnets in sequence).

The canzone was important in the development of the ode (q.v.) in England. The classical ode, like the canzone, was an elevated poem of praise, and both were associated with song; but, when English poets began to assimilate the classical ode into their literary tradition, it was the canzone's intricacy of form that suggested to many poets ways of composing their odes. "With its complex stanza shape and its alternations of long and short rhyming lines," the canzone provided "the actual source of much English composition in the ode form—far more in fact than the practice of Pindar or of Horace" (John Heath-Stubbs, *The Ode,* 1969). In other words, a continental form was naturalized by English poets, mainly during the early seventeenth century, to emulate the effect of classical odes.

Bibliography

Ivy L. Mumford, "The Canzone in Sixteenth-Century English Verse with Particular Reference to Wyatt's Renderings from Petrarch's Canzoniere," *EM,* 11 (1960), 21–32.

Character:

"A witty and facetious description of the nature and qualities of some person, or sort of person" (Ralph Johnson, *The Scholar's Guide from the Accidence to the University,* 1665).

As a short, prose sketch, in praise or blame of a representative human type, the character was a minor genre in seventeenth-century English literature; and while Johnson's definition appears in a late grammar school manual, it accurately summarizes the intentions of the character writers who popularized the genre. The "strong lines" (q.v.) of much character writing associated the prose of this genre with that of the Senecan style (q.v.).

After his definition, Johnson offers instructions on how to write a character; the three "rules," he says, are:

1. Chuse a Subject, *viz.* such sort of men as will admit of variety of observation, such be, drunkards, usurers, lyars, taylors, excise-men, travellers, pedlars, merchants, tapsters, lawyers, an upstart gentleman, a young Justice, a Constable, an Alderman, and the like.

2. Express their natures, qualities, conditions, practices, tools, desires, aims or ends, by witty Allegories, or Allusions, to things or terms in nature, or art, of like nature and resemblance, still striving for wit and pleasantness, together with tart nipping jerks about the vices or miscarriages.

3. Conclude with some witty and neat passage.

Although Johnson's instructions apply more to the creation of satiric characters than idealized ones, his remarks do point out the characteristics of a genre that encouraged great variety of detail in a short space, a pithy style, and unexpected and paradoxical turns of thought.

29

The best-known characters of the early seventeenth century are those found in Joseph Hall's *Characters of Virtues and Vices* (1608); in a work known as the Overburian collection, by Sir Thomas Overbury and others (1614); and in John Earle's *Micro-cosmography* (1628). All of these went through several editions; but the most popular was the Overburian collection, which grew from twenty-two sketches in the first edition of 1614 to eighty-two in 1622 and which went through seventeen editions by 1664. Most contributors to the Overburian collection remain anonymous; but among those now generally regarded as authors of characters are John Donne, Thomas Dekker, and John Webster.

Some characters depict human types with either admirable or reprehensible psychological or moral habits. Hall, for example, in prefatory comments to his 1608 edition, says that his characters, like those of ancient "Morall Philosophers," are "speaking pictures, or living images, whereby the ruder multitude might even by their sense learn to know virtue and discern what to detest." Other characters depict types of a particular social status or profession. Whatever the particular focus, the character writer treats human beings as belonging to more or less fixed groups. The definition given in the 1622 edition of the Overburian collection stresses the way in which the character, although imagined as alive and individual, is typical of his group. The definition reads: "To square out a Character by our English levell, it is a picture (reall or personall) quaintly drawne, in various colours, all of them heightened by one shadowing. It is a quicke and softe touch of many strings, all shutting up in one musicall cloze: It is wits descant on any plaine song [variations on a common theme]."

Like "strong-lined" poets of the same period, character writers often display their wit through highly wrought, ingenious conceits (q.v.); and like verse satirists (*see* Satire), they avoid a smooth, lyric cadence. Major syntactic devices include brevity and abruptness in members of a period, the frequent omission of usual connectives, antithesis of thought, and a lack of symmetry in the parts of the period. Such devices were associated with what contemporaries called a prose style of "strong lines."

As a genre, the character has its literary origin in the work of a single classical writer and teacher, Theophrastus (c. 373–284 B.C.). The thirty characters left by Theophrastus are all discussions of unattractive moral or psychological qualities. These discussions ridicule a person like the flatterer or the distrustful man who departs from the mean of virtue and proper behavior. Each sketch briefly defines the quality under discussion and then illustrates with objective details the speech and actions of a person guilty of that extreme.

In 1608 when Hall published his twenty-four characters, he departed from Theophrastan models by giving eight of his types admirable qualities. In one of them, *The Good Magistrate,* he departed even further by focusing on the magistrate's profession. Other seventeenth-century writers continued to create a range of psychological types, and soon characters depicting professional and social classes also became popular. Naturally moral and psychological qualities became mixed within characters of a social or vocational type. Some of the best of Earle's types relate to college life ("A Young Gentleman of the University is one that comes there to wear a gown, and to say hereafter, he has been at the university").

Almost invariably, the organization of these sketches is threefold. They begin with a definition of the type, often employing a metaphor or paradox. Hall, for example, writes, "The inconstant man treads upon a moving earth, and keeps no pace"; and the Overburian "Affected Traveller" is called a "speaking fashion." After the witty introduction comes the central development, the sentences often beginning with "he" or "she." This section of description draws upon appropriate details from the type's mannerisms, behavior, habits of speech and dress, and his thoughts, attitudes, and motives. In other words, the type is anatomized (*see* Anatomy) in as many aspects as possible to illustrate his essential quality. In contrast to Theophrastus who simply stops at this point, English character writers conclude their sketches with a strikingly phrased sentence, epigrammatic in quality. The sketch of the Overburian affected traveler concludes: "In a word, his religion is fashion, and both body and soule are governed by fame, he loves most voices above truth."

Although collections of characters did not appear in any great number until the early seventeenth century, Tudor school training included the description of human types. Every educated person was thoroughly familiar with such devices as *descriptio personae,* one of several rhetorical schemes that outlined for writers and speakers various ways of describing a person and that provided a much-desired variation or fullness of expression (*see* Copia). One rhetoric book defines *descriptio* as the creation of "cunning and curious Images . . . made so like to the persons which they present, that they do not onely make a likely shew of life, but also by outward countenance of the inward spirite and affection" (Henry Peacham, *The Garden of Eloquence,* 1593).

Bibliography

Edward C. Baldwin, "The Relation of the English 'Character' to Its Greek Prototype," *PMLA,* 18 (1903), 412-23; G. S. Gordon, "Theophrastus and His Imitators," *English Literature and the Classics,* ed. Gordon (1912), pp. 49-86; E. N. S. Thompson, "Character Books," *Literary Bypaths of the Renaissance* (1924), pp. 1-27; Gwendolen Murphy, ed., "Introduction: Development of the Character," *A Cabinet of Characters* (1925), pp. v-xxxvi; W. J. Paylor, ed., "Introduction," *The Overburian Characters* (1936), pp. v–xxxi; William G. Crane, "The Essay and the Character," *Wit and Rhetoric in the Renaissance: The Formal Basis of Elizabethan Prose Style* (1937), pp. 132–61; Wendell Clausen, "The Beginnings of English Character-Writing in the Early Seventeenth Century," *PQ,* 25 (1946), 32–45; Benjamin Boyce, *The Theophrastan Character in England to 1642* (1947); Rudolf Kirk, "The Literary Form of the *Characters," Heaven Upon Earth and Characters of Virtues and Vices* by Joseph Hall, ed. Kirk (1948), pp. 1–18; Benjamin Boyce, *The Polemic Character 1640–1661* (1955); F. P. Wilson, "A Survey," *Seventeenth Century Prose* (1960), pp. 1–25; Robert Adolph, "Character and Biography," *The Rise of Modern Prose Style* (1968), pp. 256–62; Charles R. Forker, " 'Wit's descant on any plain Song': The Prose Characters of John Webster," *MLQ,* 30 (1969), 33–52; Ronald J. Corthell, "Joseph Hall's *Characters of Vertues and Vices*: A 'Novum Repertum,' " *SP,* 76 (1979), 28–35.

Ciceronian style:

The dominant literary prose style of Tudor writers, modeled on that of the Roman orator Cicero, and typically identified with fullness of expression, syntactical symmetry, and rhetorical devices of repetition. The expansive flow, the aural emphasis, of much sixteenth-century prose was directed by the profound belief that Ciceronian polish, balance, and amplification of ideas (*see* Copia) were requirements of artistic discourse; thus the Ciceronian style is a search for "choisenesse of the Phrase, and the round and cleane composition of the sentence, and the sweet falling of the clauses, and the varying and illustration of . . . workes with tropes and figures" (Sir Francis Bacon, *The Advancement of Learning,* 1605).

No Latin writer carried more authority for sixteenth-century rhetoricians than Cicero. He is "the prince of Oratours" in whom "it seemeth that Eloquence hath sette her glorious Throne, most richly and preciousely adourned for all men to wonder at, but no man to approche at," says Thomas Elyot (*The Governor,* 1531). George Puttenham calls him "the wisest of any Roman writer" (*The Art of English Poesy,* 1589). As a model for oratorical prose style Cicero's works furnished sixteenth-century prose writers with detailed directions for success in both Latin and the vernacular. In the international effort to "correct" the "barbarisms" of late Medieval Latin, Cicero was the fountain of pure Latin undefiled. At its extremes this neo-Latin movement found some practitioners who would use only the Ciceronian lexicon with Cicero's very formulae and cadences, and Ciceronian rhetoric was the foundation of school training in rhetoric (q.v.). A work ascribed to Cicero, the *Rhetorica ad Herennium,* and Cicero's *Topica* were basic elementary texts; the *Institutio oratoria* of Quintilian, Cicero's disciple, was commonly used as an advanced rhetoric.

Since Latin orators like Cicero and Quintilian made the close examination of figures of speech an integral part of the art of rhetoric, English prose theorists also stressed the figures as central to a writer's ability to command a popular audience (*see* Elocutio). Word order is not careless, but always the product of design. Roger Ascham's emphasis is typical; "Ye know not, what hurt ye do to learning, that care not for wordes, but for matter, and so make a devorse betwixt the tong and the hart," he says (*The Schoolmaster,* 1570). Later prose theorists like Sir Francis Bacon would call for more matter and less art, but Ciceronians assumed that effective discourse requires a plentitude of words in a sonorous arrangement, "the sweet falling of the clauses." "But yet what helpeth it though we can finde good reasons, and knowe howe to place theim, if we have not apte wordes, and picked sentences, to commende the whole matter," says Thomas Wilson (*The Art of Rhetoric,* 1553).

The expressive function of the Ciceronian writer is achieved by the careful arrangement of words into patterns, both visual and aural; and his main figures are based on parallelism of sound and sense. These figures are to be found in contemporary rhetoric books with their emphasis upon "exornation" ("a gorgiousse beautifiynge of the tongue"), which opened the way for sentence structures with "equal members" (the balanced antithetical sentence "when the one halfe of the sentence answereth to the other"); "gradation" ("when we reherse the worde that goeth nexte before": "Labour getteth learnyng, learnyng getteth fame, fame getteth honour, etc."); "progression" (the cumulation of short main clauses leading to a climax); "contrarietie" (antithesis of opposites as in "To his friende, he is churlishe, to his foe he is gentle"); "conversion" (a series of sentences with like endings); and "repetition" (a series of sentences with like opening words) (quotations from Wilson).

The appeal of Ciceronian prose is enhanced by the conscious use of rhythms. Cicero in *De oratore* recommends to orators a sonorous and smooth syntax with a rhythmical word order. Rhythm articulates the period and defines its close. Cicero warns that prose rhythms should not become verse, but nevertheless he desires a word order to resemble verse in having a rhythmical cadence. Sentence endings (*clausulae*) are rhythmically most important, though the rest of the period is not to be neglected. Prose should be enclosed within the reins of form and balance, though not tied together by a definite metrical law. In this vein, John Rainolds's academic apology for poetry, the *Oratio in laudem artis poeticae,* assigns to Ciceronian rhetoric a virtue he claims was taken from the poets: "Rhetoric is cleverly couched in certain rhythms which both constrain more tightly the thread of the oration by the strength of their bonds and suffuse more pleasantly the minds of the audience with the sweetness of their measures. . . . Cicero would lie fallen and Isocrates would be frigid if their works fluctuated with sentences both vast and gaping and loose and disjointed. So it is, oratory attains all its adornment, all its strength, from the choice arrangement of rhythms" (c. 1572, trans. Walter Allen, Jr.).

Thus the tone of Ciceronian prose is one of artful premeditation. Every idea seems to split into its component elements that are then balanced so as to sharpen the sense of division among them. Below is a diagram of one period in the Ciceronian manner from Sir Philip Sidney's *Arcadia* (1590) in which Sidney's speaker renders the balance between past convictions and present accusations with a careful parallelism and repetition of "the sea," "the pirates," and "evil fortune" in each half of the period, and a strong contrast between the disapproving "I" and the condemned "thyself."

```
Heretofore I have  accused the sea
                   condemned the pirates
             and  hated the evil fortune
                   that deprived me of thee;
but now thyself is the sea
                   which drowns my comfort
             thyself is the pirate
                   that robs thyself of me
             thy own will becomes my evil fortune.
```

In one respect, the Latin Ciceronian style was modified by English writers. The Roman style, in its most elevated form, not only employed symmetrical regularities, but also suspended the verb, and hence the complete development of an idea, until the very end of a period. This syntactical device was not often imitated by English writers, but they did think of their composition as similarly "circular" or "rounded" in the sense that all members of a period refer to a central or climactic member, so that they point forward or back to the central member and give it appropriate emphasis.

By the end of the sixteenth century the excesses of the Ciceronian style became a subject of controversy. Critics found it deficient in wit and *sententiae*, too oratorical in its verbal amplitude and rhythmical cadences. With a condemnation of those who "studie words and not matter" (*The Advancement of Learning*), anti-Ciceronians, led by Bacon, turned to new Latin models for imitation and developed a prose style they called Senecan (*see* Senecan style) or Attic. Yet even then, Ciceronian prose was the norm in relation to which the "new" style defined itself.

Bibliography

George P. Krapp, "The Courtly Writers," *The Rise of English Literary Prose* (1915), pp. 271–384; Daniel C. Boughner, "Notes on Hooker's Prose," *RES*, 15 (1939), 194–200; P. A. Duhamel, "Sidney's *Arcadia* and Elizabethan Rhetoric," *SP*, 45 (1948), 134–50; Austen Warren, "The Style of Sir Thomas Browne," *Kenyon Review*, 13 (1951), 674–87; James Sutherland, "Apes and Peacocks," *On English Prose* (1957), pp. 31–56; Walter F. Staton, "The Characters of Style in Elizabethan Prose," *JEGP,* 57 (1958), 197–207; Lorna Challis, "The Use of Oratory in Sidney's *Arcadia,"* *SP,* 62 (1965), 561–76; Ian A. Gordon, "The Impact of Humanist Latinity," *The Movement of English Prose* (1966), pp. 73–83; Brian Vickers, *The Artistry of Shakespeare's Prose* (1968), pp. 35–51; Thomas M. Greene, "Roger Ascham: The Perfect End of Shooting," *ELH,* 36 (1969), 609–25; Georges Edelen, "Hooker's Style," *Studies in Richard Hooker,* ed. W. Speed Hill (1972), 241–77; Michael West, " 'Not without Dust and Heat': A Ciceronianism in Milton's *Areopagitica,"* *RES,* 29 (1978), 181–85; Alvin Vos, " 'Good Matter and Good Utterance': The Character of English Ciceronianism," *SEL,* 19 (1979), 3–18.

Comedy:

"Here's a sweet comedy. 'T begins with *O Dolentis* and concludes with ha, ha, he!" (words of a character in Cyril Tourneur's *Atheist's Tragedy,* c. 1609). In theory and in practice, the happy ending—"all's well that ends well"—was widely accepted by Renaissance playwrights as defining most clearly the difference between comedy and tragedy (q.v.). William Webbe expresses this traditional distinction when he points out that writers of tragedy create "sorrowful and lamentable histories" with calamities that increased "worse and worse till they came to the most woeful plight that might be devised," while comedies "were directed to a contrary end, which beginning doubtfully, drew to some trouble or turmoil, and by some lucky chance always ended to the joy and appeasement of all parties" (*A Discourse of English Poetry,* 1586). Similarly the made-up plot of comedy contrasted with that of tragedy in which the plot was typically linked to history, real or supposed.

Within this loose generic frame, English comedy was primarily conditioned by three traditions of comic drama to which individual playwrights responded in varying degrees. These are the traditions or practices of the native drama of the late Middle Ages, the drama of Greece and Rome, and contemporary Italian modifications of Greco-Roman comedy.

The late medieval vernacular drama of England was not organized around formal constructs like "comedy" and "tragedy." It comprised, for the most part, an amateur civic and religious drama that traditionally presented scenes from biblical history, allegorical moral plays that concerned themselves with the life of the individual Christian and corresponded to a great body of sermon literature and moral discourse, secular interludes of social recreation, and dramatized stories of chivalric quest and romantic adventure. All these plays were written in rhymed verse.

Religious drama was systematically suppressed from the early years of Elizabeth's accession; and the popular, secular drama recrystallized around "new" theories of genre, although the moral play continued in a modified form. Art forms are conservative, however, and much of the old dramatic tradition (alternately didactic and bawdy, serious and farcical) was integrated into the popular, professional theater to condition the nature of English comedy.

Some conventions and tendencies of the older religious drama that appear in comedy of the late sixteenth and early seventeenth centuries include: the satiric presentation of human fallibility with a theme of forgiveness; divisions of characters by "estates"; and a broad tradition of verbal and physical horseplay, burlesque, and grotesquerie, especially as these qualities were embodied in Vice figures, the bawdy, vulgar minions of the devil with names like "Backbiter" and "Myscheff" whose antics were broad inversions of orthodox, social norms (see Morall).

Although documentation is weak, there is good reason to believe that plays of chivalric and romantic adventure also had a persistent hold upon the practice of playwrights and the response of audiences. Few English texts of romantic drama survive from before Elizabeth's reign, but stories of knightly trials and far-wandering heroines were beloved in literary romances and on the continental stage through the late Middle Ages. Many embodied time-honored folktales bearing on the theme of the hidden watchfulness of fortune and the triumph of human ingenuity over the accidents of life, themes we would locate today as essentially those of comedy. In the early Elizabethan period the evidence of recorded titles shows that roughly a third of the players' repertoire must have consisted of plays of this type.

Three such plays that have survived contain plot motifs of knights and clowns, a wandering maiden, magical charms, disguises and recognition: *Clyomon and Clamydes* (c. 1570); *Common Conditions* (1576); and *The Rare Triumphs of Love and Fortune* (1582). Stephen Gosson, a virulent critic of plays, complains in the 1580s that: "Sometime you shall see nothing but the adventures of an amorous knight, passing from countrie to countrie for the love of his lady, encountring many a terible monster made of broune paper, and at his retorne is so wonderfully changed, that he can not be knowne but by some posie in his tablet, or by a broken ring" (*Plays Confuted,* 1582).

Besides the native English tradition, playwrights from the middle of the sixteenth century forward also began to make use of the conventions of classical comedy, particularly as they found them in the works of the Latin playwrights Terence and Plautus. Studied in the schools and then imitated in plays written in both Latin and English on the school stage, the Romans decisively affected the practice of late Elizabethan playwrights like Shakespeare and Ben Jonson. Roman comedies introduced an approach to dramatic structure that was foreign to the medieval, native theater. In contrast to the staging of impressive moments in a loose chronological sequence, Roman playwrights had created plays with a concentration on the climax of a story; each play was a tightly wrought action with the careful unfolding of causal connections between its incidents as the plot advances. Action was located in a single setting (often a street) and the time of the play's action was close to that of its actual playing time. *Hamlet*'s Polonius distinguishes between the classical kind of play and the looser, native kind of drama as "the scene individable" and "the poem unlimited" (II, ii). Also central to the classical tradition of comedy were motifs to do with the trickster and with "deceptions," guile, falsehood, adroitness—a vision of life as a comedy of "errors."

Italian comedy of the sixteenth century also shaped the practice of English playwrights. This was particularly so of the *commedia eruditia,* the "learned," amateur comedy of the courts (as opposed to the improvisational, professional *commedia d'ell arte* of the streets). While they had a sophisticated interest in Latin models, playwrights of Italy recast classical comedy to suit Italian taste. In so doing, they introduced to the European comic stage a repertoire of strategies that was very much their own: double and even triple plots of great technical virtuosity; plots of erotic intrigue in a citizen world; and the use of vernacular prose as a medium for comedy. Comedy in Italy had become a central event of courtly festival; amateur comedies were produced to celebrate royal entries, weddings, and births, and were part of the celebration of Carnival (the weeks before Lent devoted in Italy and other Roman Catholic countries to revelry and riotous amusement). During these times of celebration temporary theaters were built in the great houses for the entertainment of the court or for court shows the populace could witness. The spirit of Italian Carnival—the sense of sexual release, practical jokes, and masquerade—became the spirit of Italian courtly comedy. And while the amateur playwrights looked at the plot structure of Plautus and Terence and observed the unities of the "scene undividable," they invariably portrayed a contemporary citizen life in settings familiar to their audience. Comic action began to take place before stage scenery representing streets with buildings such as private homes, a church, a tavern, and a brothel. In striving to be "natural," to follow the injunction that comedy is to be a "mirror of the times," Italian playwrights rejected the tradition that the language of plays should rhyme and made vernacular prose their medium for comedy.

No Italian practice is more decisively related to English comedy than the use of prose as a convention on the stage. As early as 1566 George Gascoigne translated Ariosto's *I suppositi* into English prose under the title of *Supposes*. In the 1580s John Lyly, writing for the court, converted the style of his own prose romances into a highly wrought stage prose; and writers for the public playhouses began to transfer a racy, colloquial chatter to the mouths of stage clowns and rustics. By the turn of the century, Ben

Jonson had established prose as a convention for a host of later city comedies about London life.

During the last half of the sixteenth century and the early decades of the seventeenth century, the impact of Italian comedy on the popular stage was reinforced in England by a movement at Cambridge University to present neo-Latin plays in imitation of models from the Italian vernacular. This use of Italian comedy, either in Latin translations or in original dramas in Latin modeled upon it, was unique at Cambridge, occurring evidently in no other place in Renaissance Europe.

The practice of English playwrights was eclectic and varied, responsive to first one facet and then another of classical or Italian practice while they never completely abandoned native traditions of romance. In contrast, English rhetoricians and other theorists of dramatic genres were comparatively single minded and consistent in their discussions of comedy. Over and over they rehearsed the postulates of Cicero that comedy is "the imitation of life, the mirror of custom, the image of truth" and of Horace that poetry should both delight and instruct. Ignoring the fantastic or farcical or festive elements that had marked comedy from the time of the Greeks, rhetoricians stressed its corrective function and realistic surface. It is a form "wherein ivell is nat taught but discovered to intent that men beholdynge the promptnes of youth unto vice: the snares of harlotts & baudes laide for yonge myndes: the disceipte of servantes: the chaunces of fortune contrary to mennes expectation: they beinge thereof warned: may prepare them selfe to resist or prevente occasion" (Sir Thomas Elyot, *The Governor,* 1531). Comedy was to depict the "common errors of our life, which the playwrights representeth in the most ridiculous and scorneful sort" (Sir Philip Sidney, *An Apology for Poetry,* 1595). In this view comedy is to be more or less satiric, a social "medicine of cherries," an instrument for moral correction. The relation of comedy to celebration and its imitation of human vitality and fortune overcome are rarely addressed. Many practicing playwrights did, of course, stress the corrective, satirical function of comedy—or at least they made a perfunctory acknowledgment of such a function—but others self-consciously denied the view that comedy is to "instruct." John Lyly cheerfully acknowledges a hedonistic conception of comedy; the aim of comedy he maintains should be "to move inward delight" (Prologue in *Sappho and Phao,* c. 1584). And the often satiric John Marston seems perversely to deny his own practice when he insists in the prologue to *The Dutch Courtesan* that "We strive not to instruct, but to delight" (c. 1604).

Rhetoricians and other critics also emphasized a conception of comedy inherited from Greco-Roman tradition that differentiated comedy from tragedy by the rank of its characters. Comedy was to deal with the incidents of everyday life and with characters taken from the middle class. Comedy

40

is not an affair of princes, but of the middle class and its servants. George Puttenham takes this for granted. Comedies debate, he says, "the matters of the world . . . but never medling with an Princes matters nor such high personages, but commonly of marchants, souldiers, artificers, good honest householders, and also of unthrifty youthes, yong damsels, old nurses, bawds, brokers, ruffians and parasites, with such like, in whose behaviors lyeth in effect the whole course and trade of mans life" (*The Art of English Poesy,* 1589).

Similarly the rank of characters was to be distinguished carefully by language; each character was not only to behave but also to speak in a manner appropriate to his role and class, so that "by his common talk you / May his nature rightly know" (Richard Edwards, Prologue in *Damon and Pythias,* 1565?). The language of comedy was to be a collection of verbal contrasts that defined dramatic types (*see* Decorum).

As a result of stern imperatives that identified comedy with social correction, the question of laughter from the audience was treated over and over. If the function of comedy is corrective, playwrights must not be seduced by their powers to move an audience to easy laughter. Laughter is not to be an end in itself. While some playwrights defend comedies full of "harmless mirth" (Thomas Heywood, *An Apology for Actors,* 1612), others denounce the "moving of laughter" as a "fault in Comedie, a kind of turpitude, that depraves some part of a mans nature without a disease" (Ben Jonson, *Timber, or Discoveries,* 1641).

The unanimity of rhetoricians in assigning comedy a realistic surface was not total, however; the old romance tradition of native drama received a vague critical sanction in an ancient distinction between comedy and tragedy to be found in the influential commentaries on the works of Terence by the fourth-century grammarian Donatus. Donatus makes Homer's *Iliad* the model for tragedy and his *Odyssey* the model for comedy. Such a distinction is rehearsed by William Webbe, who says, "Thys distinction [between tragedy and comedy] grewe . . . by immitation of the workes of Homer: for out of hys *Iliads,* the Tragedy wryters founde dreadfull events . . . and the other out of hys *Odyssea* tooke arguments of delight, and pleasant ending after dangerous and troublesome doubtes." But the Odyssean vision of journey, encounter, and personal triumph over fortune received no developed analysis in England. "Correct" playwrights scorned comedies of love and adventure. George Whetstone, for example, denounces the writer of romantic drama who "in three howers ronnes he throwe the worlde: marryes, gets Children, makes Children men, men to conquer kingdomes, murder Monsters, and bringeth Gods from Heaven, and fetcheth Divels from Hel" (*Dedicatory Epistle, Promos and Cassandra,* 1578).

Ancient gods and devils have more to do with the nature of English

Renaissance comedy, however, than its contemporary theorists were generally prepared to recognize. There is a close interplay between social and artistic forms in Renaissance culture; and in many ways its art develops the underlying configurations in the social life of the culture. As Italian *commedia eruditia* reflects its association with Carnival, English comedy also suggests a bond with festivals developed from antiquity. Rhetoricians themselves glimpsed an association between Greco-Roman comedy and religious harvest rites, of "feasting" and "procession" (Webbe). But that such celebrations continued to inform comic practice is barely noticed. Yet some comedies, like Jonson's *A Tale of a Tub* (c. 1596) and George Chapman's *May Day* (c. 1602), depict events that occur on a particular holiday. Others, like Shakespeare's *Twelfth Night* (c. 1600), refer their audiences to holiday occasions. And the social form of Elizabethan holiday seems to have contributed to the dramatic form of some of Shakespeare's comedies, with their recurring pattern of confusion, clarification, and festive celebration. In a still more oblique way, the role reversals present in so many English comedies may have a sanction in ancient social rituals that involve a reversal or abandonment of everyday social positions: the Feast of Fools, the Boy Bishop, and English Shrovetide when "Both men and women chaunge their weede, the man in maydes array. / And wanton wenches drest like men, doe travell by the way" (quoted in Donaldson, *The World Upside-Down*). On the comic stage such role reversals and the flouting of normal social functions create a dramatic image of "the world turned upside down" that is associated with holiday from the time of Roman Saturnalia to English "Carnevalls and Shrove-tuesdays liberty of Servants" (Thomas Hobbes, *Leviathan*, 1651).

Bibliography

Ashley H. Thorndike, *English Comedy* (1929); L. C. Knights, *Drama & Society in the Age of Jonson* (1937); Oscar J. Campbell, *Comicall Satyre and Shakespeare's "Troilus and Cressida"* (1938); T. W. Baldwin, *Shakspere's Five-Act Structure* (1947); Alfred Harbage, *As They Liked It: An Essay on Shakespeare and Morality* (1947); E. C. Pettet, *Shakespeare and the Romance Tradition* (1949); Nevill Coghill, "The Basis of Shakespearian Comedy: A Study in Medieval Affinities," *E&S*, 3 (1950), 1–28; Marvin T. Herrick, *Comic Theory in the Sixteenth Century* (1950); Alfred Harbage, *Shakespeare and the Rival Traditions* (1952); Susanne K. Langer, "The Great Dramatic Forms: The Comic Rhythm," *Feeling and Form* (1953), pp. 326–50; Madeleine Doran, *Endeavors of Art: A Study of Form in Elizabethan Drama* (1954); C. L. Barber, *Shakespeare's Festive Comedy: A Study of Dramatic Form in Its Relation to Social Custom* (1959); Jonas A. Barish, *Ben Jonson and the Language of Prose Comedy* (1960); Ernest W.

Talbert, "Aspects of the Comic," *Elizabethan Drama and Shakespeare's Early Plays* (1963), pp. 7–60; Northrop Frye, *A Natural Perspective: The Development of Shakespearean Comedy and Romance* (1965); Richard Hosely, "The Formal Influence of Plautus and Terence," *Elizabethan Theatre*, eds. J. R. Brown and B. Harris, Stratford-upon-Avon Studies, 9 (1966), 131–45; Joe Lee Davis, *The Sons of Ben: Jonsonian Comedy in Caroline England* (1967); Brian Gibbons, *Jacobean City Comedy: A Study of Satiric Plays by Jonson, Marston and Middleton* (1968); Ian Donaldson, *The World Upside-Down: Comedy from Jonson to Fielding* (1970); Sylvia D. Feldman, *The Morality-Patterned Comedy of the Renaissance* (1970); Alan C. Dessen, *Jonson's Moral Comedy* (1971); William G. McCollom, *The Divine Average: A View of Comedy* (1971); Howard M. Felperin, *Shakespearean Romance* (1972); Thomas McFarland, *Shakespeare's Pastoral Comedies* (1972); Kenneth Muir, "Didacticism in Shakespearean Comedy: Renaissance Theory and Practice," *Review of National Literatures*, 3 (1972), 39–53; M. C. Bradbrook, *The Growth and Structure of Elizabethan Comedy* (rev. ed., 1973); Alexander Leggatt, *Citizen Comedy in the Age of Shakespeare* (1973); Leo Salingar, *Shakespeare and the Traditions of Comedy* (1974); John Weld, *Meaning in Comedy: Studies in Elizabethan Romantic Comedy* (1975); L. A. Beaurline, *Jonson and Elizabethan Comedy: Essays in Dramatic Rhetoric* (1978); Anthony Caputi, *Buffo: The Genius of Vulgar Comedy* (1978); Maurice Charney, *Comedy High and Low: An Introduction to the Experience of Comedy* (1978); W. D. Howarth, ed., *Comic Drama: The European Heritage* (1978); R. Chris Hassel, Jr., *Renaissance Drama & the English Church Year* (1979); George E. Rowe, Jr., *Thomas Middleton and the New Comedy Tradition* (1979).

Common-place:

In the rhetorical tradition inherited by Renaissance writers, a reference to a passage of conventional wisdom selected for insertion in a longer verbal structure. The flow of common-places in discourse was closely associated with the rhetorical ideal of amplification, which Henry Peacham defines as "those figures and formes of speech which the reason of man, the principal part and power of his minde, hath by long and diligent search found out, to the admirable utterance of his knowledge, and the glory of his wisdom" (*The Garden of Eloquence,* 1593). The term *common-place* also referred to subject topics or categories ("seats") that served as recall devices for "finding" the matter of one's discourse; as such the common-place was thought of as a "nest" or "room" in which memorable material is stored. Still a third application of this term was as the designation for a particular school exercise, a short oration describing the good or evil of a situation, the facts of which are established: "an Oracion, dilatyng and amplifying good or evill, which is incident or lodged in any man" (Richard Rainold, *The Foundation of Rhetoric,* 1563).

The traditions of the common-places are reflected in Renaissance poetry and prose of all kinds to a degree not yet completely understood. Certainly the common-places not only sanction the pervasive quotation of authorities, which is so marked a characteristic of contemporary literature, but also condition in some ways its structural organization by providing accepted methods of developing a given subject or theme.

The use of the word *place* (Greek: *topos;* Latin: *locus*) has a revealing history in rhetoric (q.v.). It comes from the memory system devised by rhetoricians before Aristotle to train speakers to remember material for their speeches. According to Cicero, the poet Simonides was the inventor of this system. Simonides developed a theory of "places" out of a personal experience. He noticed that he was able to identify mutilated corpses by recalling where each guest at a banquet table had been sitting before a roof collapsed and crushed the guests beyond recognition. Simonides inferred,

44

says Cicero, that persons desiring to train their memory must select localities, form mental images of the facts or items they wish to remember, and store those images in the localities. The places chosen by a speaker as the basis of his memory system could be any set of physical arrangements, the rooms of a house, for example, or the stages of a long journey. In time, the places as images were transformed into places as subject topics and as memorable matter.

As a subject topic, the common-place is a heading, an abstract category, a key notion, that a writer or speaker uses to find what is available in his store of knowledge on any given subject. For example, Leonard Cox in *The Art or Craft of Rhetoric* (1532) lists the places from which the praise of a person is developed as: birth, childhood, adolescence, manhood, old age, death, and what follows after death. We can understand Cox's list of places as a list of preselected ideas to be considered and taken up by a speaker.

Speaking of the common-places for an "oracion demonstrative of a dede," Thomas Wilson says, "these places helpe wonderfully, to set out any matter, and to amplifie it to the uttermoste, not onely in praising or dispraisyng, but also in all other causes where any advisement is to be used." The places he suggests are: "(1) [the deed] is honest, (2) it is possible, (3) easie to be doen, (4) hard to be doen, (5) possible to be doen, (6) impossible to be doen" (*The Art of Rhetoric*, 1553). The places of epideictic rhetoric (q.v.), in particular, came to be subsumed under poetic practice.

As subject topics, the common-places originated in the rhetoric and dialectic of ancient Greece and Rome. Aristotle calls common-places the "seats of arguments" and thinks of them as psychological areas or locales in which arguments are grouped according to their kinds and from which they can be drawn. He lists four common-places: possible and impossible, more or less, past fact and future fact, and magnification and minimization. Later orators, including Cicero and Quintilian, expanded the number and kinds of subject topics.

Also subsumed into the protean traditions of the common-place were certain formulae or motifs of composition, poetic or oratorical. (Some students of the history of rhetoric do not classify these as common-places, but such formulae seem to function as subject categories to be developed by poet or orator in much the same way that other subject headings do.) These would include such formulae as: "inability to cope with the subject"; "we must stop for night is coming on"; the "arms and letter" formula that develops the respective merits of valor and learning.

While the common-place as a subject heading was important, the common-place as a prepared passage of traditional wisdom was also significant in Renaissance rhetoric. Here the omnivorous nature of the rhetorical tradition brought into its service proverbs, apothegms, *sententiae* (q.v.), and other generalized statements of all kinds on standard topics. The use of such statements had a particular association with the praise of virtue and the denunciation of vice. Sixteenth-century rhetoric books, especially those written in Latin, rehearse over and over the association of the common-place with praise and blame. In practice, however, the term covered not only those amplifications of an oration to be considered under praise or blame, but also those appropriate to a wide range of rhetorical intentions.

One of the most influential of all sixteenth-century rhetoric books, the *De copia verborum* by Erasmus (1512), shows students how common-places or *sententiae* (Erasmus uses the terms synonymously) can be drawn from *exempla* so that "the stuff of speech will be ready to hand, as if safe nests had been built, whence you can take what you wish." From the example of the cheerful death of Socrates one could draw the common-place that "death should not be feared by the good man." Since Socrates was accused through the envy of Anytus and Melitus, two of the most corrupt citizens of Athens, one could draw the common-place that "truth creates hatred" or "outstanding virtue wins envy" (*De copia,* trans. Donald B. King and H. David Rix).

As moral generalizations, common-places were originally used by a school of Greek orators, the Sophists, as building blocks for their orations. They wrote down or memorized ahead of time passages to have ready for their speeches. By skillful manipulation any subject could be reduced to the generalizations that the Sophist had prepared. Thus speakers were continually engaged in a systematic exploration of universal rather than particular problems. It was from the persistent use of these common-places that both ancient education and, consequently, the whole of classical literature derived their permanent emphasis on general ideas and universal moral themes. As Sir Thomas Browne rather wearily observes: "There is a certain list of vices commited in all Ages, and declaimed against by all Authors, which will last as long as humane nature; which, digested into common places, may serve for any Theme, and never be out of date until Dooms-day" (*Pseudodoxica Epidemica,* 1646).

Collecting of common-places was part of the educational training of all students. In the words of a contemporary schoolmaster, boys were taught to refer everything they read to some common-place (topic) such as virtue, vice, learning, patience, adversity, prosperity, war, peace: "And if thou perceyve any thynge taken of the wyse sort, to be spoken quiklye, gravely, lernedlye, wyttilye, comely, beare it in mynd, that thou mayst, whan thou shalte have occasion, to use the same. Thou shalte have always at hande a paper boke, wherin thou shalt write such notable thynges, as thou redest thy selfe, or herest of other men worthy to be noted, be it other feate [fitting] sentence, or word, mete for familier speech, that thou maist have it in redynes" (Joannes Vives, *An Introduction to Wisdom,* trans. Sir Richard Morison, 1540; quoted in Mohl). Collections of common-places were called common-place books, "copie" books or copybooks; the purpose of this "notebook and heading" method of education was to furnish the minds of students with an abundance of material or "copie" (*see* Copia).

Besides the common-place books made by schoolboys and the many personal collections kept by adults, there were also unnumbered popular, printed collections of quotations in both Latin and English which a writer or speaker could draw upon for the amplification of his composition. The most massive and influential of such books were those of Erasmus. And general anthologies were supplemented by collections restricted to such things as proverbs, anecdotes, examples, and even similes. From Sir Thomas More to John Milton, authors turned to the collections for ideas, phrases, illustrations, and even plots.

The extensive use of citations and quotations in Renaissance literature is a vivid reminder of the widespread training in the noting of common-places. Sir Francis Bacon maintains that "for the disposition and Collo-cation of that Knowledge which wee preserve in Writing: It consisteth in a good Digest of Common Places, wherein I am not ignorant of the prejudice imputed to the use of *Common-Place Bookes,* as causing retardation of Reading, and some sloth or relaxation of Memorie. But . . . I hould the Entrie of Commonplaces to bee a matter of great use and essence in studying; as that which assureth copie of Invention and contracteth Judgment to a strength" (*The Advancement of Learning,* 1605). It is evident from his common-place book that John Milton, for example, made entries in it throughout his life, and that he drew upon material from his common-place book for both his prose and poetic works. Under headings such as "Of the Good Man," "Of Civil War," and "Of the Knowledge of Litera-ture," he kept careful notes on appropriate matter from other writers.

Bibliography

Rosemond Tuve, "The Criterion of Significancy," *Elizabethan and Meta-physical Imagery* (1947), pp. 145–79; Donald Lemen Clark, *John Milton at St. Paul's School: A Study of Ancient Rhetoric in English Renaissance Education* (1948); Ernst Robert Curtius, *European Literature and the Latin Middle Ages,* trans. Willard R. Trask (1953); Joan Marie Lechner, *Renais-sance Concepts of the Commonplaces* (1962); Frances A. Yates, *The Art of Memory* (1966); Ruth Mohl, *John Milton and His Commonplace Book* (1969); Walter J. Ong, "Tudor Writings on Rhetoric, Poetic, and Literary Theory," *Rhetoric, Romance, and Technology* (1971), pp. 48–103; John G. Rechtien, "John Foxe's *Comprehensive Collection of Commonplaces:* A Renaissance Memory System for Students and Theologians," *Sixteenth Century Journal,* 9 (1978), 83–89.

Complaint:

"Poeticall lamentations" (George Puttenham, *The Art of English Poesy,* 1589); a lyric or narrative poem of a plaintive or lamentative nature. Such poems continued a medieval tradition of poetic lamentation, particularly as meditations on the vanity of the world or tales of the fall of the great. Elizabethan poets extended this tradition of "poeticall lamentations" by emphasizing the topic of unfortunate love.

Complaints generally take the form of a monologue or speech, based on rhetorical figures associated with "faining" a person such as *prosopopoeia:* "a forme of speech by which the Orator faineth a person and maketh him speake much or little according to comelinesse" (Henry Peacham, *The Garden of Eloquence,* 1593), where the function is "to complaine, to accuse, to reprehend, to confirm and to commend." In a lyrical complaint the speaker bemoans his unhappy state caused by a personal misfortune or by the larger sorrowful condition of the world. The narrative complaints, also called "mirrors," "laments," and "tragedies" by English writers, are tales of the downfall of a mighty person, real or legendary. Often the account of the fall supposedly has been related by a ghost appearing to the poet in a dream or vision; the poet then writes his complaint to fulfill a promise to the ghost and to warn the world of the moral, religious, or political lesson conveyed by the fall. The narrative complaint reaches its highest development in the 1590s in a group of amorous complaints, a minor genre to which such poets as Samuel Daniel, Michael Drayton and Shakespeare contributed.

All complaint poems belong to a strain of lamentation that reaches back into the Middle Ages. This strain spreads in several directions: into love poetry of the plaintive Petrarchan manner; into meditations upon the vanity of life and the inevitability of decay; into elegies for the dead; into verse satires that rail against the vice and folly of mankind; and into the many stories of the fall of the great from power and fame. Puttenham

48

indicates the broad sweep of subject matter for all "poeticall lamentations" when he writes: "Nowe are the causes of mans sorrowes many: the death of his parents, friends, allies, children . . . the overthrowes and discomforts in battell, the subversions of townes and cities, the desolations of countreis, the losse of goods and wordly promotions, honour and good renowne, finally, the travails and torments of love forlorne or ill bestowed, either by disgrace, deniall, delay, and twenty other ways, that well experienced lovers could recite." Such occasions as these Puttenham hardly need say are "altogether contrary to rejoising."

The unhappy note of the lyrical monologues of the many love complaints in the Petrarchan vein is one of the most familiar of such poetic lamentations. Here, by convention, the lover bewails his state because of the unresponsiveness of his beloved. Many of these lyric complaints take the stanzaic form of the sonnet (q.v.), and a number carry the word *complaint* in their titles, as in Sir Thomas Wyatt's *Complaint for true love unrequited* or the Earl of Surrey's *Complaint of a lover rebuked.* Both these complaints first appeared in Tottel's *Miscellany* (1557), an influential poetic miscellany that was the wellspring for a later Elizabethan vogue for amorous lyric poetry.

Generally of a less personal nature are the meditative complaints in which lyric poets lament the sorrows of the world, especially the unstable and transitory conditions of life. In some of these poems the complaint merges with satire (q.v.) to urge correction of man's foolish and vicious behavior. In others the tone is simply that of a woeful outcry. As it had been in medieval poetry, the theme of *contemptus mundi* (contempt for the world) is common in such complaints, with the poet often rejecting all temporal pleasures in favor of eternal ones. In a volume of melancholic lamentations Edmund Spenser's Melpomene, the muse of tragedy, voices a typical sentiment, "Ah wretched world the den of wickednesse, / Deformed with filth and fowle iniquitie" (*The Tears of the Muses, Complaints,* 1591); and the printer of that volume of Spenser's "sundrie small poemes" says that he has "imprinted [them] altogeather, for that they al seeme to containe like matter of argument in them, being all complaints and meditations of the worlds vanitie, verie grave and profitable."

Narrative complaints relate the downfall of illustrious persons. Drawing upon mythological, biblical, and historical materials, the narrative poets tell of famous people who have fallen from high position, either through the vagaries of fortune or through the consequences of wrongdoing. Often didactic, such narrative complaints provide "mirrors" or examples of dangerous behavior as warnings to both princes and their subjects. They descend from late medieval mirror literature like Boccaccio's *De casibus virorum illustrium,* Chaucer's *The Monk's Tale,* and John Lydgate's *Fall of Princes.* Because of their historical material, their high moral purpose, and their rehearsal of the fall of the mighty from high position, these narrative complaints are often referred to by poets as "tragedies."

Narrative complaints appear both as collections of tales and as single poems. The best known of the collections is the *Mirror for Magistrates,* a compilation by various authors. That this work went through nine editions between 1555 and 1610 and prompted a good number of imitations testifies to the appeal of lamentative narrative poetry. Although some of the tales in the *Mirror* treat figures from the legendary past of England and even some contemporary figures, most of them relate historical events between the reign of Richard II through that of Richard III (1377-1485). In the preface to the edition of 1559, the editor William Baldwin makes clear the instructional purpose of the *Mirror* when, addressing "the nobility and all other in office," he says: "For here as in a loking-glas, you shall see (if any vice be in you) howe the like hath bene punished in other heretofore, whereby, admonished, I trust it will be a good occasion to move you to the sooner amendment. This is the chiefest ende whye it [the *Mirror*] is set furth, which God graunt it may attaine." Generally regarded as the best of the contributions to this compendium are those by Thomas Sackville in the 1563 edition, where in an induction, the figure of Sorrow appears to the poet and leads him through gloomy scenes to Hell where he hears the *Lament of Henry, Duke of Buckingham.*

The half century of success of the *Mirror for Magistrates* helped to spur the composition of the many single complaint poems of the latter part of Elizabeth's reign. As in the complaints of the collections, individual poems continue to relate didactic tales of woe. Following the tradition of the *Mirror* a vision or dream often frames the tale.

In one group of single complaints, largely confined to the last decade of the sixteenth century, the interest of narrative poets shifted to stories of unfortunate love. In these stories, historical events, still mainly English, are subordinate to the misfortunes in love of historical persons. In contrast to the male speaker of the lyrical Petrarchan complaints, the central figure is frequently a forsaken woman. As Edmund Spenser (*Colin Clout's Come Home Again,* 1595) says of Samuel Daniel's *The Complaint of Rosamond* (1592), the single complaints of this kind combine "Tragick plaints and passionate mischance."

The vogue for the single amorous complaint—and for what in effect was a new kind of poetry for late Elizabethans—was set by Daniel's lament of the young and beautiful Rosamond. The mistress of Henry II, Rosamond, had been forced to drink poison by his queen. Her complaint tells of yielding to the allurements of wealth and royal favor and of her remorse at the time of death. Daniel's poem, like those of other writers in the genre, generally avoids a moralistic tone and tempers the grimness of the usual narrative lament by including romantic sentiment and pathos, elaborate descriptions of beauty, and some of the mythological embellishments in the Ovidian manner.

Bibliography

Lily B. Campbell, *Tudor Conceptions of History and Tragedy in "A Mirror for Magistrates"* (1936); Willard Farnham, *"The Mirror for Magistrates"* and "The Progeny of the *Mirror," The Medieval Heritage of Elizabethan Tragedy* (1936), pp. 271–339; Lily B. Campbell, ed., "Introduction," *The Mirror for Magistrates* (1938), pp. 3–60; Homer Nearing, *English Historical Poetry, 1599–1641* (1945); Louise R. Zocca, "The Historical Material," *Elizabethan Narrative Poetry* (1950), pp. 3–93; Hallett Smith, "Ovidian Poetry," *Elizabethan Poetry* (1952), pp. 64–130; John Peter, *Complaint and Satire in Early English Literature* (1956); Maurice Evans, "Historical Poetry," *English Poetry in the Sixteenth Century* (2nd ed., 1967), pp. 123–34; Ronald Primeau, "Daniel and the *Mirror* Tradition: Dramatic Irony in *The Complaint of Rosamond," SEL, 15 (1975), 21–36.*

Conceit:

During the Elizabethan period and early seventeenth century, a term, often spelled *conceipt,* carrying the general meaning of idea, concept, or thought. It derives from the Italian *concetto* (concept). Ben Jonson says that the "conceits of the mind are Pictures of things, and the tongue is the Interpreter of those Pictures" (*Timber, or Discoveries,* 1641). In literary contexts, writers also used *conceit* to refer to the ideas in a poem, as when Thomas Nashe praises the "deepe conceit" of the "divine Master [Edmund] *Spencer*" (preface to Robert Greene's *Menaphon,* 1589). It also referred to the imagination of a poet, as Sir Philip Sidney does when he speaks of the "high flying libertie of conceit propper to the Poet" (*An Apology for Poetry,* 1595).

During the last half of the seventeenth century the term *conceit* was extended to apply not only to an idea but particularly to a witty idea or surprising similitude. Such similitudes were denigrated as "metaphors far-fet" (Jonson, *Timber, or Discoveries*) by many earlier poets. But in 1675 Edward Phillips reports that many discriminating readers rank John Cleveland as the greatest English poet because "his Conceits were out of the common road, and Wittily far-fetch't" (*Theatrum Poetarum*). Other readers looked with less favor on conceits or surprising similitudes; and John Dennis claims that a "wantonness of Wit" prompted Abraham Cowley to "roam about the Universe, and return home laden with rich, but far-fetch't Conceits" (preface, *The Passion of Byblis,* 1692).

Unlike the usual metaphor, where an obvious and close resemblance exists between vehicle and tenor, a conceit stresses a similarity between highly dissimilar elements that must be discovered through thought. In this way, the general meaning of *thought* or *idea* and an emphasis on intellectual activity carry over into the literary use of *conceit* to designate a similitude based on unusual relationships. In a conceit a poet must make the reader see what is not obvious; the poet must convince the reader that things that are dissimilar do resemble each other. The immediate effect of such metaphors is to elicit from the reader a sense of wonder or of surprise in conceding likeness while being strongly conscious of unlikeness.

Conceits, then, are a product of intellectual ingenuity, a capacity for finding likenesses in the apparently unlike. In *Richard II* (c. 1595) Shakespeare's poet-king, meditating in prison after his deposition, confronts this challenge to his mental faculty. He says:

> I have been studying how I may
>   compare
> This prison where I live unto the world.
> And for because the world is populous,
> And here is not a creature but myself,
> I cannot do it.

Unwilling to concede that he cannot find a similarity between the prison and the world, he continues:

> Yet I'll hammer it out.
> My brain I'll prove the female to my soul,
> My soul the father, and these two beget
> A generation of still breeding thoughts. (V, v)

To "hammer out" the similarity between dissimilarities is what the concettist does, and he asks in effect that his readers also use their intelligence.

The highly unusual metaphor, or as Cowley calls it "some odde Similitude" (*Ode of Wit*, 1656), had posed questions in rhetorical-poetic theory since classical times. Aristotle, for example, in the *Rhetoric* calls metaphor the primary tool for poets; he advises that metaphors should conform to a mean, and not be either too obvious or too "difficult to take in." But he also says that since "Men admire what is remote," speakers "should give our language a foreign air" and "It is metaphor above all that gives . . . a foreign air." Aristotle even believed a certain amount of obscurity was permissible, because "metaphor is a kind of enigma," and "clever enigmas furnish good metaphors." Later classical rhetoricians, such as Cicero and Quintilian, repeated such injunctions without clarifying the difference between appropriate similitudes and those that stretched too far.

English critical theory similarly valued the metaphor (Greek, "transference") as a poet's major device and warned against those of a too unusual nature. Henry Peacham, for example, in *The Garden of Eloquence* (1593), turns first to *metaphoria* in his discussion of figures; he defines it as an "artificial translation of one word, from the proper signification, to another not proper, but yet nigh and like." The poet, Peacham says, uses two faculties, his memory, "the treasure house of mans knowledge," and his

53

"discreete judgement," to create a "fit similitude." "Apt metaphors," he continues, "give pleasant light to darke things, thereby removing unprofitable and odious obscuritie." "By the aptnesse of their proportion, and nearenesse of affinitie, they worke in the hearer many effects, they obtaine allowance [agreement] of his judgement, they move his affections. . . . they are forcible to perswade . . . to commend or dispraise" and "they leave such a firme impression in the memory, as is not lightly forgotten." But, he warns, "the similitude" should "be not farre fetcht, as from strange things unknowne to the hearer, as if one should take *Metaphors* from the parts of a ship, and apply them among husbandmen which never came at the sea, he shall obscure the thing that he would faineth make evident."

Peacham's caution against the "farre fetcht" echoes throughout discussions of metaphors in the late sixteenth and early seventeenth centuries. Ben Jonson, for example, warns that "metaphors far-fet hinder to be understood" (*Timber, or Discoveries,*). In the late seventeenth century "farre fetcht" became the key term in debate over conceits. When a "farre fetcht" metaphor was "apt" and when it became "some odde Similitude" was, however, a matter of personal judgment. Thomas Hobbes, for example, argues that the more learned the poet the more likely his metaphors are to be conceits: "from *Knowing much,* proceedeth the admirable variety and novelty of Metaphors and Similitudes, which are not possible to be lighted on in the compass of a narrow knowledge." Thus Hobbes finds nothing objectionable when the poems of an educated writer used "far fetch't but withal apt, instructive, and comly similitudes" (*Answer to Davenant,* 1650).

English poets' frequent search into the recondite for their conceits reflects an extension of a traditional analogical habit of mind. The universe was generally thought of as a vast network of universal correspondences or analogies that united all the seemingly heterogeneous elements of experience; and since, as Sir Thomas Browne says in *Religio Medici* (1643), the world is God's "universal and public manuscript," in its way a kind of divine and witty poem, the poet of sufficient insight could discover relationships hidden to those of a duller mind. John Donne, for example, in his lyric *Air and Angels* (1633) draws upon an abstruse branch of theology known as angelology to demonstrate a difference he sees "Twixt women's love, and men's." In short a theory of universal correspondence prepared both poets and readers of the late sixteenth and early seventeenth centuries for unusual analogies. The search for the "far-fet" within this vast network of symbolic correspondences is probably what led a later English critic to speak of the "occult" when he describes the wit of metaphysical poets as "a kind of *discordia concors;* a combination of dissimilar images, or discovery of occult resemblances in things apparently unlike" (Samuel Johnson, *Cowley, Lives of the Poets,* 1779).

Theoretical discussion of the conceit was not an interest in England until late in the seventeenth century and contemporary critical commentary on the nature of the conceit is to be found only on the continent. Among major writers on the theory of the conceit are Baltasar Gracián (*Arte de ingenio,* 1642) in Spain and Matteo Pellegrini (*Delle acutezze,* 1639), Pierfrancesco Minozzi (*Gli sfogamenti dell'ingegno,* 1641), Cardinal Sforza-Pallavicino (*Trattato del dialogo e dello stile,* 1646), and Emmanuele Tesauro (*Il cannochiale aristotelico,* 1654), in Italy. Despite minor differences, these writers shifted the emphasis in criticism from discussions of appropriate poetic subject matter and the nature of imitation to matters of form. Form was for them the key to the aesthetic pleasure of a poem; and form in a poem was the result of a poet's *ingegno* or wit, a nondiscursive type of human understanding that discovers similitudes and creates metaphors. Having found an unforeseen relationship between two phenomena, the business of the concettist was to develop all possible similarities and to give them eloquent expression. Pallavicino, for example, in *Trattato* says that the main function of a conceit is to show how things that appear unconnected are really similar and to arouse thereby a certain sensation of wonder. The wonder elicited was not, however, to be that of shock at the perverse or extravagant, but a wonder at the insight produced by the new similitude.

The conceits of English Renaissance poetry are often spoken of today as being of two types, the brief or condensed and the extended. The brief conceit is "a telescoped image that develops the thought by rapid association or sudden contrast" (Williamson). Shakespeare's Cleopatra in *Antony and Cleopatra* (c. 1607), uses such a conceit of telling brevity when she refers to her earlier love for Julius Caesar as having been during "My salad days, / When I was green in judgment." An extended conceit is one in which analogy is subject to detailed and ingenious development, often throughout an entire poem. For example, in the sonnet entitled *The lover compareth his state to a ship in perilous storm tossed on the sea* (1557), Sir Thomas Wyatt finds similarities between a lover and a ship and between the many mental torments of unrequited love and the physical distresses occasioned by a fierce storm at sea.

As a rhetorical device, conceits are especially associated with poems in the Petrarchan mode, usually love sonnets, and with what was called in its own day a poetry of "strong lines" (q.v.) and is known today as "metaphysical poetry." The elaborate comparisons in Elizabethan love poetry in the Petrarchan mode are generally ones in which physical qualities or experiences are described in terms of physical objects. The slightest resemblance seems one upon which the poet can build his metaphor. Hyperbole is the norm. A common way of organizing conceits describing the lady's beauty is the *blazon* or catalogue. A favorite device for ordering conceits describing the lover's malady is oxymoron, a bringing together of contradictory terms.

In contrast to Petrarchan analogies, the conceits of the metaphysical poets utilize knowledge and experience from many areas—the highly learned and esoteric as well as the surprisingly mundane. Typically, the metaphysical conceit avoids images with established poetic association, such as those of classical mythology and of the Petrarchan tradition; but when it does make use of such imagery, the metaphysical conceit tends to stress a startling resemblance. Donne's speaker in *The Flea* (1633), for example, is, like the Petrarchan lover, envious of any object close to his beloved; but that object here is not a glove, but a flea. Often the metaphysical conceit is used to define a psychological state or an attitude, or is a rhetorical means of persuasion or "proof" in a speaker's argument.

Bibliography

M. B. Ogle, "The Classical Origin and Tradition of Literary Conceits," *American Journal of Philology,* 34 (1913), 125–52; Raymond M. Alden, "The Lyrical Conceit of the Elizabethans," *SP,* 14 (1917), 129–52; Raymond M. Alden, "The Lyrical Conceits of the 'Metaphysical Poets,' " *SP,* 17 (1920), 183–98; Kathleen M. Lea, "Conceits," *MLR,* 20 (1925), 389–406; George Williamson, *The Donne Tradition* (1930); Lu Emily Pearson, *Elizabethan Love Conventions* (1933); George Williamson, "Strong Lines," *ES,* 18 (1936), 152–59; Lisle Cecil John, *The Elizabethan Sonnet Sequences: Studies in Conventional Conceits* (1938); George R. Potter, "A Protest against the Term *Conceit,*" *PQ,* 20 (1941), 474–83; Frances A. Yates, "The Emblematic Conceit in Giordano Bruno's *De Gli Eroici Furori* and in the Elizabethan Sonnet Sequences," *JWCI,* 6 (1943), 101–21; Rosemond Tuve, *Elizabethan and Metaphysical Imagery* (1947); Rosemary Freeman, *English Emblem Books* (1948); Ernst Robert Curtius, "Mannerism," *European Literature and the Latin Middle Ages,* trans. Willard R. Trask (1953), pp. 273–301; Odette de Mourgues, *Metaphysical, Baroque & Precieux Poetry* (1953); T. N. Marsh, "Elizabethan Wit in Metaphor and Conceit: Sidney, Shakespeare, Donne," *EM,* 13 (1962), 25–29; Joseph Anthony Mazzeo, "A Seventeenth-Century Theory of Metaphysical Poetry" and "Metaphysical Poetry and the Poetic of Correspondence," *Renaissance and Seventeenth-Century Studies* (1964), pp. 29–59; Mario Praz, *Studies in Seventeenth-Century Imagery,* (2nd ed., 1964); Donald L. Guss, *John Donne, Petrarchist: Italianate Conceits and Love Theory in "The Songs and Sonets"* (1966); Jay L. Halio, "The Metaphor of Conception and Elizabethan Theories of the Imagination," *Neophil,* 50 (1966), 454–61; Don Cameron Allen, *Image and Meaning: Metaphoric Traditions in Renaissance Poetry* (1968); Earl Miner,

The Metaphysical Mode from Donne to Cowley (1969); K. K. Ruthven, *The Conceit* (1969); Robert J. Bauer, "A Phenomenon of Epistemology in the Renaissance," *JHI,* 31 (1970), 281–88; Earl Miner, ed., *Seventeenth Century Imagery: Essays on Uses of Figurative Language from Donne to Farquhar* (1971); Forrest G. Robinson, *The Shape of Things Known: Sidney's "Apology" in Its Philosophical Tradition* (1972); S. K. Heninger, Jr., "Metaphor as Cosmic Correspondence," *Touches of Sweet Harmony: Pythagorean Cosmology and Renaissance Poetics* (1974), pp. 325–63; Alastair Fowler, *Conceitful Thought* (1975) Melissa C. Wanamaker, *Discordia Concors: The Wit of Metaphysical Poetry* (1975).

Copia:

"Varietie of discourse, as the fittest and forciblest accesse into the capacitie of the vulgar sort" (Sir Francis Bacon, *The Advancement of Learning,* 1605). In the rhetorical-poetic systems of the sixteenth and early seventeenth centuries, copia was achieved by amplifying an idea, by a heaping of figures, as a strategy for moving a popular audience. "Sentences [*see* Sententia] gathered and heaped together commend muche the matter," says Thomas Wilson (*The Art of Rhetoric,* 1553).

One of the most widely used textbooks of rhetoric (q.v.) in Tudor schools was Desiderius Erasmus's *De duplici copia verborum ac rerum* (1512), designed to assist students in acquiring elegance and variety of expression in Latin composition. So popular was *De copia* that it had over 150 printings by a variety of printers both English and continental in the sixteenth century alone. Its plan was probably suggested to Erasmus by a passage in the tenth book of Quintilian's *Institutio oratoria,* the first chapter of which bore the title "De copia verborum" in editions of the work printed in the lifetime of Erasmus, and by the phrase "copia rerum ac verborum" (echoing a similar phrase in Book III of Cicero's *De oratore*) appearing early in the chapter. While Quintilian barely discusses either copia of words (*verba*) or of ideas (*res*), Erasmus supplies the details omitted by his great predecessor, claiming to be the first to think through and develop his subject. By way of illustrating copia, Erasmus presents 150 variations of one clause (*tuae literae me magnopere deluctarunt,* your letter has delighted me very much).

Sixteenth-century rhetoricians emphasize copia as the central thrust of their systems. Richard Rainold's *Foundation of Rhetoric* (1563), for example, describes rhetoric as that which "dilateth and setteth out small thynges or woordes, in soche sorte, with soche aboundaunce and plentuousnes, bothe of woordes and wittie invencion, with soche goodlie disposicion, in soche a infinite sorte . . . that the moste stonie and hard hartes, can not but bee incensed, inflamed, and moved thereto."

To "dilate" with abundance and plenty, one studied the figures of speech (*see* Elocutio). Erasmus would vary words, for example, with synonyms, enallage (a small change in the same word), antonomasia (change of name, as Pelides for Achilles), periphrasis, metaphor, allegory, metonymy, and hyperbole. Ways to vary thought are achieved by figures such as the treatment of a generalized idea with length and detail; recounting causes; enumerating circumstances; descriptions of all kinds; "exempla" such as fables, proverbs, parables, narratives; and by drawing from common-places (q.v.), such as "class" and "species."

Typically, rhetoric books list the figure of amplification as a figure that itself encompasses the smaller figures of variation. As a figure, amplification consists in "augmentynge and diminishynge of anye matter, and that divers wayes" (Wilson). To amplify is "to be well stored with much copienesse" (Wilson). Henry Peacham, speaking of the figures of speech, "whereof the whole body of Amplificacion consisteth," says they are the "mighty and plentifull streams of copious eloquence, which are continually fed and filled with ye perpetuall and pleasant springs of man's wit" (*The Garden of Eloquence,* 1593).

The function of amplification is to move the feelings of an audience. Speakers or writers who can "bothe copiouslie dilate any matter or sentence, by pleasauntnes and swetenes of . . . their wittie and ingenious oracion can drawe unto theim the hartes of a multitude," "pluck downe and extirpate affections and perturbacions of people," "move pitee and compassion," "alter the counsaill of kynges" (Rainold). In a similar vein Peacham says the function of amplification is "the moving of affections"; "a stirring, or forcying of the mynde, either to desier, or elles to detest, and lothe anything, more vehemently then by nature we are commonly wonte to doe."

The power to amplify an idea is a particular requirement for poets writing an heroic poem or tragedy; rhetoric books often make amplification a coordinate of the "high" or "mighty" style. In Thomas Wilson's description of the "three styles" of discourse, for example, he associates the "mighty kind" with "vehement figures" that are the figures of amplification, noting that in the "lowe kind" of style the orator will not "use any amplifications."

In the energetic sixteenth-century debate over the use of the vernacular (*see* Vulgar language) rather than Latin or Greek for serious literary efforts, a recurring issue was the ability of the English language to supply enough words for fullness of discourse. It was sometimes contended that English was lacking in "the Trew Paterne of Eloquence" (Roger Ascham, *The Schoolmaster,* 1570). Claims for copia in English belong to the last quarter of the sixteenth century. Writing about 1595 Richard Carew in *The Excellency of English* confidently believes that English meets the requisites of language in its "Copiousness" ("that wee maye expresse the meaning of our mindes . . . fullye, so as others may thoroughlie conceive us"). By 1626 Michael Drayton can praise his native language as that "plenteous *English*" (*To My Most Dearly-Loved Friend Henry Reynolds*).

Contemporary critics noticed that the emphasis upon copia could become an emphasis upon mere wordiness. Ben Jonson derides poor poets "who utter all they can thinke, with a kind of violence, and indisposition; without relation . . . to any fitnesse. . . . Now because they speake all they can (however unfitly) they are thought to have the greater copy" (*Timber, or Discoveries,* 1641). In a similar vein Bacon, attacking "vaine affectations" of learning, condemns excesses of "copie of speech" in which the inclination is rather towards "copie" than "weight."

Bibliography

William G. Crane, *Wit and Rhetoric in the Renaissance: The Formal Basis of Elizabethan Prose Style* (1937); Madeleine Doran, "Eloquence and 'Copy,'" *Endeavors of Art: A Study of Form in Elizabethan Drama* (1954), pp. 24–52; Donald B. King and H. David Rix, "Introduction," *Desiderius Erasmus of Rotterdam: On Copia of Words and Ideas,* trans. King and Rix (1963), pp. 1–8; Mary E. Hazard, "An Essay to Amplify 'Ornament': Some Renaissance Theory and Practice," *SEL,* 16 (1976), 15–32.

Couplet:

"Two verses rhyming together" (William Webbe, *A Discourse of English Poetry,* 1586). Describing the various placements of end rhymes in verses, or the "proportion of distance," George Puttenham writes, "the first distance . . . goeth all by *distick* or couples [pair] of verses agreeing in one cadence, and do passe so speedily away and so often returne agayne, as their tunes are never lost, nor out of eare, one couple [one verse] supplying another so nye and so suddenly." He adds, "this is the most vulgar [native] proportion of distance or situation, such as used *Chaucer* in his Canterbury tales, and *Gower* in all his workes" (*The Art of English Poesy,* 1589).

English poets, of course, varied the metrical length of their couplets. Webbe reports that the "longest verse in length, which I have seene used in English consisteth of sixteene syllables, eache two verses rhyming together," but "thys kynde is not very much used." The "most acustomed of all other," he continues, is "an other kynd" of rhymed couplet "where eche verse hath fourteene syllables" (*A Discourse of English Poetry*). But the preference of poets was even then shifting to either the iambic tetrameter or the iambic pentameter couplet, with the closed decasyllablic couplet the most frequently used form. The preference for the decasyllabic line was itself a preference for what Samuel Daniel calls "our old accustomed measure of five feet" (*A Defense of Rhyme,* 1603).

Couplets may be either "open" or "closed." In an open couplet the thought and syntax carry over from one set of rhymed lines to the next, so that its most striking characteristic is that of a forward thrust. In contrast, in a closed couplet the thought and syntax are complete within the rhymed lines.

The closed decasyllabic couplet was evolved "by and large from the efforts of many Elizabethan poets (among them Christopher Marlowe, Sir John Harington, Michael Drayton, Thomas Heywood, Joseph Hall and, of course, Donne and Jonson) to reproduce in English the effects of the Latin elegiac distitch, especially as it had been employed by Ovid in his *Amores* and *Heroides* and by Martial in his *Epigrammaton*" (Piper). The Latin elegiac distich is a pair of unrhymed lines, one in dactylic hexameter and the other in pentameter. The most distinguishing feature of this distich is its second or pentameter line; it is composed of two exactly equal metrical halves, and is divided in the middle by a caesura. Metrically, the Latin elegiac distich presents a regular hierarchy of pauses, the strongest at the close of the distich, the next strongest at the end of the first line, and the third strongest at the midpoints of each of the two lines. It was such effects as these that English poets sought to imitate in their closed decasyllabic couplets. English practice in the vernacular also tended to use strong pauses both within and at the end of lines. The rhythm created by these pauses lends itself particularly to the rhetorical features of inversion, parallelism, and antithesis. Ben Jonson, in his conversations with William Drummond of Hawthornden, distinguishes closed couplets as "the bravest sort of verses, expecially when they are broken, like Hexameters," his reference apparently being to the regular hierarchy of pauses.

As units of versification, couplets appeared in contemporary poetry in two ways. On the one hand, the couplet was a subordinate element within an established stanza form. Two stanzas popular with narrative poets, rhyme royal and ottava rima (qq.v.), conclude with couplets, which generally offer a summation of thought or action or make an epigrammatic comment. On the other hand, the couplet was sometimes the sole unit of poetic composition. It could stand alone as an individual poem (despite Puttenham's claim that "a *distick* or couple of verses is not to be accompted a staffe [stanza]." The two-line epigram (q.v.) was a favorite for witty expression.

Because of Chaucer's use of the decasyllabic couplet in his *Canterbury Tales,* a native tradition associated that couplet with long narrative poetry. However, since his couplets, supposedly careless about their caesuras, were felt to lack metrical dignity, theorists like Puttenham and George Gascoigne speak condescendingly of them as "but riding ryme" and associate them only with "a merie tale" (Gascoigne, *Certain Notes of Instruction,* 1575). Daniel also criticizes the use of couplets in long poems. He writes: "I must confesse that to mine owne eare those continuall cadences of couplets used in long and continued Poemes are verie tyresome and unpleasing, by reason that still, me thinks, they run on with a sound of one nature, and a kinde of certaintie which stuffs the delight rather than entertaines it. But yet, notwithstanding, I must not out of mine owne daintinesse condemne this kinde of writing, which peradventure to another may seeme most delightfull; and many worthy compositions we see to have passed with commendation in that kinde."

Late Elizabethan and early seventeenth-century poets extended the use of couplets beyond narrative discourse, whether "merie" or not. As the

Latin elegiac distich was naturalized, it became an important unit of composition in a variety of "long and continued" poems—satires, verse epistles, and complimentary and occasional poems. These kinds of poems are similar to the ones for which classical writers had used the elegiac distich. In other words, poets came to think of the decasyllabic couplet as particularly appropriate for those poems for which decorum (q.v.) required a conversational style. Still other poets, like John Milton in his companion poems of praise *L'Allegro* and *Il Penseroso* (1645), made similar use of iambic tetrameter couplets.

Bibliography

John S. P. Tatlock, "Origin of the Closed Couplet in English," *The Nation,* 98 (April 9, 1914), 390; E. C. Knowlton, "Origin of the Closed Couplet in English," *The Nation,* 99 (July 30, 1914), 134; Paull Franklin Baum, "Heroic Couplet," *The Principles of English Versification* (1922), pp. 93–102; George Pope Shannon, "Nicholas Grimald's Heroic Couplet and the Latin Elegiac Distich," *PMLA,* 45 (1930), 532–42; Ruth C. Wallerstein, "The Development of the Rhetoric and Metre of the Heroic Couplet, especially 1625–1645," *PMLA,* 50 (1935), 166–209; Barbara Herrnstein Smith, "The Rhymed Couplet," *Poetic Closure: A Study of How Poems End* (1968), pp. 70–78; William Bowman Piper, *The Heroic Couplet* (1969).

Decorum:

"The Greekes call this good grace of every thing in his kinde, το πρεπον, the Latines *decorum:* we in our vulgar call it . . . *decencie* . . . we call it also *comelynesse,*" says George Puttenham (*The Art of English Poesy,* 1589). It is, he continues, a "lovely conformitie, or proportion, or conveniencie." As "the line & levell for al good makers to do their business by," decorum is a criterion in terms of which all other questions of polished discourse could be understood in the sixteenth and early seventeenth centuries. As a conceptual frame, decorum controlled a poet's adjustment of character, genre, and style to what was "apt" or "fitting." E. K.'s epistle to Gabriel Harvey (1579) in commendation of Spenser's *Shepherd's Calendar* praises the poet for his "dewe observing of Decorum everye where, in personages, in seasons, in matter, in speach."

In its most common English usage decorum implied a concern for language appropriate to character with an unquestioned emphasis upon character types in all kinds of fictions. At its most extreme, decorum would decree that a character in a fiction must act and speak according to his sex, age, nation or city, art or profession, and nature; it implies consistency of speech and action according to character. Richard Edwards's *Damon and Pythias* (c. 1565) insists upon this kind of propriety; the Prologue is describing that which "our author" learned from Horace "from whom he doth not swerve, / In all such kind of exercise *decorum* to observe."

> The olde man is sober, the younge man rashe, the lover triumphyng in joyes,
> The Matron grave, the Harlat wilde, and full of wanton toys.
> Whiche all in one course they no wise doo agree;
> So correspondent to their kinde their speeches ought to bee.

In a similar vein Ben Jonson says one must choose words "according to the persons wee make speake, or the things wee speake of. Some are of the Campe, some of the Councell-board, some of the Shop, some of the

Sheepe-coat, some of the Pulpit, some of the Barre, &c." (*Timber, or Discoveries,* 1641). He complains of Guarini's pastoral play that "Guarini, in his Pastor Fido, kept not decorum, in making Shepherds speeke as well as himself could" (*Conversations with Drummond,* 1619).

Behind such references to decorum extends a rhetorical-poetic tradition that emphasizes audience expectation in relation to types and traditional heroes. It assumes a conservative consistency with established social forms. During the late Middle Ages, the *locus classicus* for this notion of decorum was Horace's *Ars poetica.* Horace offers poets advice on men speaking as they should in the view of an audience and on consistency of character:

> If now the phrase of him that speaks, shall flow
> In sound, quite from his fortune; both the rout,
> And *Roman* Gentry, will with laughter shout.
> (trans. Ben Jonson,
Horace his Art of Poetry, 1640)

Poets should make Medea "wild, fierce, impetuous," Ixion "trecherous," "griev'd *Orestes* sad." If the poet creates a new character, "look he keep his state / Unto the last, as when he first went forth, / Still to be like himselfe, and hold his worth."

Aristotelian and Ciceronian rhetoric (q.v.) also encouraged a prescriptive understanding of character and language in relation to audience. Aristotle's *Rhetoric* reminds readers that "the use of maxims is appropriate only to elderly men, and in handling subjects in which the speaker is experienced. For a young man to use them is—like telling stories—unbecoming." In Book III of the *Rhetoric* he says that "each class of men, each type of disposition, will have its own appropriate way of letting the truth appear." Under class he includes differences of age, of sex, of nationality. Ciceronian rhetoric books encourage a similar emphasis upon congruence of character type and the language assigned to that type: "The same style and the same thoughts must not be used in portraying every condition in life, or every rank, position or age." Propriety "depends on the subject under discussion, and on the character of both the speaker and the audience" (Cicero, *Orator*).

When Aristotle's *Poetics* was rediscovered in Italy in the very late fifteenth century, many of his remarks were taken to reinforce Horatian conceptions of decorum. Passages from the *Ars poetica* and the *Poetics* were set forth in parallel columns to make their resemblances clearer. The belief became current that Horace knew Aristotle's work, used it as his source and guide, and meant to do no more than paraphrase it in verse. Thus when Aristotle says in the fifteenth book of the *Poetics* that a character must be true to life and that he must be consistent, his remarks were understood in the light of theories of Horatian decorum. Similarly when Aristotle tells his readers that valor in a woman is inappropriate, he seemed to be fully Horatian.

It is this powerful tradition that firmly welds conceptions of character to a decorum of style. And the first criterion proposed by rhetoricians for style is that of "styles"; poets must use a style appropriate to the general subject matter and to the degree of nobility of the persons represented. Sir Philip Sidney speaks of this as "peizing each syllable of each word by just proportion according to the dignity of the subject" (*An Apology for Poetry*, 1595). Thus Puttenham mocks a translator of Virgil's *Aeneid* who "said that *AEneas* was fayne to trudge out of Troy; which terme became better to be spoken of a beggar, or of a rogue, or a lackey: for so wee use to say to such maner of people, be trudging hence." He rehearses a traditional view when he says that "in all decencie the stile ought to conforme with the nature of the subject, otherwise . . . a writer will seeme to observe no *decorum* at all." There are three styles, says Puttenham, summarizing the Horatian-Ciceronian tradition; these are "the high, meane and base style." The high style is advanced by "wordes, phrases, sentences, and figures, high, loftie, eloquent, & magnifick in proportion"; mean matters are "caried with all wordes and speaches of smothnesse and pleasant moderation, & finally the base things to be beholden within their teder, by a low, myld, and simple maner of utterance, creeping rather than clyming & marching rather than mounting upwardes."

Distinctions among styles are sometimes based on their degree of amplification (*see* Copia). Thomas Wilson says, for example, that in the high or "mighty kinde" we use "vehement figures" (figures of amplification). In the low style, he says, "we use no Metaphores, nor translated wordes, nor yet use any amplifications, but go plainlye to worke, and speake altogether in commune wordes" (*The Art of Rhetoric*, 1553).

With the co-relations between subject and style of the Three Styles, the concept of decorum in all poetic matters radiated into critical decisions of every kind. Few elements of concern could not be discussed under the question of "appropriateness." If all poetic matters could be reduced to the Three Styles, then they could also be reduced to questions of diction. One of the ways of considering poetry was to consider it exclusively in terms of words or expression. And decorum was related to genre as genre was related to subject matter. Genre concerned with "high" subjects required a "high" style. Thus an influential Italian critic develops seven different kinds of decorum: the first being that of the Ciceronian Three Styles. Then he goes on to develop the decorum of style according to the speaker; a decorum of style according to the auditor (the "dignity" of the person being addressed); the character of style according to the "places" of rhetoric; style according to the emotions of the orator or the characters of whom he speaks; and a decorum according to whether one is beginning, narrating, or concluding a speech. His last category is that of decorum according to purpose, such as persuading, comforting, or attacking (Antonio Minturno, *L'arte poetica,* 1564).

Invoked as principle, decorum inevitably raises questions of verisimilitude (*see* Imitation). The Horatian emphasis is upon a poet's creation of character in relation to audience expectation, and hierarchical social conventions. It continually points outward to recognitions of what is "higher" and what is "lower." Sometimes decorum can be invoked on the basis of naturalistic realism or "truth to nature." In the preface to his 1591 translation of *Orlando Furioso,* Sir John Harington, fending off a potential charge of obscenity, reminds his readers that there is "so meet a decorum in the persons of those that speake lasciviously." An Italian critic can defend the soliloquy in tragedy because, he says, great men do not discuss their private affairs with the multitude, but they speak in soliloquy as they would in their houses (Giraldi Cinthio, *Didone,* 1543).

Because of its relation to "nature," however, decorum as a concept carried with it all the ambiguity and instability of any large principle. What is "apt" and "fitting" is not always easy to locate or to locate with unanimous agreement. After struggling with the term, and associating it with "proportion" and "good construction," Puttenham reports: "But, sir, all this being by them [poets] very well conceived, there remainyed a greater difficultie to know what this proportion, volubilitie, good construction, and the rest were." If decorum was, as John Milton says "the grand master peece to observe" (*Of Education,* 1644), the complex adjustment of a poem to style, genre, and verisimilitude finally turns on decisions subject to an individual poet's interpretations, rather than a simple reliance on "rules."

Bibliography

Vernon Hall, Jr., *Renaissance Literary Criticism: A Study of Its Social Content* (1945); Marvin T. Herrick, *The Fusion of Horatian and Aristotelian Literary Criticism, 1531–1555* (1946); Rosemond Tuve, *Elizabethan and Metaphysical Imagery* (1947); Kester Svendsen, "Epic Address and Reference and the Principle of Decorum in *Paradise Lost,*" *PQ,* 28 (1949), 185–206; Maurice B. MacNamee, *Literary Decorum in Francis Bacon* (1950); Madeleine Doran, *Endeavors of Art: A Study of Form in Elizabethan Drama* (1954); A. C. Hamilton, "The Modern Study of Renaissance English Literature," *MLQ,* 26 (1965), 150–83; Thomas Kranidas, *The Fierce Equation: A Study of Milton's Decorum* (1965); Annabel Patterson, *Hermogenes and the Renaissance: Seven Ideas of Style* (1970); T. McAlindon, *Shakespeare and Decorum* (1973).

Echo poem:

A "kind of Poem imitating the resounding Rocks, wherein the last Syllables of a sentence repeated, give answer to a question in the same, or a divers, and sometime a contrary sence" (Ralph Johnson, *A Scholar's Guide,* 1665). An echo poem was a poem in which the closing syllables of one line are repeated, as by an echo, in the following line to offer a reply or a comment. The poem is composed of a series of such couplets. The first line of the couplet often asks a question, but may only make a statement. The repeated syllables in the echo line usually make up that entire second line.

The echo device is as old as the *Greek Anthology.* Like their Italian and French contemporaries, English poets of the late sixteenth and seventeenth centuries often associated echo poems with eclogues (q.v.) and pastoral plays (*see* Pastoral). A common theme in such poems is unrequited love.

Eclogue:

"The pastorall Poesie . . . we commonly call by the name of *Eglogue* and *Bucolick*" (George Puttenham, *The Art of English Poesy,* 1589); a formal pastoral poem. In one of the first English dictionaries, *A Table Alphabetical* (1604), Robert Cawdrey defines an *eglogue* simply as "a talking together." More specifically, William Webbe calls eclogues "Goteheardes tales, because they bee comonly Dialogues or speeches framed or supposed betweene Sheepeheardes, Neteheardes, Goteheardes, or such like simple men." He continues by saying that although the subject matter pastoral poets "take in hand seemeth commonlie in appearaunce rude and homely, as the usuall talke of simple clownes, yet doo they [poets] indeede utter in the same much pleasaunt and profitable delight," and that although pastoral poets write in "homely manner," yet "indeede with great pythe and learned judgment" (*A Discourse of English Poetry,* 1586).

In content, a Renaissance eclogue follows the literary conventions of the pastoral mode, which derive in large part from such classical poets as "*Theocritus* in Greeke, and . . . *Virgill* in Latin" (Webbe). Their pastoral poems, called idyls and eclogues, served as models for many English poets; and this heritage of classical eclogues, as well as the example of influential Italian poets, made pastoral poetry a respected genre throughout the late sixteenth and early seventeenth centuries. The work that did the most to naturalize the pastoral poem in England was Edmund Spenser's *The Shepherd's Calendar* (1579).

What English poets inherited was a fictive social microcosm with its own setting and characters and its own particular literary formulae and topics. The pastoral tradition delineates the shepherd-speaker of the eclogues as a dweller in an idealized world who guards his flocks carefully, but who has more than ample time to engage in singing matches and debates and in contemplative dialogue. The *locus amoenus* (pleasant or lovely place) is Arcadia (or Eden in the Christian pastoral), a land of endless delights, lush crops, and fair weather.

In form, an eclogue is a quasi-dramatic poem, usually a dialogue; it is often set in a descriptive or narrative frame. In his remarks on pastoral poetry and its adaptability to a protean variety of subjects, Puttenham stresses the dramatic mode of the eclogue. He says classical writers of eclogues attempted "nothing so high" as the writers of tragedy and comedy, but instead "in base and humble stile by manner of Dialogue, uttered the private and familiar talke of the meanest sort of men, as shepheardes, heywards, and such like."

Through the speeches of the eclogue, poets in the *personae* of shepherds discourse on many subjects. As Puttenham says, the "poet devised the *Eglogue* long after the other *dramatick* poems not of purpose to counterfait or represent the rusticall manner of loves and communication, but under the vaile of homely persons and in rude speeches to insinuate and glaunce at greater matters, and such as perchance had not bene safe to have been disclosed in any other sort, which may be perceived by the Eglogues of *Virgill,* in which are treated by figure matters of greater importance then the loves of *Titirus* and *Corydon.*" Puttenham knows, as did the other English poets, that throughout its long history the pastoral eclogue, especially through the influence of Virgil, had been used as a vehicle for much more than the celebration of the "green world," of the simple and good life of the countryside. Michael Drayton, in the preface to his *Pastorals* (1619), says much the same thing in his remark, "The subject of Pastorals, as the language of it[,] ought to be poor, silly [crude], & of the coursest Woofe in appearance. Nevertheless, the most High, and most Noble Matters of the World may bee shaddowed in them, and for certaine sometimes are."

The prologue to a collection of eclogues by Alexander Barclay, published posthumously in 1570, also stresses the variety of subjects traditionally associated with the form:

> That five Egloges this whole treatise doth holde,
> To imitation of other Poetes olde.
> In whiche Egloges shepheardes thou mayst see
> In homely language not passing their degree
> Sometime disputing of courtly misery,
> Sometime of Venus' disceatful tiranny,
> Sometime commending love honest and laudable,
> Sometime despising love false and deceyvable,
> Sometime despising and blaming avarise,
> Sometime exciting vertue to exercise,
> Sometime of warre abhorring the outrage,
> And of the same time the manifolde damage,
> And other matters, as after shall appeare
> To their great pleasure which shall them reade or heare.

As Barclay indicates, the intention of a poet in his eclogues is conditioned by the rhetorical categories of praise ("commending") or blame ("despising").

Many topics are traditional in "the usuall talke" of eclogue poets in their guise as shepherds, particularly the praise of nature, the praise of a beloved (a shepherdess or nymph), or the praise of another worthy person, often an actual person of the contemporary world. The birth of Christ was believed to be an especially appropriate topic for the eclogue. Drayton remarks, for example, that "in the Angels Song to Shepheardes at our Saviours Nativitie Pastorall Poesie seems consecrated" (preface, *Pastorals*). In still other eclogues praise couples with lament for a dead person, imaginary or real (*see* Elegy). The topic of praise for the dead, like that of the beloved, was an established element of the eclogue tradition from its earliest beginnings in the idyls of Theocritus.

The subject matter of English eclogues is not confined to the "private and familiar talke" of shepherds, however. As Drayton had said, eclogues often discourse on "the most High, and most Noble Matters of the World." The inherited classical and Christian tradition invested the English shepherd-speaker with the symbolic roles of archetypal poet and priest. In these roles almost no subject of contemporary life eludes his purview for commentary and for satire; and within a context of simplicity the pastoral poet "shaddowed" the most serious subjects. In other words, in many Renaissance eclogues idyllic descriptions of life in Arcadia are of less importance than those "greater matters" upon which the shepherd-speaker in his roles as poet-singer and "good shepherd" or priest reflects. As poet-singer, he can comment upon the nature and function of poetry, the state of contemporary poetry and poets, and the relationship between art and nature. As the "good shepherd," he can speak of philosophical, social, ethical, and religious matters. From the vantage point of a golden world, he is especially sensitive to abuses in the state and church; he can, in Webbe's words, "enveigh grievously against abuses," and pastoral poems are often heavily satiric (*see* Satire). Thus pastoral poetry meets the Renaissance requirement of teaching by delighting. Puttenham, for example, holds that the eclogue will "enforme morall discipline, for the amendment of mans behaviour."

Beyond its varied subject matter, the English eclogue acquired a complexity and vitality from tensions implied in its essential contrasts—contrasts between the ways of the city and court and those of the country, between the active and contemplative life, and between the cultivated and the simple. The pastoral mode is "a mode for the juxtaposition of contending values and perspectives. . .a critical exploration and counterbalancing of attitudes . . . and experiences" (Cullen). English pastoral poets whose tastes, values, and learning were associated with the center of things, the court and the city, had no real desire to be exiled to the actual countryside. Yet, by donning shepherd's weeds and by entering a golden world of literary convention, the courtly pastoral poet gained the advantage of at least a double perspective upon reality. On the one hand, for example, he could satirize the corruptions of the court and church by extolling the honesty and goodness of the shepherd, and on the other he could make abundantly clear the limited existence and vision of the countryside and hence praise the learning and graces of the court and city. This double perspective also informed the eclogue poet's attitudes towards time, nature, art, and love. The rhetorical feature that perhaps most allows for this double perspective as well as for the poet's freedom to "glaunce" at serious matters in a context of simplicity is that of the eclogue's double speakers and double audiences. One set of speakers and audience is that of the fictive Arcadian world; the other is that of the poet himself and his more sophisticated reading audience.

Despite its adaptability and complexity, however, Renaissance theorists and poets thought of the pastoral poem as a humble kind of lyric poetry. Because of the rustic speaker, decorum (q.v.) required that the style of the eclogue be "homely" or low; and because the rustic setting only allowed the poet to "figure" or "shadow" the "greater matters," the pastoral poem could not be accorded a high rank in the hierarchy of poetic kinds. According to E. K. in his prefatory comments to *The Shepherd's Calendar,* eclogues are a fit kind of poetry for young poets to "trye theyr habilities." Like "young birdes, that be newly crept out of the nest," poets need "first to prove theyr tender wyngs, before they make a greater flyght."

Within the larger history of pastoral literature the quasi-dramatic form of the eclogue is generally regarded as a major formative influence in the development of the formal pastoral play, a distinct kind of play that grew up and flourished in the Renaissance (*see* Pastoral). Most pastoral plays are Italian or French, but there are a few significant examples of the genre in England during the first decades of the seventeenth century. The eclogue made its contribution to this genre during the fifteenth century in Italy when its popularity extended to theatrical presentations in court revels. A dialogue between shepherds, which could be read, could also be staged. The Italian pastoral dramatist Giovanni Baptista Guarini in *Il verato secondo* (1593) recognizes the inherent dramatic nature of the eclogue. He writes, "The eclogue is nothing but a short discussion between shepherds, differing in no other manner from that sort of scene which the Latins call dialogue, except in so far as being whole and independent, possessing within itself both beginning and end" (quoted in Greg).

Bibliography

Martha H. Shackford, "A definition of the Pastoral Idyll," *PMLA,* 19 (1904), 583–92; Walter W. Greg, *Pastoral Poetry and Pastoral Drama*

(1906); Wilfred P. Mustard, "Later Echoes of the Greek Bucolic Poets," *American Journal of Philology,* 30 (1909), 245–83; Herbert E. Cory, "The Golden Age of the Spenserian Pastoral," *PMLA,* 25 (1910), 241–67; Merritt Y. Hughes, "Spenser and the Greek Pastoral Triad," *SP,* 20 (1923), 184–215; E. K. Chambers, "The English Pastoral," *Sir Thomas Wyatt and Some Collected Studies* (1933), pp. 146–80; Frank Kermode, ed., "Introduction," *English Pastoral Poetry* (1952), pp. 11–44; Hallett Smith, "Pastoral Poetry," *Elizabethan Poetry* (1952), pp. 1–63; Ernst R. Curtius, "The Ideal Landscape," *European Literature and the Latin Middle Ages,* trans. Willard R. Trask (1953), pp. 183–202; Bruno Snell, *The Discovery of the Mind: The Greek Origins of European Thought,* trans. T. G. Rosenmeyer (1960); S. K. Heninger, Jr., "The Renaissance Perversion of Pastoral," *JHI,* 22 (1961), 254–61; Edward William Tayler, *Nature and Art in Renaissance Literature* (1964); W. Leonard Grant, *Neo-Latin Literature and the Pastoral* (1965); Richard Cody, *The Landscape of the Mind: Pastoralism and Platonic Theory in Tasso's "Aminta" and Shakespeare's Early Comedies* (1969); Joan Grundy, "Pastoral Poetry," *The Spenserian Poets* (1969), pp. 72–106; Harry Levin, *The Myth of the Golden Age in the Renaissance* (1969); Thomas G. Rosenmeyer, *The Green Cabinet: Theocritus and the European Pastoral Lyric* (1969); Patrick Cullen, *Spenser, Marvell, and Renaissance Pastoral* (1970); Donald M. Friedman, *Marvell's Pastoral Art* (1970); Peter V. Marinelli, *Pastoral* (1971); Harold E. Toliver, *Pastoral Forms and Attitudes* (1971); Paul Alpers, "The Eclogue Tradition and the Nature of Pastoral," *CE,* 34 (1972), 352–71; Charles W. Hieatt, "The Integrity of Pastoral: A Basis for Definition," *Genre,* 5 (1972), 1–30; Laurence Lerner, *The Uses of Nostalgia: Studies in Pastoral Poetry* (1972); Niels Bugge Hansen, *That pleasant place: The Representation of Ideal Landscape in English Literature from the 14th to the 17th Century* (1973); Raymond Williams, "Pastoral and Counter-Pastoral," *The Country and the City* (1973), pp. 13–34; Renato Poggioli, *The Oaten Flute: Essays on Pastoral Poetry and the Pastoral Ideal* (1975); Paul Alpers, *The Singer of Eclogues* (1979); Marion Meilaender, "Marvell's Pastoral Poetry: Fullfillment of a Tradition," *Genre,* 12 (1979), 181–201; Joseph Wittreich, "From Pastoral to Prophecy: The Genres of *Lycidas,*" *MiltonS,* 13 (1979), 59–80.

Elegy:

"A mournful song used at funeralls" (Henry Cockeram, *The English Dictionary*, 1623). More largely a Renaissance elegy was a lyric meditation associated with a tone of lament on subjects as various as love, friendship, and death. Sometimes the term was applied by poets to sensuous love poetry in the Ovidian manner.

The classical elegy, as opposed to the Renaissance kind, is identified by its medium, the elegiac distich, a pair of unrhymed dactylic lines, the first line of which is a hexameter of six long syllables and the second of which is, roughly, a pentameter line of five long syllables (*see* Couplet). The Latin elegus means simply one distich of a dactylic hexameter line followed by a pentameter line. George Puttenham calls these quantitative verses "a limping Pentameter after a lustie Exameter" (*The Art of English Poesy*, 1589).

The elegiac distich was used for a wide variety of poetry in classical Rome; but, if there was a predominant theme in Latin poems written in the elegiac distich, it was that of love. Catullus, for example, uses the elegiac distich for a cycle of short poems centered upon the poet's relationship with his mistress, and Ovid makes the elegiac distich the medium for poetry in a variety of genres (*Heroides, Ars amatoria, Amores, Tristia*) in all of which the dominating theme is love.

Some English poets attempted to render the Latin elegiac distich in English quantitative verse, but they met with little success (*see* Vulgar language). Samuel Daniel in *A Defense of Rhyme* (1603) dismisses their effort as a failure, commenting that their imitations are "no other than our old accustomed measure of five feet." And there does seem to be a tacit response by poets to the Latin elegiac distich that equates it with the effects of the rhymed pentameter couplet. A rhymed pair of verses rendered the two lines of the elegiac distich, and a vague tradition made the five-stress line in English the rough equivalent of the Latin dactylic hexameter. Christopher Marlowe translates Ovid's elegiacs of the *Amores* into closed couplets, and many other, though not all, English elegies use the rhymed pentameter couplet. Some French poets of the sixteenth century also used the pentameter couplet as the equivalent of the elegiac distich, and a contemporary Italian critic says the elegy is characterized by its own rather free form of pentameter (Julius Caesar Scaliger, *Poetices libri septem,* 1561).

It was the Ovidian treatment of love in the elegiac distich that accounts primarily for a group of "sportive" love poems called elegies by their authors. With the Ovidian model in mind William Webbe associates the elegy with "light matters" and "much pleasant daliance" (*A Discourse of English Poetry,* 1586). Theoretically, however, the subject matter of the elegy was no more restricted for English poets than had been the use of the elegiac distich by their Latin and Greek models; and English poets assign the title *elegy* to almost any kind of lyric meditation. Shakespeare, for example, has the lovesick Orlando hang "elegies on brambles—all, forsooth, deifying the name of Rosalind" in *As You Like It* (c. 1599). Edmund Spenser mourns the loss of friends in *Daphnaida: An Elegie upon the death of the noble and virtuous Douglas Howard* (1591) and in *Astrophel: A Pastorall Elegie* (1595) written to commemorate the death of Sir Philip Sidney. Sir John Davies's *Nosce Teipsum in Two Elegies* (1599) is a disquisition on the human soul and its attributes. Michael Drayton's *Elegies upon Sundry Occasions* (1627) includes *To Henry Reynolds, Esquire, of Poets & Poesie,* which is a critical estimate of important writers, living and dead.

A tradition that identified the origin of the elegiac distich with lamentation controlled the tone of many Renaissance elegies. Such a tradition had its *locus classicus* for Renaissance writers in the assertion by Horace in the *Ars poetica* (11, 75–78) that the elegiac distich had its genesis in an expression of sorrow (*querimonia*). Sidney rehearses the Horatian formula when he refers to "the lamenting Elegiack, which in a kinde hart would moove rather pitty then blame, who bewailes with the great Philosopher *Heraclitus* the weakenes of mankind, and the wretchednes of the world" (*An Apology for Poetry,* 1595). The "Englished" elegy became in one degree or another, a lyric of lament, whether its subject was the weakness of all mankind, the problems of love, or the death of a single person. Puttenham associates the classical "elegiack" with poets "who sought the favor of faire Ladies, and coveted to bemone their estates at large & the perplexities of love in certain pitious verse." Sir John Harington, reviewing contemporary practice, says of the elegy that "it is still mourning" (*A Brief Apology for Poetry,* 1591). Francis Meres identifies the elegy with poets who "bewaile and bemoane the perplexities of Love" (*Palladis Tamia,* 1598).

In its association with lament, the term *elegy* became a classical label for a poem written in a native, generic tradition, the complaint (q.v.). George Gascoigne, in the dedicatory letter to his *Complaint of Philomene* (1576) calls the poem "an Elegye or sorrowefull song." Michael Drayton's sonnet cycle *Idea's Mirror* (1594) also identifies the elegy with the complaint:

"Reade heere, (sweet Mayd) the story of my wo . . . My lives complaint in doleful Elegies."

The Renaissance elegy finds its sanction for the use of the pastoral mode in traditions of the classical eclogue (q.v.) which often made lamentation its dominant theme. The archetype for the pastoral elegy is the first *Idyl* of the Greek poet Theocritus: here a poet-speaker laments the early death of another poet, young Daphnis, with the fiction that Thyrsis, who sings the lament, was, as Daphnis had been before him, the most famous of the rustic poets. Following Theocritus, bucolic poets of the Alexandrine age composed other lamentative eclogues, particularly Bion's *Lament for Adonis* and Moschus's lament for his fellow-poet, *Lament for Bion,* which extended the use of pastoral imagery to mourn the death of a real person. Virgil's "lofty" Latin eclogues (themselves often imitative of Theocritus and the other Greek bucolic poets) almost defined the nature of the pastoral elegy as Renaissance writers came to think of it. Virgil's *Eclogue X,* for example, is a love lament in imitation of Theocritus's *Idyl I.* It employs motifs later poets accepted as conventional: an invocation to the Sicilian muse; the absence of nymphs from their accustomed haunts; the sympathetic lamentation of nature; a procession of mourners. Other traditional motifs include: "with fairest flowers . . . I'll sweeten thy sad grave"; "the riddle of this painful earth" (resentment at cruel fate that blasts life in the bud); and "peace, peace! he is not dead."

A number of English elegies, particularly memorial verses on the death of the great, subordinated lamentation to celebration. As occasional poetry for a ceremonial event, such as a funeral, elegies are firmly linked to the rhetorical controls of the epideictic kinds (*see* Epideictic rhetoric). While lament is part of their intention, such elegies typically follow a pattern of praise, lament, and consolation, with both praise and consolation overshadowing lamentation.

Traditionally (in a form going back to funeral songs described by Greek rhetoricians) the funeral oration or poem was divided into three main sections: the *epainos* (praise of the individual), the *threnos* (song of lament), and *paramuthia* (the consolation). Scaliger, whose treatises on poetry were well known to many English writers, reviews the dual possibility of the elegy—its potential emphasis upon lament or upon celebration. The material of the elegy, he says, may be either "lugubrious" as in the commiserations of lovers, or "celebratory," as in songs of thanks or of successful amatory conquest. To eternize their subject, poets tended to follow the topics of praise that were outlined in the rhetoric books: the birth and infancy of the subject; childhood; adolescence; manhood; old age; and circumstances of death. The four virtues of prudence, temperance, fortitude, and justice received particular attention as appropriate for eulogy; while chief among the topics of consolation were variations on such formulae as: "he is not dead"; "death is common to all"; "he was too good for us";

"he died for our sins"; and "immoderate mourning is not natural."

It was only fitfully that the funeral or memorial elegy became primarily a poem of lamentation or, as Cockeram says above, "a mourneful song used at funeralls." Some hint of this increasingly restrictive conception of the elegy can be found in the contrasts between Puttenham's words in 1589 and those of Izaak Walton in 1633. Puttenham assumes that in classical practice funeral songs were called "Epicedia if they were song by many, and Monodia if they were uttered by one alone." He does not think of "the doleful ditty" as an elegy. But the posthumous 1633 edition of John Donne's poetry, *Poems with Elegies on the Author's Death,* entitles one section of this volume *Epicedes and Obsequies,* while many of the individual poems have the term *elegy* in their titles. Izaak Walton's *An Elegie upon Dr. Donne* in this collection avoids panegyric and is confined to lamentation with the statement that he would "write no *Encomium,* but an *Elegie.*"

Bibliography

James Holly Hanford, "The Pastoral Elegy and Milton's *Lycidas," PMLA,* 25 (1910), 403–47; George Norlin, "The Conventions of the Pastoral Elegy," *American Journal of Philology,* 32 (1911), 294–312; Pauline Aiken, *The Influence of the Latin Elegists on English Lyric Poetry 1600–1650* (1932); Thomas P. Harrison, Jr., "Spenser and the Earlier Pastoral Elegy," *Texas Studies in English,* 13 (1933), 36–53; Francis W. Weitzmann, "Notes on the Elizabethan *Elegie," PMLA,* 50 (1935), 435–43; Thomas P. Harrison, ed., "Introduction," *The Pastoral Elegy: An Anthology* (1939), pp. 1–24; Kathryn Anderson McEuen, *Classical Influence upon the Tribe of Ben* (1939); Ruth Wallerstein, "The Laureate Hearse," *Studies in Seventeeth-Century Poetic* (1950), pp. 3–148; A. L. Bennett, "The Principal Rhetorical Conventions in the Renaissance Personal Elegy," *SP,* 51 (1954), 107–26; J. B. Leishman, "Epigrams, Elegies, Satires, Verse Letters," *The Monarch of Wit* (3rd ed., 1957), pp. 50–106; O. B. Hardison, Jr., "The Topics of Elegy," *The Enduring Monument* (1962), pp. 113–62; W. Leonard Grant, *Neo-Latin Literature and the Pastoral* (1965); Robert Ralston Cawley, "The Elegy" and "Peacham and the Elegy," *Henry Peacham: His Contribution to English Poetry* (1971), pp. 69–113; R. J. Lyall, "Tradition and Innovation in Alexander Barclay's 'Towre of Vertue and Honoure,' " *RES,* 23 (1972), 1–18; Avon Jack Murphy, "The Critical Elegy of Earlier Seventeenth-Century England," *Genre,* 5 (1972), 75–105; C. W. Jentoft, "Surrey's Five Elegies: Rhetoric, Structure, and the Poetry of Praise," *PMLA,* 91 (1976), 23–32; Ellen Zetrel Lambert, *Placing Sorrow: A Study of the Pastoral Elegy Convention from Theocritus to Milton* (1976); Alan Armstrong, "The Apprenticeship of John Donne: Ovid and the *Elegies," ELH,* 44 (1977), 419–42; Alan J. Peacock, "Ben Jonson's *Elegies* and Roman Elegy," *Etudes Anglaises,* 32 (1979), 20–27.

Elocutio:

"That part of Rhetorique whereby not onely wordes are aptly used, but also sentences are in right order framed. . . . Elocucion getteth wordes to set furthe invencion, & with suche beautie commendeth the matter, that reason seemeth to be clad in purple"; it is "gorgious talke" to "tell our conceipte [idea]" (Thomas Wilson, *The Art of Rhetoric,* 1553). The third in the traditional quintet of arts which comprised the skill of the orator (invention, disposition, elocution, memory, and delivery), *elocutio* addressed itself to questions of style (*see* Rhetoric).

The Renaissance emphasis upon style is unparalleled in Western history. To sixteenth-century rhetoricians, the efficacy of an artful style is associated with civilization itself. Puttenham, equating the poet with the orator, says that it was he "that by good & pleasant perswasions first reduced the wilde and beastly people into publicke societies and civilitie of life, insinuating unto them, under fictions with sweete and coloured speeches, many wholesome lessons and doctrines" (*The Art of English Poesy,* 1589). Thomas Lodge is even more emphatic about the power of *elocutio:* "A man may baule till his voice be hoarse, exhort with teares till his tongue ake and his eyes be drie, repeate that hee woulde perswade, till his stalenes dooth secretlie call for a Cloake bagge, and yet move no more then if he had been all that while mute, if his speech be not seasoned with eloquence, and adorned with elocutions assistance" (*The Anatomy of Absurdity,* 1589).

Thomas Wilson, following Quintilian, divides the art of *elocutio* into four parts: "plainess" (using correct English words); "apteness" or perspicuity (the appropriate choice of words for one's subject); "composicion" (ordering words and clauses) and "exornation" or embellishment (the use of the figures of speech, "the coloures of Rhetorique"). Of these the first three are assumed to be necessary but ready accomplishments; but it is by the polish and embellishment of his style that the speaker or writer recommends himself in his proper character.

A figure of speech is any artful deviation from a supposed flow of careless, everyday speech. This definition, familiar to Renaissance writers, is derived from Quintilian who says a figure is "any deviation, either in thought or expression, from the ordinary and simple method of speaking, a change analogous to the different positions our bodies assume when we sit down, lie down, or look back" *(Institutio oratoria,* IX, I, 10, trans. John S. Watson). The most widely used classical handbook in Renaissance schools, *Rhetorica ad Herennium,* required students to learn some sixty-five figures. Other rhetorics pushed the number to around two hundred. The figures were closely connected with the process of invention, of finding and elaborating ideas. They were not considered to be mere decorative additions to expression, but the pattern of thought itself. Thus rhetoricians define the figures as giving clarity and liveliness to thought. They are the primary means to invest language with the power to move and persuade a popular audience. The affection of the rhetoricians for the figures is ardent. Henry Peacham says they are "the principal instruments" by which eloquence "allureth" men's "minds and affections." They are "as stars to give light, as cordials to comfort, as harmony to delight, as pitiful spectacles to move sorrowfull passions, and as orient colours to beautifie reason." To Thomas Wilson they are "as starres" or "floures in a garden."

Not all rhetoricians describe and classify the figures in identical ways. Peacham's *The Garden of Eloquence,* 1593 edition, is used here to demonstrate the close examination of the figures that Renaissance rhetoricians encouraged. *The Garden of Eloquence* itself makes use of citations from many Latin sources, particularly the works of Quintilian, Cicero, and the *Ad Herennium;* many of these citations were probably found by Peacham in the earlier sixteenth-century compilations, Joannes Susenbrotus's *Epitome troporum ac schematum* (1540) and Erasmus's *De copia.*

Peacham is typical and traditional when he divides the figures into two large classes: the tropes and the schemes *(schemate).* A trope "translates" a word or sentence from one signification to another; a scheme is a change in word order or arrangement of ideas.

The tropes of words are *metaphor, onomatopoeia, catachresis, synecdoche, metonymia, antonomasia, metalepsis,* and *antiphrasis.* Peacham devotes twelve closely written pages to the word *metaphor* alone, considering the places from "whence translations may be taken": from the senses (by the sense of tasting "we may by sweetnesse signifie pleasure, by bitternesse griefe of mind, or crueltie of speech, and by sowernesse severitie"); from the living to things without life ("by this place the sea is sayd to swallow, the wind or tempests to rage, the frost to bite, the ground to thirst"); or from the four elements ("with translations taken from the nature and propertie of fire we say a man of an inflamed mind, the flaming desire of malice doth seldome die till it be quenched with blood, kindle not wrath, lest thou beest not able to quench it: an evill name is the smoke of sinne").

Onomatopoeia, the second trope of words, he defines as a "forme of speech whereby the Orator or speaker maketh and faineth a name to something, imitating the sound or voyce of that it signifieth, or else whereby he affecteth a word derived from the name of a person, or from the originall of the thing which it doth expresse." His examples of imitation of sound include "a hurliburly, signifying a tumult or uprore: likewise, rushing, lumbring, ratling, blustring." *Catachresis* is "a forme of speech whereby the speaker or writer wanting a proper word, borroweth the next or the likest to the thing that he would signifie. . . .An example of Moses, The drinke, the pure blood of the grapes, here the prophet putteth this word blood for juyce." Peacham defines *synecdoche* as "an understanding, and it is a forme of speech by which the Orator signifieth more or lesse by a word, which the proper signification doth not expresse: and it is by putting the whole for the part, or the part for the whole. . . . An example of the holy Scriptures: All the world came to heare the wisdome of Salomon, understanding a great part of the world, and not all the world, as it is expressed." *Metonimia* is "called of the Latines Transnominatio"; "it is a forme of speech, wherby the Orator putteth one thing for another, which by nature are nigh knit together." In this manner "we use to put the chaine for bondage, the key for office, the rod for correction, and the crosse for persecution." *Antonomasia* is "a forme of speech by which the Orator for a proper name putteth another, as some name of dignity, office, profession, science or trade. By this figure when the Orator speaketh to a king or a Prince, he saith, your Grace, your Highnesse, or your Majestie: to a Nobleman, your Lordship, your Honor." By this figure, says Peacham, the orator "boweth (as it were) the knee of his speech." *Metalepsis* is a figure by which the speaker "in one word expressed, signifieth another word or thing removed from it by certaine degrees. Virgil by eares of corne signifieth sommers, & by sommers, yeares." *Antiphrasis* is especially valuable "to reprehend vice and mock folly." It is "a forme of speech which by a word exprest doth signifie the contrary: as when the speaker sayth, wisely or wittily, understanding the contrary. Also to say, You are alwayes my friend, meaning, mine enemie."

Under the tropes of sentences, Peacham places ten figures: *allegoria, aenigma, paroemia, hyperbole, asteismus, ironia, charientismus, sarcasmus, mycterismus,* and *diasyrmus. Allegoria* is "a forme of speech which expresseth one thing in words, and another in sense"; "an Allegorie is called a continued Metaphore" (*see* Allegory). An *aenigma* is a kind of allegory "which for the darknesse, the sense may hardly be gathered." *Paroemia* is the proverb, "a sentence or forme of speech much used, and commonly knowen"; it must be "witty" and "well proportioned" and "commended by antiquitie and learning." *Hyperbole* is "a sentence or saying surmounting the truth onely for the cause of increasing or diminishing, not with the purpose to deceive by speaking untruly." *Asteismus* is "a wittie jesting in civill manner, and gracing of speech with some merie conceipt: it is usually taken for any mirth or pleasant speech which is voyd of rusticall simplicitie & rudenesse." *Ironia* is a trope in which "one contrarie [meaning] is understood by another. . . . to reprove by derision . . . and also to jest and move mirth by opposing contraries." *Charientismus* is "a forme of speech which mitigateth hard matters with pleasant words": "Salomon commendeth that answer which may turne away displeasure and pacifie wrath." In contrast, *sarcasmus* is "a bitter kind of derision, most commonly used of an enemie"; "this figure is like to most bitter corrections in Physicke." *Mycterismus* is "a privie kind of mocke . . . yet not so privie but that it may well be perceived." An example: "To one that demanded of Demonax the philosopher if Philosophers did use to eate sweet cakes, Demonax made this answer, Doest thou thinke (quoth he) that bees gather their hony for fooles onely?" Lastly, *diasyrmus* is "a Trope by which the arguments of an adversarie are either depraved or rejected." This figure is "for the most part made either by some base similitude, or by some ridiculous example, to which the adversaries objection or argument is compared."

In contrast to the limited number of tropes, there are many schemes. The schemes, which involve a deviation from the ordinary pattern or arrangement of words and ideas, are divided by Peacham into three orders. The first order pertains more to words than to sentences. It is significant to the Renaissance concern with effects upon style that Peacham associates the figures of the first order with "harmonie and pleasant proportion," in contrast to "gravitie and dignitie." Here are the figures of repetition "by which one word may . . . be rehearsed in diverse clauses, and may ten maner of wayes be pleasantly repeated: and likewise one and the same letter by Paroemion [alliteration] may be repeated in the beginning of diverse words." *Epanaphora* is a figure of repetition, for example, in which diverse clauses begin with the same word: "The Lord sitteth above the water floods. The Lord remaineth a king for ever. The Lord shall give strength unto his people. The Lord shall give his people the blessing of peace." The figures of omission also belong to Peacham's first order of schemes. In these figures "is some word omitted, which a full construction doth require, which notwithstanding hath by the omission a pleasant grace of beautie." The figures of omission include, for example, *asyndeton* "which keepeth the parts of speech together without the helpe of any conjunction": "An example of Caesar, where he saith, I came, I saw, I overcame." The figures of conjunction are also in the first order; these figures "do joyne the parts of our speech together, either by conjunction of Grammer, or by similitude of sound." *Homeoptoton* is a figure of conjunction; it is a "setting of diverse nownes in one sentence which ende alike with the same letter or same syllable: thus. We came into Cilicia, and then spied out Africa: and after that came with his armie into Sardinia." The last group of schemes in the first order are the "figures of separation"; these are schemes that "do separate words & clauses one from another, either by distinguishing the sound, or by separating the sense." Peacham puts the figure *compar* in this class: "a forme of speech which maketh the members of an oration to be almost of a just number of sillables, yet the equalitie of those members or parts, are not to be measured upon our fingers, as if they were verses, but to bee tried by a secret sence of the eare." An example of the figure is: "See that equitié flow as the water, and righteousnesse as a mightie streame."

The second order of schemes includes the "figures of sentences" or the figures of affection (passion). These are contrasted with the figures of words in the first order: "the figures of wordes are as it were effeminate, and musicall, the figures of sentences are manly, and martiall." Again the order is broken down into four groups: figures of exclamation, figures of moderation, figures of consultation, and figures of concession. Under the figures of exclamation are such figures as *ecphonesis* ("a forme of speech by which the orator . . . bursteth forth into an exclamation or outcrie, signifying thereby the vehement affection or passion of his mind. . . . O Death, where is thy sting? O Grave where is thy victorie?"); *eulogia* ("a forme of speech by which the Orator pronounceth a blessing uppon some person for the goodnesse that is in him or her"); *mempsis* ("a forme of speech by which the Orator maketh a complaint, and craveth helpe"); *threnos* ("by which the Orator lamenteth some person or people for the miserie they suffer, or the speaker his owne calamitie. . . . Why died not I in the birth? Why did not I perish as soone as I came out of the wombe?"); *euche* ("a solemne promise or vow"); *thaumasmus* ("by which the Orator declareth how much hee marvelleth at some thing"); or *paeanismus* ("the speaker useth to expresse his joy, either for the cause of some good thing obtained, or some evil avoyded").

The figures of moderation are less passionate than those of exclamation. Peacham includes figures like *martyria* ("a forme of speech by which the Orator or Speaker confirmeth some thing by his own experience") and *euphemismus* ("a Prognostication of good") in this category.

The figures of consultation are those which "by reason of their forme and interrogation seeme to consult and deliberate with the hearers." The figures of this order are of "great strength and force," says Peacham. They are "mighty, and also most apt to confirme or confute, to praise or dispraise, to accuse or defend, and briefly they are most fit formes for a most earnest and vehement oration." These would include *interrogatio* ("a demaunding or asking . . . And as the wise men did, saying: Where is he that is borne king of the Jewes?"); *erotema* ("by which the Orator doth affirme or deny something strongly. An example of Esay: Are you not children of Adultery and a seed of dissimulation?") and *aporia* ("by which the speaker sheweth that he doubteth, either where to begin for the multitude of matters or what to do or say in some strange and doubtfull thing").

The last group in the "figures of affections or schemes of sentences" is made up of figures of permission, "such formes of speech as do after a sort commit the cause in hand ... to the consideration and judgments of others." These are figures such as *synchoresis* ("a forme of speech by which the Orator trusting strongly to his cause, giveth leave to the Judges or his adversaries, to consider of it with indifferencie. . . . An example of Cicero: But now Judges I leave the whole, and most lawfull right of my cause, which I have declared, and commit it unto you to judge and determine it, as reason and wisedome shall direct you"), and *apostrophe* ("by which the Orator turneth suddenly from the former frame of his speech to another").

The Garden of Eloquence defines a third order of rhetorical schemes that, like those above, are considered figures of sentences; but the figures of the third order are particularly associated with amplification (*see* Copia), and some rhetoric books take them up before a detailed discussion of other schemes. Wilson, for example, following Quintilian, discusses amplification before he describes the other figures. In this third order Peacham describes four categories of figures "which for the most part do both amplifie and garnish matters, and causes." They are "artificiall and cunning instruments apt and ready." Amplification itself is a figure, "devised to increase causes and to augment the Oration with words and sentences" to move an audience. To amplify is "a singular art, and mighty to delight and perswade the mindes of men." The matters of amplification ought to be "great, excellent, good, or notorious, evill, cruel, horrible, marvellous, pleasant, or pittifull: after which may follow and that worthily, desire, hatred, feare, admiration, hope, gladnesse, mirth, pittie, weeping, and such like affections."

The four groups into which the figures of amplification are divided are: distribution, description, comparison, and collection. Distribution includes those figures by which we "dilate and spread abroad the generall kinde, by reckoning up the speciall kindes, the whole by dividing it into parts, and the subject by rehearsing the accidents." These are, in a general way, the figures of analysis such as *diaeresis* ("which divideth the generall kind into the special kinds. . . . whereof this saying of Job may be an example: Aske the cattaile, and they shall inform thee, the fowles of the aire & they shall tel thee, the increase of the earth, and it shal shew thee, or the fishes of the sea, and they shal certifie thee") and *symphoresis* ("otherwise Congeries . . . by which the Orator doth multiply and heape manie words together, signifying diverse things of like nature. An example of the Scripture: Thus all thinges were mixed together with blood, manslaughter, theft, and deceit, corruption, and unfaithfulnesse, sedition, perjury, disquieting of good men, unthankfulnesse, defiling of soules, changing of byrth, disorder in marriage, adultry, and uncleannesse").

The second of the four groups of schemes assigned to amplification is *descriptio,* "when the Orator by a diligent gathering together of circumstances, and by a fit and naturall application of them, doth expresse and set forth a thing so plainly and lively, that it seemeth rather painted in tables, then declared with words." Here belong great figures like *prosographia* (by which the "very person of a man as of a fained, is by his form, nature, maners, studies, doings, affections, and such other circumstances" set before the "eies of the hearer"); *mimesis* ("whereby the Orator counterfaiteth not onely what one said, but also his utterance, pronunciation, and gesture, imitating every thing as it was"); *topographia* (q.v.) ("an evident and true description of a place"); and *icon* ("a forme of speech which painteth out the image of a person or thing, by comparing forme with forme, qualitie with qualitie, and one likenesse with another"). Here also are the *epithet, periphrasis, digression,* and *encomium.*

Also under amplification is the category of figures of comparison. *Comparatio* may "stand as a generall head and principall of many figures, but namely of those which do tend . . . to amplifie or diminish by forme of comparisen, as either from the greater to the lesse, from the lesse to the greater, from equall to equall, or by opposition of contraries." This class includes figures such as *antithesis, similitude,* and *auxesis* ("by which the Orator amplifieth by putting a greater word for a lesse, as to call a proude man Lucifer").

The last of the "four streams of copious eloquence" which Peacham locates under amplification is that of *collectio* so called because such figures leave the sense to be "collected" by the hearer. *Collectio* includes such figures as *metastasis* ("by which we turne backe those thinges that are objected against us, to them which laid them to us"); *procatalepsis* ("by which the Orator, perceiving aforehand what might be objected against him, and hurt him, doth confute it before it be spoken"); *paradigma* ("the same which the Latines call Exemplum and we in English an example, and in Rhetoricke it is called the rehearsall of a deede or saying past and applying of it to our purpose, whereof there be two kindes, the one true which is taken from Chronicles & histories of credit. . . . The other kinde of example is fained by Poets and inventors of fables for delectations sake"); *exegesis* ("an added interpretation"); *exposition* ("when we abide still in one place, and yet seeme to speake diverse things, many times repeating one sentence [idea] but yet with other words, sentences . . . and figures"); and *sententia* (q.v.).

Bibliography

Miriam Joseph Rauh, *Shakespeare's Use of the Arts of Language* (1947); Rosemond Tuve, *Elizabethan and Metaphysical Imagery* (1947); Richard A. Lanham, *A Handlist of Rhetorical Terms* (1968); Lee A. Sonnino, *A Handbook to Sixteenth-Century Rhetoric* (1968); Edward P. J. Corbett, "Style," *Classical Rhetoric for the Modern Student* (2nd ed., 1971), pp. 414–593; Warren Taylor, *Tudor Figures of Rhetoric* (1972); Daniel Javitch, *Poetry and Courtliness in Renaissance England* (1978), pp. 50–75; Barbara K. Lewalski, "The Poetic Texture of Scripture: Tropes and Figures for the Religious Lyric," *Protestant Poetics and the Seventeeth-Century Religious Lyric* (1979), pp. 72–110.

Emblem:

"A sweet and morall Symbole, which consists of picture and words, by which some weighty sentence [thought] is declared" (Thomas Blount in his translation of a French work by Henri Estienne, *The Art of Making Devices,* 1646); a combination of a motto, picture, and short poem, which together expounded a moral or ethical theme.

In testimony to the force of the visual image as a vehicle for serious instruction, Francis Bacon says, "Emblem reduceth conceits intellectual to images sensible, which strike the memory more" (*De augmentis scientiarum,* 1640). Appearing in collections known as emblem books, emblem poems were a kind of Renaissance pictorial poetry which welded the ancient art of poetry to the new art of engraving. Although emblem books were more numerous on the continent than in England, emblem poetry attracted English poets in the late sixteenth century and remained popular well into the seventeenth century.

English writers used the word *emblem* variously. Sometimes it referred to the picture alone; Francis Quarles, for example, in *To the Reader* of his *Emblems* (1635) writes, "An Embleme is but a silent Parable," At other times *emblem* referred to both the picture and the accompanying motto and explanatory poem as it does in Blount's definition above.

All three components—the picture, the motto (the word or *vox*), and the poetic text—were considered essential to emblem poetry. Without the text, the pictures were "dumb showes" or "dumb figures"; without the woodcut or engraving, poetic texts were "naked emblems." The physical eyes were to work with the "eye" of the mind so that the reader might profit from the double medium of picture and poetry. Neither the picture nor the poem could be an extraneous ornament without destroying the serious intention of the emblem poet. George Wither tells his readers, for example, that when they have "heeded" the pictures with their "*Eyes of sense,*" they should then "Consider, what may gather'd be from thence, / And, what your *Eye of Understanding* sees" (*A Collection of Emblems,* 1635). And in an

86

injunction to readers in his translation of a French emblem book in 1633, Henry Hawkins points to the close connection between image and language (and in a larger sense between the arts of painting and poetry in the Renaissance; *see* Ut pictura poesis). Hawkins says,"If you eye wel and marke these silent Poesies, give eare to these speaking pictures."

The first emblem book, *Emblemata* (1531), a Latin work by the Venetian lawyer Andrea Alciati, established the pattern of three components and the tight relationship between picture and poetry for all Renaissance emblem books. Written in part under the influence of a contemporary interest in Egyptian hieroglyphics and the pseudoscience that surrounded them, Alciati's emblem book went through countless editions and served as a principal model for imitation by later writers; its woodcuts were often borrowed and given new poetic texts.

The motto above the picture is a kind of label announcing the meaning of an emblem poem. Single words may express some virtue or vice to be elaborated upon by picture and poem. Frequently classical tags or proverbs serve as mottoes. For example, one of Alciati's four-line poems and its woodcut, Aeneas carrying his father Anchises out of burning Troy, develops the motto *Pietas filiorum in parentis;* and one of Wither's couplets above a picture of a prince set against a detailed symbolic background reads, "A Princes most ennobling Parts, / Are Skill in Armes, and Love to Arts."

The picture beneath the motto is always symbolic, not naturalistic. The picture may be relatively simple, showing an object or a personification, or it may be highly complicated, such as a detailed landscape scene. The picture may also suggest a narrative. Classical tales were frequent subjects for allegories in emblem books. The narrative scenes usually depict events that could not possibly subsist together at one time; but in such pictures it is the symbolic value of the many details that matters, not verisimilitude to a given dramatic moment. Generally speaking, the more complicated the picture in its details, the more necessary it is for the poem to explicate the symbolism of the objects or the events of the picture. Something of the wide range of possible subject matter for pictures is suggested in the prefatory remarks of the first English emblem book, *A Choice of Emblems* (1586) by Geoffrey Whitney. Whitney claims that his emblems are of three kinds: *"Historicall,* as representing the actes of some noble persons, being matter of historie. *Naturall,* as in expressing the natures of creatures, for example, the love of the yonge Storkes, to the oulde, or of suche like. *Morall,* pertaining to vertue and instruction of life, which is the chiefe of the three, and the other two maye bee in some sorte drawen into this head. For, all doe tende unto discipline, and morall preceptes of living." Sometimes the relationship between the picture and the word is an intrinsic one, as in the case of a picture of a skull; at other times the relationship is arbitrary and assigned by the emblem writer. Over the years several emblem writers used the same plates but gave different meanings and applications to the pictures.

Printed beneath the picture is the poem. Most of the poems are relatively short, often an epigram (q.v.) or a sonnet (q.v.). Whatever its length, the poem explicates the picture or makes an application of the moral idea, or does both. The symbolic value of details that might not be readily understood in a complicated picture and even the highly unusual significance of a fairly simple picture are clarified in the poetic text. Almost without fail the poem, as Whitney says, leaves the reader with "morall preceptes of living," or, in the words of Wither, a "wholsome nourishment to strengthen the constitution of a Good-Life." Occasionally some emblem writers added a second, and longer, poem or wrote a prose commentary to elaborate even further on the moral meaning that the reader was to "see" on the page.

For all Renaissance poets, nature was itself a kind of emblem book and each event of history a kind of symbol, all inscribed by the Creator with meanings that the diligent might discover. Francis Quarles repeats this belief when, in defending the symbolic profundity of his *Emblems,* he says, "And, indeed, what are the Heavens, the Earth, nay every creature, but Hierogliphicks and Emblemes of His Glory." Thus Renaissance readers of emblem books were asked to discover correspondences between visual images and moral ideas, which at first viewing might seem to have little, if anything, to do with each other. Emblematists depended on their readers to measure the importance of an object or a scene by its symbolic meaning, not by the nature of the thing itself. To follow an emblem writer through his poetic exposition of the relationship between the picture and its significances required "wit" or intelligence.

Bibliography

E. N. S. Thompson, "Emblem Book," *Literary Bypaths of the Renaissance* (1924), pp. 29–67; Erwin Panofsky, *Studies in Iconology: Humanistic Themes in the Art of the Renaissance* (1939); D. J. Gordon, "The Imagery of Ben Jonson's *The Masque of Blacknesse* and *The Masque of Beautie*," *JWCI,* 6 (1943), 122–41; D. J. Gordon, "*Hymenaei:* Ben Jonson's Masque of Union," *JWCI,* 8 (1945), 107–45; Henri Stegemeier, "Problems in Emblem Literature," *JEGP,* 45 (1946), 26–37; Samuel C. Chew, *The Virtues Reconciled: An Iconographic Study* (1947); Rosemary Freeman, *English Emblem Books* (1948); E. H. Gombrich, " 'Icones Symbolicae,' The Visual Image in Neoplatonic Thought," *JWCI,* 11 (1948), 163–92; Walter J. Ong, "From Allegory to Diagram in the Renaissance Mind: A Study in the Significance of the Allegorical Tableau," *JAAC,* 17 (1959), 423–40; Robert J. Clements, *Picta Poesis: Literary and Humanistic Theory in Renaissance Emblem Books*

(1960); Samuel C. Chew, *The Pilgrimage of Life* (1962); Mario Praz, *Studies in Seventeenth-Century Imagery* (2nd. ed., 1964); Dieter Mehl, *The Elizabethan Dumb Show* (1966); Lloyd Goldman, "Samuel Daniel's *Delia* and the Emblem Tradition," *JEGP*, 67 (1968), 49–63; Hessel Miedema, "The term *Emblema* in Alciati," *JWCI*, 31 (1968), 234–50; Dieter Mehl, "Emblems in English Renaissance Drama," *RenD* n.s., 2 (1969), 39–57; Marc F. Bertonasco, "Crashaw and the Emblem," *Crashaw and the Baroque* (1971), pp. 6–42; Rosalie L. Colie, "Small Forms: Multo in Parvo," *The Resources of Kind: Genre-Theory in the Renaissance,* ed. Barbara K. Lewalski (1973), pp. 32–75; John Doebler, *Shakespeare's Speaking Pictures: Studies in Iconic Imagery* (1974); Dieter Mehl, "Emblematic Theatre," *Anglia,* 95 (1977), 130–38; Shahla Anand, *Of Costliest Emblem: "Paradise Lost" and the Emblem Tradition* (1978); Barbara K. Lewalski, "Emblems and the Religious Lyric: George Herbert and Protestant Emblematics," *HUSL,* 6 (1978), 32–56; Margery Corbett and Ronald Lightbown, *The Comely Frontispiece: The Emblematic Title-page in England 1550–1660* (1979); Peter M. Daly, *Literature in the Light of the Emblem: Structural Parallels between the Emblem and Literature in the Sixteenth and Seventeenth Centuries* (1979); John M. Steadman, "The Iconographical Approach," *Nature Into Myth: Medieval and Renaissance Moral Symbols* (1979), pp. 23–45.

Encomium:

That branch of epideictic rhetoric (q.v.) concerned with praise: "that forme of speech by which the Orator doth highly commend to his hearers, some person or thing in respect of their worthy deserts & vertues" (Henry Peacham, *The Garden of Eloquence,* 1593). More loosely, an encomium was any laudatory discourse or eulogy.

In classical rhetoric, the definition of encomium is more restricted than it is in the vocabulary of English writers. In Greek usage an encomium was a poem or speech in praise of a living person before a select group. In this sense it contrasted with the epitaph (q.v.), which praised the dead.

Reviewing classical practices, George Puttenham also notes a distinction between praise of the "immortal gods" in hymns and those "ballades of praise called *Encomia*" that laud "great Princes and heroicke personages" (*The Art of English Poesy,* 1589). "We call them carols of honour," he says.

The decorum (q.v.) of idealized types is firmly embedded in the rhetoric books that review encomia. Peacham says, for example, that princes are to be praised for the "wisdom, religion, justice, mercy, clemency, providence, blessed government, liberality." Judges are to be praised for "their wisedome, feare of God, learning, care of equitie, for regarding the cause without respecting the person." The pastor is to be praised for his "learning, gravitie, good life, apt gifts of teaching, care of his flocke"; and military officers are to be praised for "their experience, providence, fidelitie, for their courage and fortitude in fight, and for their modestie and mercie in victorie."

The power of the encomium to reinforce virtuous behavior and to render homage to virtuous men makes it central to a didactic theory of rhetoric and poetics. As a "forme of speech, which doth speaketh while the vertuous man doth live, and also liveth when the vertuous man is dead" (Peacham), the encomium fits easily with the traditional Horatian formula that poetry should "teach goodnes and delight the learners" of it (Sir Philip Sidney, *An Apology for Poetry,* 1595). At the same time the encomium makes poets the guardians of "fame," since it is in their power to either praise or denigrate.

90

Epideictic rhetoric:

A repertoire of topics and controls belonging to the epideictic or demonstrative oration that "standeth either in praise, or dispraise of some one man, or some one thyng, or of some one deede doen" (Thomas Wilson, *The Art of Rhetoric,* 1553). The tradition of epideictic rhetoric included praise and dispraise of a wide variety of subjects: "There are diverse thynges whiche are praised, and dispraised, as menne, Countreis, Citees, Places, Beastes, Hilles, Rivers, Houses, Castles, dedes doen by worthy menne, and pollicies invented by great warriers, but moste commonly men are praised, for diverse respectes, before any of the other thynges are taken in hande" (Wilson). The norms of epideictic rhetoric were inextricably assimilated into Renaissance conceptions of poetic function, subject matter, and development. Sir Philip Sidney, for example, takes it as given that a poet's work "in commendation or disprayse must ever holde an high authority" (*An Apology for Poetry,* 1595).

The Greco-Roman tradition divided oratory into three types: judicial or forensic oratory, designed to persuade on the basis of what is just; deliberative or political oratory, which advises or dissuades by arguing what is advantageous in a given cause; and demonstrative or epideictic oratory, which praises or blames on the basis of what is honorable. Epideictic rhetoric is treated as occasional oratory, primarily associated with ceremonial gatherings, such as patriotic festivals, commemorations, and funerals.

Like the other two types of oratory, epideictic is a means of persuasion. By showing, through the praise of a person, for example, that his actions were noble, honorable, and the source of his fame, the orator moves men to emulate those actions; and by censuring the actions of a man as ignoble and the cause of his infamy, the orator moves his audience to avoid dishonorable actions. The moral efficacy of praise and blame has an early source in Plato's *Republic* where Socrates excepts from expulsion in the perfect commonwealth those poets who make hymns to the gods and praises of famous men (X). Aristotle's *Rhetoric* encourages orators to heighten the effect of both virtue and infamy so that an audience cannot help but follow an implied course of action. The need for such heightening leads Aristotle to characterize amplification as the primary rhetorical tool of the epideictic oration.

A long rhetorical tradition treated all poetry as occasional discourse. All poetic genres were divided between the great epideictic divisions of praise or blame. The early rhetoric books, such as those of Hermogenes and Quintilian and the *Rhetorica ad Herennium,* codified epideictic theory in relation to poetry, and sixteenth-century rhetoricians, both continental and English, simply continued the process. So George Puttenham speaks of poets as "the trumpetters of all praise and also of slaunder (not slaunder, but well deserved reproch)" *(The Art of English Poesy,* 1589).

The subject matter of epideictic orations also became that of the poetic genres. By late antiquity, most of the themes associated with lyric (q.v.) poetry, for example, were parallel with lists of epideictic subjects to be used as material for rhetorical exercises. One list of epideictic types includes the following: praise of a country by situation, advantages of climate, products; praise of its founders, festivals, buildings; praise of a city; praise of a ruler; speech on debarking; speech on departing; marriage hymn; funeral oration; farewell speech; the plaint (it is to be brief and emotional); the paradoxical encomium; and the panegyric (Menander's list of epideictic types in *Peri epideiktikon;* cited in Burgess, *Epideictic Literature*). The epideictic also extended to poetry in conventional praises of seasons, gardens, and love.

Epideictic theory not only gave the poet broad lists of things worth praising, but even the possible amplifications (*see* Copia) for each individual subject. Leonard Cox's rhetoric book, *The Art or Craft of Rhetoric,* (1530) tells a speaker that praise of a person, for example, should be presented "after the fasshyon of an hystorye" and should be drawn from the following places (*see* Common-place): the subject's birth, childhood, adolescence, adulthood, old age, death, and events after his death. Each place is then amplified, so that, for example, in treating his subject's birth an orator would note his ancestry and events at or near the time of his nativity. Following Quintilian, Thomas Wilson's *Art of Rhetoric* (1553) suggests that "mannes state" would include his service to king and country, his wise counsels, the goodness of his wit, while the earlier "strypling age" could include praise of his skill in languages, his prowess in poetry, weaponry, riding, tilting, music, and painting.

Similarly, the epideictic tradition provided a sanctioned set of topics or common-places for English poetry that poets shaped and reshaped at will: for example, "inexpressibility," according to which the speaker proclaims his inability to do justice to his superlative subject; "outdoing," whereby the subject is said to surpass any with whom he can be compared; and "universal renown," whereby all mankind is said to honor the person in question.

The rhetorical tradition is fairly consistent in its alignment of genres with the categories of praise and blame. The hymn (q.v.) and the ode (q.v.) are treated as "praises," as were most other lyrics. Sidney speaks of the lyric which "giveth praise, the reward of vertue, to vertuous acts." The heroic poem (q.v.) is consistently described as a kind of praise. An influential fourth-century commentary on Virgil's *Aeneid* speaks of it as nothing other than epideictic (Tiberius Claudius Donatus, *Interpretations Virgilianae*). Virgil's poem is a praise of Aeneas, and this association is rehearsed in almost all references to the heroic poem. Edmund Spenser speaks of *The Faerie Queene* (1590) as a song of "Knights and Ladies gentle deeds; / Whose prayses having slept in silence long, / Me . . . the sacred Muse areeds / To blazon broad emongst her learned throng."

Occasional poems, such as the elegy, the epigram, and the epitaph (qq.v.), are described as giving either praise or censure. Tragedy (q.v.) is sometimes spoken of as a praise and sometimes as a dispraise, partly as the result of a twelfth-century paraphrase of Aristotle's *Poetics,* the *Paraphrase of Averroës.* With an absolute misunderstanding of Aristotle's actual treatise, Averroës assigns to Aristotle the notion that tragedy is a praise and that comedy contrasts with it as a dispraise. As a result, some sixteenth-century commentators repeated the notion that tragedy is a praise of great men. Generally, however, tragedy is described as a dispraise. Tragedy reprehends "the evil and outragious behaviours of Princes," says George Puttenham. Sidney describes it as that which "openeth the greatest wounds, and sheweth forth the Ulcers that are covered with tissue."

Comedy and satire (qq.v.) are genres also associated with reprehension. Puttenham, reviewing classical practice, says there were "three kinds of poems reprehensive, to wit, the *Satyre,* the *Comedie,* and the *Tragedie.*" Satire was "the first and most bitter invective against vice and vicious men." Comedy glanced "at every abuse," Sidney makes similar assumptions about contemporary genres. Satire, he says, makes a man "laugh at folly" and "to laugh at himselfe." Comedy imitates "the common errors of our life," so that one can find "his own actions contemptibly set forth."

Bibliography

Theodore C. Burgess, "Epideictic Literature," *University of Chicago Studies in Classical Philology,* 3 (1902), 89–261; Ernst R. Curtius, *European Literature and the Latin Middle Ages,* trans. Willard R. Trask (1953), pp. 154–82; O. B. Hardison, Jr., *The Enduring Monument: A Study of the Idea of Praise in Renaissance Literary Theory and Practice* (1962); Warren L.

Chernaik, "Waller's *Panegyric to My Lord Protector* and the Poetry of Praise," *SEL,* 4 (1964), 109–24; A. Leigh DeNeef, "Epideictic Rhetoric and the Renaissance Lyric," *JMRS,* 3 (1973), 203–31; Barbara K. Lewalski, "Donne's Poetry of Compliment: The Speaker's Stance and the Topoi of Praise," *Seventeenth-Century Imagery,* ed. Earl Miner (1971), pp. 45–67; Barbara K. Lewalski, *Donne's "Anniversaries" and the Poetry of Praise* (1973); Thomas H. Cain, *Praise in "The Faerie Queene"* (1978).

Epigram:

A "wittie and short" poem "which under a fained name doe . . . praise or taxe some particular person or thing" (Henry Cockeram, *The English Dictionary,* 1623). Historically, the first poetic epigrams, those of archaic Greece, were inscriptions marked on tombs, road-signs, and votive tablets: hence the traditional emphasis upon brevity in the literary form.

One of the epideictic kinds (*see* Epideictic rhetoric), the epigram was distinguished not only by its brevity but also by its role as a vehicle for praise or vituperation. George Puttenham describes it as "a pretty fashioned poeme short and sweete (as we are wont to say) . . . in which every mery conceited man might without any long studie or tedious ambage, make his frend sport, and anger his foe, and give a prettie nip, or shew a sharpe conceit in few verses" (*The Art of English Poesy,* 1589). When Cockeram says that an epigram operates under a "fained name," he is referring to the fact that poets, both as a matter of protection and as part of the claims of the genre, often invent names for the object of their "blame." Thus Ben Jonson addresses one of his epigrams to "Gut" and another to "Sir Voluptuous Beast." In contrast, epigrams of praise generally complimented their subject by actual name.

A treatise on the epigram by an Italian critic suggests that one kind of "praise" associated with the epigram comes from its bravura effects as a reflection of the poet's skill. The first "end" of the epigram, he says, is with respect to the poet himself "to whom it brings praise and glory" (Tommaso Correa, *De toto eo poematis genere, quod epigramma vulgo dicitur Libellus,* 1569, trans. Bernard Weinberg). The epigram requires, says Correa, great art, great wit, sharpness of talent, becoming brevity, and a certain dexterity and discernment.

Writing epigrams in Latin was a school exercise in the sixteenth and seventeenth centuries. Ralph Johnson's *A Scholar's Guide* (1665), for example, recommends epigrams as "poetical exercises" appropriate for young students; the epigram is to be "a short but witty poem, facetiously expressing the nature or quality of an action, thing, or person . . . comprized within a *Distich* or two, or three at most." Students were often given a "theme" (proverb or phrase) such as *Tempus edax rerum* (Time the devourer of things) to be given restatement, application, or comment as an epigram. This treatment of epigram as a reflection on a theme is carried over into printed collections of epigrams that sometimes have each poem headed by a phrase or proverb, often in Latin though the poem itself is in English. And sometimes scholars were required to paraphrase or vary a complete epigram from the *Greek Anthology,* or from Martial or some other Latin source. The practice of paraphrasing and varying a topic in all possible ways is made a tour de force in John Stockwood's important school textbook *Progymnasma Scholasticum* (1597) in which Stockwood demonstrates 450 ways to vary one "Disticke or couple of Verses" (*see* Copia).

In theory, the range of subject matter for the epigram is almost endless. Its tradition includes amatory, funeral, and patriotic praises as well as scurrilous and even coprophilic reprehensions. Thomas Bastard opens his collection of epigrams (*Chrestoleros,* 1598) with a list of subjects that suggests the epigram's range: "I Speake of wants, of frauds, of policies, / Of manners, and of vertues, and of times, / Of unthrifts, and of frends, and enimies . . . Of Warrs, of captaynes, Nobles, Princes, Kings, / Asia, Europe, and all the world beside." Puttenham is less inclusive, contending that the epigram is a praise or reprehension of the "meaner sort" (middle range of subjects) in contrast to hymns that praise the "immortal gods" or "historicall reports of great gravitie and majestie."

The form of the epigram is fairly consistent. Typically a specific person, real or fictional, is either spoken to or spoken of; and the body of the poem leads to a witty concluding comment or question. The conclusion frequently employs surprise achieved by extreme compression, antitheses, puns, paradoxes, or unusual metaphors. Puttenham recommends two figures in particular for the epigram: *prosonomasia,* a figure by which "ye play with a couple of words or names much resembling each other" and *epithonema* or *acclamatio* ("consenting close"), which is a final cry of assent to or approval of the thing narrated or proved. One writer compares the epigram to a scorpion "because as the Sting of the Scorpion lyeth in the tayl, so the force and vertue of an Epigram is in the conclusion."

The epigram rivaled the sonnet (q.v.) in popularity. As a short lyric (q.v.) poem of praise, the sonnet shares part of the traditional purpose assigned to the epigram; mid–sixteenth-century poets sometimes use the terms interchangeably. By the end of the century, however, the sonnet is treated as different from the epigram. Sir John Harington, who wrote a collection of poems under the title *Elegant and Witty Epigrams* (1618), suggests that the contrast between the two poetic types is primarily one of tone:

Once, by mishap, two Poets fell a-squaring,
The Sonnet, and our Epigram comparing;
And *Faustus,* having long demurd upon it,
Yet, at the last, gave sentence for the Sonnet,
Now, for such censure, this his chiefe defence is,
Their sugred taste best likes his likresse senses.
   Well, though I grant Sugar may please the taste,
   Yet let my verse have salt to make it last.

Harington is reminding his readers of the epithets commonly associated with the amorous and highly figured sonnet, "sugred" and "sweet," and of the fact that sweet food spoils faster than salted. In a similar vein, a rhetorical treatise familiar to late sixteeth-century readers, the *Art of Rhetoric* by Hermogenes, associates the epigram with "Subtlety," a style in which humble material is given sharpness and acuteness, with diction that is only a mild departure from common usage.

The very short epigram praising (or sometimes scorning) a dead person becomes an epitaph (q.v.). Other very short epigrams shade into gnomic verse, as in this justly famous nugget from Harington, "Treason doth never prosper, whats the reason? / For if it prosper, none dare call it Treason" (*Epigrams Both Pleasant and Serious,* 1615).

Bibliography

T. K. Whipple, *Martial and the English Epigram from Sir Thomas Wyatt to Ben Jonson* (1925); Kathryn Anderson McEuen, *Classical Influence upon the Tribe of Ben: A Study of Classical Elements in the Non-Dramatic Poetry of Ben Jonson and his Circle* (1939); Hoyt H. Hudson, *The Epigram in the English Renaissance* (1947); G. R. Hamilton, *English Verse Epigram* (1965); Joseph C. Baldwin, "John Heywood and Sir John Davies: A Change in the Tradition of the Sixteenth Century Satiric Epigram," *Satire Newsletter* (1967), 16–24; Barbara Herrnstein Smith, *Poetic Closure: A Study of How Poems End* (1968), pp. 196–210; Joseph H. Summers, *The Heirs of Donne and Jonson* (1970); Robert Ralston Cawley, "The Epigram" and "Peacham and the Epigram," *Henry Peacham: His Contribution to English Poetry* (1971), pp. 21–67; William E. Sheidley, "George Tubervile's Epigrams from the Greek Anthology: A Case Study of 'Englishing,'" *SEL,* 12 (1972), 71–84; Robert J. Wichensheiser, "George Herbert and the Epigrammatic Tradition," *George Herbert Journal,* 1 (1977), 39–56; R. V. Young, Jr., "Jonson, Crashaw, and the Development of the English Epigram," *Genre,* 12 (1979), 137–52.

Epistle:

"And to describe the true definition of an Epistle or letter, it is nothing else but an Oration written, conteining the mynde of the Orator or wryter, thereby to give to understand to him or them that be absent, the same that should be declared if they were present" (William Fulwood, *The Enemy of Idleness,* 1568). And in his rhetoric for schoolboys Ralph Johnson says: "An Epistle is a Discourse wherein we talk with an absent friend, as if we were with him" (*The Scholar's Guide from the Accidence to the University,* 1665). In a prose letter, probably addressed to Sir Henry Goodyer in 1604, John Donne expresses the typical Renaissance high regard for the epistolary form, whether in verse or prose: "No other kinde of conveyance is better for knowledge or love."

As a literary genre, the epistle in verse came into prominence in English poetry during the late sixteenth and early seventeenth centuries. A Renaissance verse epistle was a poem in the form of a letter in which the "busines bee matter . . . not bare forme, or meere Ceremony" (Ben Jonson, *Timber, or Discoveries,* 1641). It was written in the conversational style traditionally considered appropriate for a serious letter addressed to a particular person.

Writing on another occasion Donne points to the personal quality and sense of immediacy of all verse epistles. He begins a verse letter to a friend: "Sir, more then kisses, letters mingle Soules; / For, thus friends absent speake" (*To Sr. Henry Wooten,* 1633). And Jonson, aware of his own intimate knowledge of the recipient of his verse epistle, says: "I know to whom I write" (*An Epistle to Master John Selden,* 1641). The claim that the basis of an epistle is personal intimacy had its roots in classical rhetoric. The first-century rhetorician Demetrius, for example, says: "It may be said that everybody reveals his own soul in his letters. In every other form of composition it is possible to discern the writer's character, but in none so clearly as in the epistolary" (cited in Palmer). English handbooks on letter writing repeat such ideas.

Tudor school training in rhetoric prepared English poets to write verse epistles. After schoolboys had learned enough Latin to compose sentences, they were set to writing short letters, which were usually organized around an assigned *sententia* (q.v.). Among letters serving as models in the schools were the verse epistles of Ovid and Horace and the prose letters of Cicero and Seneca. While providing models of style, all of these writers were especially admired for their gravity of thought. A key text on letter writing was that by Erasmus, *De conscribendis epistolis,* in which Erasmus distinguishes various types of letters and outlines their structure according to rhetorical principles. Three of his four types follow the traditional categories of oratory (epideictic, deliberative, and judicial), but he adds a fourth, non-oratorical kind, the familiar letter. In all four types Erasmus places great emphasis on the need for the letter writer to pay close attention to the relationship between the writer and his audience. Later English treatises and formularies continued to apply the ancient rules of rhetoric to letter writing.

Rhetorical tradition assigned to the familiar epistle a conversational style. Seneca, for example, defending himself against a charge of writing carelessly in his letters, says: "I prefer that my letters should be just what my conversation would be if you and I were sitting in one another's company or taking walks together,—spontaneous and easy; for my letters have nothing strained or artificial about them." But, he adds, "our conversation on matters . . . important should not be meagre and dry; for even philosophy does not renounce the company of cleverness" (*Epistulae morales,* Letter LXXV, trans. R. M. Gummere). English handbooks on letter writing continued to stress the "spontaneous and easy" quality of the "humble" or "low" style appropriate for familiar epistles. The requisites of this style are enumerated by John Hoskins in *Directions for Speech and Style* (written about 1600). Hoskins lists four requisites: brevity, that is, letters "must not be treatises or discourcings"; "perspicuitie"; "plainness," "which is . . . a kind of diligent negligence"; and "respect," the decorum that adjusts style to the social relationship between writer and recipient (as transcribed by Ben Jonson, *Timber*). Similarly, James Howell comments on the style appropriate to an epistle when he says: "It was a quaint difference the Ancients did put 'twixt a *Letter* and an *Oration,* that the one should be attird like a Woman, the other like a Man: The latter of the two is allowd large *side* robes, as long periods, parenthesis, similies, examples, and other parts of Rhetorical flourishes: But a *Letter* or *Epistle,* should be short-coated, and closely couchd; a Hungerlin [short furred robe] becomes a *Letter* more hansomly then a gown. Indeed we should write as we speak; and that's a true familiar Letter which expresseth ones mind, as if he were discoursing with the party to whom he writes in succinct and short terms" (1650 edition of *Epistolae Ho-Elianae*).

The practice of English poets distinguished between two kinds of verse epistles, each with a classical model. In one kind, the letter writer and recipient are fictive creations by the poet. Such verse epistles, amatory in subject matter, imitate Ovid's *Heroides,* verse letters mainly by deserted women to their lovers. When not known to English readers in the original, Ovid's verse epistles became available in George Tubervile's English translation of 1567. Englishmen especially admired the *Heroides* for its *sententiae* (q.v.). Henry Peacham expresses a typical praise for Ovid's verse epistles when he writes: "Among his Workes his Epistles are most worthy your reading, being his neatest peeces, every where embellished with excellent and wise Sentences; the numbers smoothly falling in, and borrowing their lustre and beauty from imitation of native and antique Simplicity" (*The Complete Gentleman,* 1622). The best known of the English fictive epistles influenced by Ovid are those by Michael Drayton, *England's Heroical Epistles.* This popular work appeared in five separate editions between 1597 and 1602 and earned Drayton the title of "our English Ovid" among his contemporaries.

The other—and more usual—kind of verse epistle is one in which the poet-writer speaks directly to a living person on a subject of concern to them both. Such verse epistles are "after the manner of Horace," as Samuel Daniel says on the second title page of *A Panegyric Congratulatory* (1603) in which appeared his *Certain Epistles.* The verse epistles of Horace, along with the prose letters of Seneca (*see* Senecan style), were the principal models for English writers speaking in their own voice to an actual person; and the familiar letters of both writers were admired for their conversational style and sententious thought. William Webbe, for example, says that Horace is "a poet not of the smoothest style, but in sharpnesse of wytt inferiour to none" (*A Discourse of English Poetry,* 1586); and Gabriel Harvey praises Horace as "A sharpe, and sententious Poet" who "after his pithy manner, comprized much in fewe wordes" (*Pierce's Supererogation,* 1593). The first clear introduction of the Horatian epistle into English poetry is the inclusion of seven verse epistles in Thomas Lodge's *A Fig for Momus* (1595). Lodge comments in the preface: "For my *Epistles,* they are in that kind, wherein no Englishman of our time hath publiquely written."

Verse epistles to living persons have for their subjects serious matters of individual, social, and political conduct. Many of them treat the two principal Horatian topics—the retired life and the nature of poetry. Their rhetorical intentions are often closely related to those of epideictic and deliberative oratory. As in epideictic rhetoric (q.v.), praise is the aim of verse epistles like those addressed by Donne to his patronesses. As in a deliberative oration (*see* Rhetoric), other verse epistles ask a recipient to consider the writer's attitude on a topic. But regardless of subject, "knowledge, or love," or of the adjustments necessitated by "respect" for the social rank of a particular recipient, verse epistles "after the manner of

Horace" are marked by a "low" style with a "kind of diligent negligence" that made it appropriate for a serious meditation with an absent friend.

Bibliography

Maude B. Hansche, *The Formative Period of English Familiar Letter-writers and Their Contribution to the English Essay* (1902); Edward Kennard Rand, *Ovid and His Influence* (1925); Jean Robertson, *The Art of Letter Writing: An Essay on the Handbooks Published in England During the Sixteenth and Seventeenth Centuries* (1943); Homer Nearing, Jr., *English Historical Poetry 1599–1641* (1945); Frederick S. Boas, *Ovid and the Elizabethans* (1947); Laurence Stapleton, "The Theme of Virtue in Donne's Verse Epistles," *SP,* 55 (1958), 187–200; Jay Arnold Levine, "The Status of the Verse Epistle before Pope," *SP,* 59 (1962), 658–84; Wesley Trimpi, "The Epistolary Tradition," *Ben Jonson's Poems: A Study of the Plain Style* (1962), pp. 60–75; W. Milgate, ed., "Donne as Moralist: The Verse Letters," *John Donne: The Satires, Epigrams and Verse Letters* (1967), pp. xxxiii–xl; Richard F. Hardin, "Convention and Design in Drayton's *Heroicall Epistles,*" *PMLA,* 83 (1968), 35–41; N. Christoph de Nagy, *Michael Drayton's "England's Heroical Epistles"* (1968); D. J. Palmer, "The Verse Epistle," *Metaphysical Poetry,* eds. Malcolm Bradbury and David Palmer, *Stratford-upon-Avon Studies,* 11 (1970), 73–99; Earl Miner, "Friendship," *The Cavalier Mode from Jonson to Cotton* (1971), pp. 250–305; Patricia Thomson, "Donne and the Poetry of Patronage: The *Verse Letters,*" *John Donne: Essays in Celebration,* ed. A. J. Smith (1972), pp. 308–23; Barbara K. Lewalski, "Contemporary Epideictic Poetry: The Speaker's Stance and the *Topoi* of Praise" and "Donne's Poetry of Compliment: Meditative Speaker and Symbolic Subject," *Donne's "Anniversaries" and the Poetry of Praise: The Creation of a Symbolic Mode* (1973), pp. 11–70; Allen Barry Cameron, "Donne's Deliberative Verse Epistles," *ELR,* 6 (1976), 369–403; Margaret Maurer, "Samuel Daniel's Poetical Epistles, Especially Those to Sir Thomas Egerton and Lucy, Countess of Bedford," *SP,* 74 (1977), 418–44.

Epitaph:

A short poem made to resemble an inscription upon a burial marker; a kind of epigram (q.v.) that functioned to "report of the dead persons estate and degree, or of his other good or bad partes, to his commendation or reproch" (George Puttenham, *The Art of English Poesy,* 1589).

Like "an inscription such as a man may commodiously write or engrave upon a tombe in a few verses," an epitaph should be "pithie, quicke, and sententious, for the passer-by to peruse and judge upon without any longer tariaunce." Puttenham takes to task the "bastard rimers" who commit the "errour" of writing too long an epitaph and hence make it unsuitable for engraving. Long commemorative verses to the dead, he says, are more appropriately made in the form of an elegy (q.v.).

Although the epitaph as a lyric (q.v.) form theoretically served both for commendation or reproach, the bias of the epitaph was in the direction of praise. Sir Philip Sidney's mock anathema on all those who scorn "the sacred misteries of Poesie" is that, lacking the poet's power to preserve and memorialize, such detractors of poetry will let their own memories "die from the earth for want of an *Epitaph*" (*An Apology for Poetry,* 1595).

Epithalamion:

"Rejoysings" composed "to celebrate marriages were called songs nuptiall or *Epithalamies*" (George Puttenham, *The Art of English Poesy,* 1589). And Randle Cotgrave's *A Dictionary of the French and English Tongues* (1611) defines an epithalamion as "A wedding Song, or Poeme: verses made, or a song sung, at a wedding, in commendation of the parties married." As a lyric (q.v.) poem, a Renaissance epithalamion celebrated a particular wedding and honored a newly married couple. Typically, these poems of praise were structured around the several events of a wedding day, from the waking of the bride to the bedding of the couple.

The word *epithalamion* derives from the Greek *thalamos,* (bed chamber) and originally designated only one of several songs actually sung during the festivities of a wedding day, this particular one being sung outside the bridal chamber on the wedding night. It is in this sense that Puttenham calls an epithalamion a "bedding ballad of the ancient times." Aware that there were other songs appropriate to the various occasions of the marriage day, he writes that this "ballade . . . was song very sweetely by Musitians at the chamber dore of the Bridegroome and Bride . . . and they were called *Epithalamies* as much to say as ballades at the bedding of the bride: for such as were song at the borde at dinner or supper were other Musickes and not properly *Epithalamies*."

Classical writers sometimes included wedding songs in their epics; Homer does so, for example, in the *Iliad.* This classical precedent lies behind the hymn of blessing, "Hail wedded Love," by the epic voice in John Milton's *Paradise Lost* (1667). It was as a separate form, however, that the epithalamion became a distinct lyric kind. Many of its conventions were created by Catullus in three nuptial songs (*Carmina,* 61, 62, 64).

Modeling his lyric poem *Epithalamion* (1595) on the pattern of Catullus, Edmund Spenser is the English poet responsible for establishing the characteristic design of the many epithalamia of the early seventeenth century (*see* Imitation). Although there were at least two English epithalamia before Spenser's, it was his poem that was echoed in the structure and motifs of later poems.

English epithalamia refer to the specific day of a wedding, with the poet selecting events from the day's activities to structure his poem. The wedding celebrated, fictive or real, is that of persons belonging to the nobility or upper class; their rank justifies the praise of them by the poet-speaker, especially if the wedding has far-reaching social or political implications. The poet-speaker often calls attention to the fact that he does not belong to the same social class as the other celebrants. He serves as something of a master of revels in that he directs the activities of the day, and he acts as a spokesman for society by offering the traditional wishes for prosperity, harmony, and increase and by interpreting the particular significance of this wedding.

An epithalamion has both a dramatic and ritualistic public quality. Much of the dramatic quality derives from the way in which the poem is structured around the joyous events of the wedding day—the awakening of the bride, the dressing (and later the undressing) of the bride, the wedding procession, the marriage ceremony, the merriment after that ceremony, and the ritual of the bedding of bride and groom. The distance that the poet-speaker keeps between himself and the day's events helps to account for the ceremonial quality of the poem. His emphasis is on the social context of the wedding. In his function as interpreter of the social significance of the marriage, he resembles the epideictic orator of classical tradition; and he too offers praise (*see* Epideictic rhetoric). Puttenham calls the epithalamist a "Civill Poet"; and he says that the subject matter of the epithalamist, "honorable matrimonie, a love by al lawes allowed," is "the highest & holiest of any ceremonie apperteining to man; a match forsooth made for ever and not for a day, a solace provided for youth, a comfort for age, a knot of alliance & amitie indissoluble."

The description of the epithalamion as a "bedding ballad" points to one of the original functions of the song, the encouragement of fertility. English poets retained this motif as an essential part of their epithalamia.

Bibliography

Robert H. Case, ed., "Introduction," *English Epithalamies* (1896), pp. vii–lx; Cortlandt Van Winkle, ed., "Introduction," *Edmund Spenser: Epithalamion* (1926), pp. 5–26; Thomas M. Greene, "Spenser and the Epithalamic Convention," *CL,* 9 (1957), 215–28; Charles C. Osgood, "Epithalamion and Prothalamion: 'and theyr eccho ring,' " *MLN,* 76 (1961), 205–208; Enid Welsford, "Introduction: Epithalamion," *Spenser: "Fowre Hymnes" & "Epithalamion": A Study of Edmund Spenser's Doctrine of Love* (1967), pp. 63–83; Leonard Forster, "Conventional Safety Valves: Alba, Pastourelle, and Epithalamium," *The Icy Fire: Five Studies in European Petrarchism* (1969), pp. 84–121; Gary M. McCowan, "Milton and the Epic Epithalamium," *MiltonS,* 5 (1973), 39–66; Sandra R. Patterson, "Spenser's *Prothalamion* and the Catullan Epithalamic Tradition," *Comitatus,* 10 (1979–80), 97–106.

Fourteener:

"Some makers write in verses of foureteene sillables giving the *Cesure* at the first eight" (George Puttenham, *The Art of English Poesy,* 1589); a line of poetry containing fourteen syllables arranged in seven iambic feet with a medial pause after the fourth foot. Although this verse was much used by mid–sixteenth-century poets, the fourteener gradually gave way to iambic pentameter as the standard long line in English prosody. Following a medieval practice, writers also sometimes divided the long line of the fourteener into two parts of alternating four and three stress lines. This form of "eight-and-sixes" is the traditional ballad meter.

Commenting on verse forms in English poetry, William Webbe, in *A Discourse of English Poetry* (1586), remarks that the longest line he has seen is a seldom-used one of sixteen syllables. Then he says, "An other kynd next in length to thys is where eche verse hath fourteene syllables, which is the most accustomed of all other, and especially used of all the translatours of the Latine Poets." This long line, he adds, "often is devyded, eche verse into two, the first having eyght sillables, the second sixe, whereof the two sixes shall always ryme, and sometimes the eyghtes, sometimes not, according to the wyll of the maker."

Although long lines of fourteen syllables exist in classical Greek and Latin poetry, these in all probability had little to do with the genesis of the English fourteener. The fourteen-syllable line that English poets had used since the thirteenth century seems to be a metrical metamorphosis of the Anglo-Saxon standard line. This line consists of four strongly stressed syllables, with any number of unstressed syllables, in two hemistichs (half lines) with two stresses each. A strong medial pause separates the half lines.

Whatever its origins, the fourteener continued to serve Renaissance poets, as it had medieval writers, for topics of a serious nature. Among the several original works using fourteener couplets is William Warner's historical narrative *Albion's England* (1586). Two important "translatours of the Latine Poets" writing in fourteeners are Arthur Golding (Ovid's

Metamorphoses, 1567) and George Chapman (Books I–II and VII–IX of the *Iliad,* 1598). Golding's work made readily available a highly popular collection of classical tales; Chapman's poem is the first major translation of Homer's epic into English.

Despite its popularity during the mid-sixteenth century, especially for narrative poetry, the fourteener could not withstand the contemporary competition of iambic pentameter as a stichic method of organizing poetic material. As Puttenham says, the fourteener becomes "tedious, for the length of the verse kepeth the eare too long from his delight, which is to heare the cadence or the tuneable accent in the ende of the verse." With its regular accents and its medial caesura, this long line passed "the bounds of good proportion."

Heroic poem:

"That princelie part of Poetrie, wherein are displaied the noble actes and valiant exploits of puissaunt Captaines, expert souldiers, wise men, with the famous reportes of auncient times, such as are the Heroycall workes of *Homer* in Greeke, and the heavenly verse of *Virgils AEneidos* in Latine" (William Webbe, *A Discourse of English Poetry,* 1586). The "heroicall" or "epick" poem was controlled primarily by the assumptions that its greatest models—the works of Homer and the *Aeneid* of Virgil—were poems based on historical events shaped by the deeds of great national heroes as exemplars of both private virtue and national success.

The role of the hero as an inspiring model of human possibility was central to the Renaissance epic. It is that poetry in which "the famous acts of Princes and the vertuous and worthy lives of our forefathers were reported" (George Puttenham, *The Art of English Poesy,* 1589). Sir Philip Sidney says of the heroic poem that it is "the best and most accomplished kinde of Poetry" since "the loftie image of such Worthies most inflameth the mind with desire to be worthy, and informes with counsel how to be worthy" (*An Apology for Poetry,* 1595). Edmund Spenser's letter to Sir Walter Raleigh explaining his plans for *The Faerie Queene* (1590) rehearses an almost identical theory of the heroic poem as exemplum. He says he has chosen "the historye of king Arthure, as most fitte for the excellency of his person, being made famous by many mens former workes. . . . In which I have followed all the antique Poets historicall, first Homere, who in the Person of Agamemnon and Ulysses hath ensampled a good governour and a vertuous man . . . then Virgil, whose like intention was to doe in the person of Aeneas: after him Ariosto comprised them both in his Orlando."

The terms *heroic* and *historicall* were virtually synonymous in discussions of narrative poetry. Even the most marvelous and mythic of the classical heroes were assumed to act in history. Pagan gods and demigods became heroes because of a traditional explanation that pagan mythology was ultimately based on fact. They were thought to be in their origin historical figures who for their benefactions to mankind were first adored and eventually worshipped by posterity. A vast body of medieval and Renaissance thought is concerned with tracing the genealogies of Saturn, Jove, Hercules, or the Trojan line back to their fountainhead in Noah. Demigods like Ulysses and Aeneas are only slightly at a tangent to the plane of reality assigned to King Arthur or Charlemagne.

The school study of an epic more narrowly conceived than the *Aeneid*, *De bello civili* by Lucan (39–65 A.D.), which treats the struggles between Pompey and Caesar, served to further weld chronicled history and the heroic together. Lucan's poem was much admired for its figures of speech and its oratorical treatment of set topics, one of the most significant being the horrors of civil dissension. Francis Meres points to the similarity between Lucan's poem and two English poems when he writes: "As Lucan hath mournefully depainted the civil wars of Pompey and Caesar: so hath [Samuel] Daniel the civill wars of Yorke and Lancaster, and [Michael] Drayton the civill wars of Edward the second and the Barons" (*Palladis Tamia,* 1598).

Webbe too assumes the relations of history and the heroic poem as he examines the success of English historians in comparison to Homer and Virgil: "To these, though wee have no English worke aunswerable, in respect of the glorious ornaments of gallant handling: yet our auncient Chroniclers and reporters of our Countrey affayres, come most neere them: and no doubt, if such regarde of our English speeche, and curious handling of our verse, had beene long since thought uppon, and from time to time been pollished and bettered by men of learning, judgement, and authority, it would ere this, have matched them in all respects." In another statement typical of the close identification between epic and historical poetry, Meres says further: "As Homer and Virgil among the Greeks and Latins are chief Heroic poets: so Spenser and Warner be our chief heroical makers." William Warner's *Albion's England* (1586), sweeping over the whole history of England from its earliest legendary beginnings to the reign of Elizabeth, was one of the most popular poems of the late sixteenth and early seventeenth centuries. Warner himself, according to Meres's contemporary account, was honored by "the best wits of both our Universities" as "our English Homer." Similarly, Puttenham, surveying earlier native literature, praises John Hardying, a medieval verse-chronicler, as "a Poet Epick or Historicall, who handled himself well according to the time and manner of his subject."

The assumption that *heroic* implied historical was not unique to English poets, but a widespread European conviction. Italian commentators like Torquato Tasso maintained that the subject of the heroic poem should be historical. Tasso says that it is not "probable" that illustrious actions like those in the epic should be unknown to history. The authority of history gains for the poet that semblance of truth necessary to deceive the reader and make him accept the poet's fictions (*Discoursi dell' arte poetica,* 1587). Joachim du Bellay, himself a poet, bluntly suggests to his compatriots that they go to the French chronicles for material for their heroic poems (*Défense et illustration de la langue française,* 1549).

Although the heroic poem was to have a historical ground, commentators also assumed that the poet was free to use his material imaginatively. As Samuel Daniel says in an apology for a breach of historical accuracy, poets need that "poeticall licence, of framing speaches to the persons of men according to their occasions" (*The Civil Wars,* 1609). The poet was to elaborate the historical event in accordance with the rules of poetic imitation. The very nature of the heroic poem—its need for magnitude and moral force—required the poet's intervention: 'Because the Acts or Events of *true Historie* have not that Magnitude which satisfieth the minde of Man, *Poesie* faineth Acts and Events Greater and More Heroicall; because *true Historie* propoundeth the successes and issues of actions not so agreable to the merits of Vertue and Vice, therefore *Poesie* faines them more just in Retribution and more according to Revealed Providence; because *true Historie* representeth Actions and Events more ordinarie and lesse interchanged, therefore *Poesie* endueth them with more Rarenesse and more unexpected and alternative Variations. So as it appeareth that *Poesie* serveth and conferreth to Magnanimitie, Moralitie, and to delectation" (Sir Francis Bacon, *The Advancement of Learning,* 1605).

The historical ground of the heroic poem was one sanction for epic poetry based on stories from the Bible. As an ever-growing number of critics opposed the imitation of classical models in all genres and favored the substitution of sacred subjects and models, the biblical subject had a strong defense on the basis of its unquestionable historical veracity in contrast to the falsity of mythology (despite the body of thought that linked myth to history). Many continental poets, under some attack for the pagan or immoral subject matter of their poems, were ready to agree that since the most excellent epic should be based on history, the best history would be that of the Christian religion, rather than feigned subject matter. Torquato Tasso, himself the author of an epic based on the First Crusade, insists, for example, that he has excluded mythological embellishments from his work (*Discoursi dell' arte poetica*). Abraham Cowley, in the invocation to his *Davideis* (1656) identifies the issue: "But Thou, Eternal Word, Hast call'd forth Me / Th'Apostle, to convert that world to Thee / T' unbind the charmes that in slight Fables lie, / And teach that Truth is truest Poesie."

The use of allegory (q.v.) in the heroic poem was closely linked to the assumption that a heroic poem was historical. Allegory further binds the heroic poem to the world of history; through allegory marvelous and magical events, like that in the *Aeneid* in which ships turn into nymphs, could be understood as figuring the "true" moral and spiritual problems of human experience. Such allegorical readings of classical epics had made them a rich source of study for centuries, and Italian epic poets who influenced English conceptions of the genre sometimes provided elaborate allegorical commentaries on their own works. Thus Tasso claims that heroic poetry consists of two elements, "the Imitation and the Allegory." The imitation presents the external actions of men. The allegory concerns the passions and opinions and characters not only insofar as these are apparent, but also and mainly in their intrinsic being, and it signifies them obscurely, with what one might call mysterious notes (*Allegoria del poema*, printed with the 1581 edition of *Gerusalemme liberata*). And in the evolving tension between a traditional ethic that exalted heroic virtue as a martial virtue and more refined ideas that made heroic virtue an ethical discrimination, allegory reconciled a pagan representation of physical combat with Christian emphasis upon moral struggle.

The belief that heroic poetry must possess magnitude, that it was to be the most comprehensive and universal of all the genres, was widespread. Vastness of design, whatever the source of the historical subject material and whatever the fashion of its treatment, is assumed to be the hallmark of the epic poem. "But as a Court of Kings Palace requires other dimensions than a private house: So the *Epick* askes a magnitude, from other Poems" (Ben Jonson, *Conversations with Drummond,* 1619). Puttenham says of the heroic that it is a "long history" and stresses its range of interests as it praises the great by "shewing their high estates, their Princely genealogies and pedigrees, marriages, aliances, and such noble exploites, as they had done in th' affaires of peace & warre to the benefit of their people and countries, by invention of any noble science or profitable Art, or by making wholesome lawes or enlarging of their dominions by honorable and just conquests, and many other wayes."

Despite the tradition that associated them with narrative length, not all heroic poems were necessarily long. Michael Drayton speaks of his own brief chronicle poems, *Piers Gaveston* and *Matilda,* as a "species of Epick or Heroick Poeme" that "describeth the act or acts of some one or other eminent Person: not with too much . . . compasse, or extension . . . and by way of Briefe, or Compendium (*Poems,* 1619). And John Milton distinguishes between the long and short epic in *The Reason of Church Government* (1642) as he refers to "that Epick form where the two poems of Homer, and those other two of Virgil and Tasso are a deffuse, and the book of Job a brief model." A complex European tradition maintained that parts of the Bible were already epic poetry and so could supply proper epic subject matter even in shorter poems based on such material. And standard Greco-Roman definitions of the poetic genres according to their metrical forms brought together in the epic category various sorts of poems using the dactylic hexameter: long poems such as the *Iliad,* brief sequels, many comparatively brief didactic poems such as the *Works and Days* of Hesiod, and even very short poems such as Theocritus's *Infant Herakles.*

In a less serious vein than that of the *Book of Job* or the *Works and Days,* another tradition aligned brief narrative poems of a witty, amatory nature with the heroic poem. A short narrative poem by the Greek poet Musaeus (c. 500 A.D.) about the loves of Hero and Leander, for example, was treated as "historicall" or "heroic" throughout Europe. George Puttenham compares Musaeus to Homer: "for as *Homer* wrate a fabulous or mixt report of the seige of Troy, and another *Ulisses* errors or wandrings, so did *Museus* compile a true treatise of the life & loves of *Leander and Hero,* both of them *Heroick,* and to none ill edification." He distinguishes the long heroic poem from "the short historicall ditty" that is not written in "long meeters or verses *Alexandrins,* according to the nature & stile of large histories."

At the end of the sixteenth century the idea of an amatory brief epic attracted the attention of a number of English poets who combined the Musaean model with subject matter taken from the Latin poet Ovid as a connoisseur of erotic experience, "of the vayne delights of love and dalliaunce" (William Webbe). The vogue for the amatory epic was initiated by Thomas Lodge with a work called *Scylla's Metamorphosis* (1589). Lodge and his successors refer their works to the traditions of the heroic poem with a variety of conventional signals, but they avoid the "grave" intentions of the epic by using either a "light" six-line stanza form (*see* Sixain) or rhymed couplets as a medium.

Given the loose generic frame of the heroic poem and the variety of poets from antiquity considered to be heroic—Homer, Virgil, Lucan, Apollonius, Lucretius—most poets signalled their epic intentions with a repertoire of formulae associated with the traditional heroic poem: an invocation to a muse; a statement about the nature of the "song" ("I sing the civill Warres, Tumultuous Broyles, / And bloody factions of a mightie Land" [Daniel, The Civil Wars, 1609]); lists and catalogues; extended similes; descriptions of battles, storms, and prophecies; the heavy use of *sententiae* and elaborate paraphrases. The use of *ottava rima* (q.v.), established as a norm in Italian heroic poetry by both Ludovico Ariosto and Torquato Tasso, also could identify a poet's epic intention and required "gravity" of style.

The *ottava rima* stanza is at a marked distance from the Greco-Roman unrhymed dactyllic hexameter as the medium (even the identifying medium) for epic poetry. Here Italian critics tended to invoke usage and European practice as a justification for their non-classical stanza (Lionardo Salviati, *Parafrasi e comento, della poetica d'Aristotile,* 1586). And they often linked *ottava rima* to the heroic grand style by defending its composition of two fours or four twos as a "texture of utmost solidity" since the number eight, according to arithmeticians, is the first of the solid or cubic numbers. A strong native tradition in England also sanctioned rhyme, "which both Custome and Nature doth most powerfully defend" as that which gives "both to the Eare and echo of a delightful report, and to the Memorie a deeper impression of what is delivered therein" (Samuel Daniel, *A Defense of Rhyme,* 1603). In contrast to the "boundlesse running on" of "the Greekes or Latines," the rhymed stanza, says Daniel, is "of that happiness, both for the disposition of the matter, the apt planting the sentence where it may best hit, the certaine close of delight with the full body of a just period well carried." *Ottava rima* or a variation of it was the English heroical norm until Milton rejected it for *Paradise Lost* where "the Measure is English Heroic Verse without Rime, as that of Homer in Greek, and of Virgil in Latin; Rime being no necessary Adjunct or true Ornament of Poem or good Verse, in longer Works especially" (preface, *Paradise Lost,* 1674).

The decorum (q.v.) of the heroic poem required that it be in a style variously termed "high," "grave," or "magnificent." Puttenham voices this conviction when he says that since the heroic poem is about "high subjects" ("the noble gests and fortunes of Princes"), it is necessarily to be rendered in a style also "high and loftie." The nature of the high style was, however, not without ambiguities. Poets like Spenser and Milton do not demonstrate identical conceptions of just how the high style is to be achieved. Milton, in particular, seems to have been heavily influenced by theories developed in Italy by Tasso.

Ciceronian rhetoric had long divided the artistic use of language into the Three Styles: high, middle, and low. Like an orator, a poet in any given discourse works within a framework of one of these styles. And a late medieval tradition discovered that the Three Styles of Cicero were analogous to the three great works of Virgil. Thus the *Aeneid,* the *Georgics,* and the *Bucolics* stood as models for the high, middle, and low styles, respectively. The thrust of this Ciceronian tradition was to equate the high style with "wordes, phrases, sentences and figures, high loftie, eloquent & magnifik in proportion." There is a recurring suggestion that the middle or mean style contrasts with the high in that the mean style aims for "smoothness" and "pleasant moderation" (Puttenham), while the high style requires more expressive force or "vehemence."

Besides the Ciceronian formula, there were other rhetorical systems that competed with it to offer stylistic models for poets. One of these that was popular in Europe in the last half of the sixteenth century was the *Art of Rhetoric* by Hermogenes. Hermogenes's *Rhetoric* analyzes discourse into seven Ideas or categories of style: Clarity, Grandeur, Beauty, Speed, Ethos

Verity, and Gravity. It stresses flexibility rather than the exclusive assignment of one style to one genre in the Ciceronian fashion. One genre can subsume many of the Ideas; different Ideas can belong in the same genre. A commentator contends, for example, that Ariosto's *Orlando furioso* (1516; revised 1532) and Tasso's *Gerusalemme liberata* (1581) were written according to different Hermogenic Ideas. Ariosto is said to be writing according to the Idea of Clarity, while Tasso's complex "rough" style is said to be written under the Idea of Grandeur (Arazio Ariosto, *Riposte ad alcun i luoghi del dialogo dell' epica poesia,* 1585).

Tasso himself equated Grandeur with the Ciceronian high style, and Hermogenes makes it clear that Grandeur is intended to stand as the foundation for any style associated with a "loftie" genre like the heroic poem. Its first requirement is a deeply serious subject to be treated with a wealth of sentence (*see* Sententia and Copia), circumlocution, and figurative brilliance. It may create a desirable and powerful obscurity. Tasso maintained that Virgilian complexity could be obtained in Italian by "drawing out" the sentences, suspending the completion of meaning, and applying metrical devices to slow down and stiffen the movement of one's verse (Prince). He aims at difficulty, defending the transposition of words out of the order of common usage, foreign borrowings, poetic mutations, and a dense consonantal texture for his heroic verse (*Discoursi del poema eroico,* 1594).

The Italian impact on English practice is also evident in the weight of Italian commentary on Aristotle's *Poetics.* Most sixteenth-century English comments on the heroic poem reflect a late medieval tradition of the heroic as historical and exemplary. Aristotle's *Poetics* was made available in a Latin translation in 1498 in Italy, and the result was a wealth of Italian criticism on the epic poem, especially in the last half of the sixteenth century. Complex polemic exchanges centered first on Dante's *Divine Comedy* considered an epic poem, followed by quarrels centered on the nature of epic and romance in relation to *Orlando furioso* and *Gerusalemme liberata.* So numerous were such debates that one Italian critic subtitled a survey of their issues "one hundred poetic controversies" (Paolo Beni, *In Aristotelis poeticam commentarii,* 1613). It is not an exaggeration to say that Italian discussions of the *Poetics* initiated modern literary criticism and directly affected the practice of English poets from Sidney to Milton. Topics included issues of plot structure, decorum of character, the nature of imitation (q.v.), the function of allegory, and the nature of genre itself.

Aristotle seemed to say that the ideal epic had but a single action, illustrious in nature, restricted in temporal scope, performed by a great hero (XXIII); Homer's *Iliad,* structured around the "wrath of Achilles," seemed to be his paradigm. The action of many men, he says, belongs not to the epic but to "pure" history.

Nonetheless, *Orlando furioso,* which was so successful that it attained some two hundred European editions in the eighty-four years after its first publication, was not at all Aristotelian in structure. It treats various actions of a multitude of knights with an intricate plot and a vast quantity of incidents and characters. Some critics maintained that successful works like *Orlando* could establish a precedent for all matters pertaining to a form. Others said that *Orlando* was not a heroic poem but a romance (q.v.) and should be judged by its own laws. Still others contended that Ariosto's intricate multiple plot was "barbaric."

Aside from plot structure, the subject of romance with its emphasis upon love and chivalry was also raised in its relation to the heroic poem. Traditional epics paid little attention to love themes, although readers did point to Aeneas's encounter with Dido in the *Aeneid* as a sanction for their presence. But Virgil says he sings of "arms and the man," while Ariosto announces that his song is to be "of Dames, of Knights, of armes, of loves delight" (*Orlando furioso,* trans. Sir John Harington, 1591). Sidney, noting that critics of poetry claim that it trained men's wit to wanton sinfulness and lustful loves, concedes that "even to the heroical, Cupid hath ambitiously climbed."

Neo-Aristotelian critics also debated the presence in the heroic poem of "marvelous" actions, a debate that came to include the nature of poetic verisimilitude and probability (*see* Apology). Aristotle had allowed room for the "marvelous" in both the epic and tragedy, with the caution that unusual actions are easier to describe than to put on stage (XXIV). He seemed to stress invention, the "feigned marvelous," a substitute world created out of the imagination, with only a shadowy relation to history. In the controversies over Aristotle's meaning, the central argument was whether *mythos* (*fabula,* "fable") meant the configuration of a lifelike action or of a nonrealistic, invented action. Was the poet's world to be entirely imagined or one "perfected," refined by judgment and decorum? Ariosto fills *Orlando* with magic and magicians, "wonders" of all kinds. Was this appropriately "marvelous"? Or was "marvelous" a reference to the role of the poet in creating a "golden world," still shadowing history but altering, changing, increasing, or diminishing events to render them as "they should be"? And is there a conflict between the romantic "marvelous" and Christian values? Tasso, condemning Ariosto, denounces enchantments and maintains that a Christian poet must use only the "Christian marvelous" (*Discoursi dell' arte poetica,* 1587).

Inevitably the nature of the hero himself became a matter for controversy in the contradictions between neo-Aristotelian poetics, which made plot the soul of the poem, and Horatian apologetics which made poetry a moral discipline in its ability to imitate the ideas of virtue and vice. Many read Aristotle's remarks in the *Poetics* in respect of character that it must be "good" to mean that a character must be virtuous. Did an evil man have any place in the epic kind? And if the hero is to be a moral exemplar, how could the traditional warrior hero of the pagan world be reconciled with the ethical ideals of Renaissance chivalry? One solution for the Christian poet was to make his heroic person an unquestionable exemplar, a "godlike" man such as Adam or Christ or another biblical figure who would be both historical and a representative of Christian virtue.

Allegory or allegorical readings of the heroic poem also seemed to resolve some of these dilemmas. Allegory could display a hero's virtues in a martial context that figures a spiritual battle. Supernatural events could be illuminated. Ariosto's many references to magical events were sometimes excused (in a Christian poem) by allegorizing them and converting the allegory into moral instruction. Thus Sir John Harington provides his translation of *Orlando furioso* with notes that furnish the allegory to the poem "because the reader may take not only delight but profit in reading" (*An Advertisement to the reader, Orlando Furioso in English Heroical Verse,* 1591). That allegory is "of some things that are merely fabulous, yet have an allegoricall sence which every bodie at the first shew cannot perceive." This is in addition to his notes on "the Historicall sence" of the poem ("the acts and notable exploits of some persons worthy memorie") and "the Morall sence" ("Profitable for the active life of man, approving vertuous actions and condemning the contrarie") (*A Preface, Orlando Furioso*). Tasso provided his own allegorical reading of *Gerusalemme liberata*. George Chapman in the *Epistle Dedicatory* to his translation of the *Odyssey* (1614) makes Homer's "marvelous" the "moral marvelous" of the heightened exemplar: the *Odyssey* is not "phantastique, or meere fictive" but "the most material, and doctrinall illations of *Truth*" both for "manly information of Manners in the yong" and "even Christian pietie, in the most grave and high-governd." If the body of the poem, "the letter or historie," says Chapman, "seemes fictive and beyond possibilitie to bring into Act: the sence then and Allegory (which is the Soule) is to be sought."

The relations between tragedy (q.v.) and epic also formed part of the Italian examination of the *Poetics*. A rhetorical tradition identified tragedy and the heroic poem as contrasting genres. Puttenham, for example, assumes a contrast between tragedy, which "taxes the great for a secret reprehension to others," and the "heroick" poem, which "praises" the great. But medieval commentators had tended to treat drama as a form of oration and read the plays of Terence and Seneca as material for study rather than performance; drama seemed to become a part of narrative poetry in general. Thus the five-act structure discovered by the commentator Donatus in the works of Terence could be applied to narrative poems. And because Aristotle emphasizes plot and treats the *Iliad* and the *Odyssey* in the same terms he uses for tragedies like *Oedipus Rex,* the study of his *Poetics* further sanctioned a confusion of epic with drama. Epic and drama resemble each other in subject matter ("noble actions" of "noble personages"), construction, and species. Each should have reversals of situation, recognitions, and scenes of suffering (XXIV). Thus while the conventional Renaissance fable for the heroic poem was that of an illustrious action with a fortunate ending, commentators could argue that the type of plot in which a heroic character suffered an unfortunate end was not necessarily inappropriate for heroic poetry. And might not the hero of an epic demonstrate some of the great crimes or sins associated with tragedy if he excelled in other qualities? It is in this vein that Milton describes his argument in *Paradise Lost* (1674) as both "tragic" and "heroic."

Bibliography

Ralph C. Williams, *The Theory of the Heroic Epic in Italian Criticism of the Sixteenth Century* (1921); Merritt Y. Hughes, *Virgil and Spenser* (1929); Lewis F. Ball, "The Background of the Minor English Renaissance Epics," *ELH,* 1 (1934), 63–89; H. T. Swedenberg, Jr., *The Theory of the Epic in England, 1650–1800* (1944); C. M. Bowra, *From Virgil to Milton* (1945); Homer Nearing, Jr., *English Historical Poetry 1599–1641* (1945); Richard H. Perkinson, "The Epic in Five Acts," *SP,* 43 (1946), 465–81; Louis R. Zocca, "Mythological Narrative Poetry," *Elizabethan Narrative Poetry* (1950), pp. 189–288; Hallett Smith, *Elizabethan Poetry* (1952); Alison I. T. Higgins, *Secular Heroic Epic Poetry of the Caroline Period* (1953); F. T. Prince, *The Italian Element in Milton's Verse* (1954); E. M. W. Tillyard, *The English Epic and Its Background* (1954); Walter Allen, Jr., "The Non-Existant Classical Epyllion," *SP,* 55 (1958), 515–18; Paul W. Miller, "The Elizabethan Minor Epic," *SP,* 55 (1958), 31–38; Edwin B. Benjamin, "Fame, Poetry, and the Order of History in the Literature of the English Renaissance," *Studies in the Renaissance,* 6 (1959), 64–84; Lily B. Campbell, *Divine Poetry and Drama in Sixteenth-Century England* (1959); Burton O. Kurth, *Milton and Christian Heroism: Biblical Epic Themes and Forms in Seventeenth-Century England* (1959); O. B. Hardison, Jr., *The Enduring Monument* (1962); Graham Hough, *A Preface to "The Faerie Queene,"* (1962); Douglas Bush, *Mythology and the Renaissance Tradition in English Poetry* (rev. ed. 1963); John Buxton, "Shakespeare: *Venus and Adonis,"* *Elizabethan Taste* (1963), pp. 295–306; Elizabeth Story Donno, ed., "Introduction," *Elizabethan Minor Epics* (1963), pp. 1–20; Thomas Greene, *The Descent from Heaven: A Study in Epic Continuity* (1963); Anthony LaBranche, "Drayton's *The Barons Warres* and the Rhetoric of Historical Poetry," *JEGP,* 62 (1963), 82–95; Robert M. Durling, *The Figure of the Poet in Renaissance Epic* (1965); A. Bartlett Giamatti, *The Earthly Paradise and the Renaissance Epic* (1966); Barbara K. Lewalski, *Milton's Brief Epic: The Genre, Meaning, and Art of "Paradise Regained"* (1966); Paul W. Miller, ed., "Introduction," *Seven Minor Epics of the English Renaissance (1596–1624)* (1967), pp. vii-xxvii; Wayne Shumaker, "*Paradise Lost* and the Italian Epic Tradition," *Th'Upright Heart and Pure,* ed. Amadeus P. Fiore (1967), pp. 87–100; John M. Steadman, *Milton and the Renaissance Hero* (1967); M. M. Reese, ed., "Introduction," *Elizabethan Verse Romances* (1968), pp. 1–23; Mark Rose, *Heroic Love: Studies in Sidney and Spenser* (1968); John M. Steadman, *Milton's Epic Characters: Image and Idol* (rev. ed., 1968); Anthony LaBranche, "Poetry, History, and Oratory: The Renaissance Historical Poem," *SEL,* 9 (1969), 1–19; John T. Shawcross, "The Style and Genre of *Paradise Lost,*" *New Essays on "Paradise Lost,"* ed. Thomas Kranidas (1969), pp. 15–33; Elizabeth Story Donno, "The Epyllion," *English Poetry and Prose, 1540–1674,* ed. Christopher Ricks (1970), pp. 82–100; Annabel M. Patterson, *Hermogenes and the Renaissance: Seven Ideas of Style* (1970); Rosalie L. Colie, *The Resources of Kind: Genre-Theory in the Renaissance,* ed. Barbara K. Lewalski (1973); Caroline Jameson, "Ovid in the Sixteenth Century," *Ovid,* ed. J. W. Binns (1973), pp. 210–42; William Nelson, *Fact or Fiction: The Dilemma of the Renaissance Storyteller* (1973); Raymond B. Waddington, "An Ovidian Epic: *Hero and Leander,*" *The Mind's Empire: Myth and Form in George Chapman's Narrative Poems* (1974), pp. 153–80; John M. Steadman, "The Arming of an Archetype: Heroic Virtue and the Conventions of Literary Epic," *Concepts of the Hero in the Middle Ages and the Renaissance,* eds. Norman T. Burns and Christopher J. Reagan (1975), pp. 147–96; S. Clark Hulse, "Elizabethan Minor Epic: Toward a Definition of Genre," *SP,* 73 (1976), 302–19; John M. Steadman, *Epic and Tragic Structure in "Paradise Lost"* (1976); William Keach, *Elizabethan Erotic Narratives* (1977), Michael O'Connell, *Mirror and Veil: The Historical Dimension of Spenser's "Faerie Queene"* (1977); Joan Malory Webber, *Milton and His Epic Tradition* (1978); Anne Lake Prescott, *French Poets and the English Renaissance: Studies in Fame and Transformation* (1978); Thomas E. Maresca, *Three English Epics: Studies in Chaucer, Spenser, and Milton* (1979); Joseph Anthony Wittreich, Jr., "Revelation's 'New' Form," *Visionary Poetics: Milton's Tradition and His Legacy* (1979), pp. 3–78.

History:

By the early seventeenth century playwrights seemed to be in loose agreement that when the term *history* was used to designate a dramatic poem, the term referred to a play based upon English history of the preceding four hundred years, particularly as that history was described in the prose chronicles of England. They were plays that "instructed such people as cannot read in the discovery of all our English chronicles" (Thomas Heywood, *An Apology for Actors,* 1612).

The chronicles were narrative prose histories, usually continuous and detailed accounts of events that "representeth a time" (Sir Francis Bacon, *The Advancement of Learning,* 1605). The most popular chronicle sources for the history play were Edward Hall's *The Union of the Two Noble and Illustrious Families of Lancaster and York* (1548); Raphael Holinshed's *Chronicles of England, Scotland and Ireland* (1578); and John Stow's *Chronicles of England from Brute . . . unto the Present Year of Christ 1580.*

Although the term *history* appears in print as a theatrical term before the 1590s, it seems to be merely a synonym for *true story* or even just *story.* For example, in 1568, *Jacob and Esau* was printed as "a newe mery and wittie comedie or enterlude . . . treating upon the Historie of Jacob and Esau." The first play to have *historie* attached to it on the title page was *The Taming of a Shrew (A pleasant, conceited Historie)* in 1594. The same year Robert Greene's *Friar Bacon* was issued as an *Honorable Historie.*

The first play based directly on English chronicle history to be published as a *history* was William Shakespeare's *The History of Henrie the Fourth,* issued in 1598. Before this, dramas that dealt with the careers of earlier English monarchs had been called *tragedies, troublesome reigns,* and *lives and deaths.* Shakespeare also established the term *chronicle history* with *The Cronicle History of Henry the fift* in its 1600 publication. After 1600, the use of the word *history* in the more general sense of *story* as a designation in play-titles and descriptions declined rapidly. All of Shakespeare's plays that are called *histories* in the Folio of 1623 are based primarily on the English chronicles and are restricted to the reigns of English rulers of the preceding four hundred years. Popular contemporary attitudes toward those reigns are suggested in the table of contents in Hall's *Two Noble and Illustrious Families:* "The unquiet tyme of King Henry the fowerth," "The victorious actes of King Henry the V," and "The Tragicall doynges of King Richard the iii." Thus it seems that Shakespeare's example established the relation between the English chronicles and history plays, and he seemed to define, in the opinion of his contemporaries, the nature of a history as a dramatic genre.

While this restriction of the term *history* to plays based on the reigns of kings from King John forward seems warranted by the actual practice of playwrights, this statement must be qualified by the vague use of the term in play titles and other references and by a lack of agreement among modern scholars about just what Elizabethan and Jacobean playwrights must have meant when they called their plays *histories.* There is not agreement among modern scholars about either the definition of the term *history play,* or, when they seem to agree, on the canon of plays to be included under such a term. The problem is further compounded by the fact that tragedies (q.v.), too, during the Renaissance were assumed to be histories, plays based on real events. And Shakespeare's plays about chronicled rulers of the remote past, such as King Lear and Macbeth, are grouped with the tragedies in the Folio of 1623.

It is suggestive of the sweeping application of the term *history* that a rhetorician like William Webbe, dividing all poetry into three kinds, comical, tragical, and historical, assigns to the last "all such matters which is indifferent between the other two [which] doo commonly occupy the pennes of poets: such are the poeticall complying of Chronicles, the freendly greetings betweene freendes, and very many sortes besides *(Discourse of English Poetry,* 1586).

Nevertheless, the history play, despite its ambiguous generic frame, is a new dramatic genre in the last part of the sixteenth century; and its appearance then seems natural, even inevitable, given the nature of contemporary literary values and the intricate relations among poetry, history, and rhetoric (q.v.). Traditionally the writing of history was thought of as a literary activity in itself. In the study of history "a yonge gentilman shal be taught to note and marke nat only the ordre and elegancie in declaration of the historie, but also the occasion of the warres, the counsailes and preparations of either part. .. the fortune and successe of the holle affaires" (Thomas Elyot, *The Governor,* 1531). One function of the study of history was the delineation of historical figures as examples of political vice and virtue for posterity to execrate or admire: "the commodites and good sequele of vertue, the discommodies and evyll conclusions of vicious licence" (Elyot). Because such historical characters were thought of as concrete instances of permanent categories, it was assumed that they would always be useful as moral exempla. The life of Richard III was a warning to all tyrants.

As a literary form, history was conditioned by the rhetorical system that was the foundation of school training. Historians relied on the procedures of the rhetorician to specify what attributes of a character were of permanent interest and worthy of note. These procedures were particularly the "topics" or "places" of demonstrative oratory (*see* Common-place). Students in Elizabethan schools were taught to analyze the materials of history as well as those of poetry in terms of such topics, essentially categories of "what to say"; they were also taught to construct "lives" of great men through the use of the "topics." Thus in praising or execrating a great man one would consider first, under the topic *genus,* his race, native country, ancestors, and parentage; second, the manner of his education; and third, under *res gestae,* his physical attributes, spiritual attitudes, and gifts of fortune. One topic of particular power was the "outdoing" topic, a description of how the hero's deeds "outdo" those of someone else. The "outdoing" topic seems to have had a structural impact on the history play itself in that it created a habit of mind that assumed a comparison of one great man with another—the "parallel" life. Thus the playwright was equipped with a comprehensive rhetorical apparatus for eliciting from his chronicle sources a set of formal devices for elaborating the characters of great men.

The very idea of history is a lodestone in Renaissance aesthetics, drawing to itself such diverse genres as the heroic verse epistle, the complaint, and the heroic poem (qq.v). Poets went to history for their subject matter, convinced of the exemplary force and effective weight of the lives of great men and women, and those theories of tragedy that assumed the value of history as a ground for the "highest" kind of drama needed only a slight refocus to provide a sanction for the history play. If, in a very loose sense, a tragedy can be thought of as a dramatized complaint, the history play can be thought of as a dramatized "heroical" or epic poem. Where the complaint, like tragedy, emphasizes the fall of a prince and his suffering in that change of fortune, the scope of the heroic poem, like that of the history play, is broader, more comprehensive, pointing beyond the destiny of an individual to that of the commonwealth.

The genesis of the Elizabethan history play is also to be found in the persistent tendency of an increasingly secular English drama to combine spectacular story with a didactic purpose. Generally the history play substitutes fact and direct statement for the allegorical presentation of political virtue and vice of the older morall plays *(see* Morall). For example, there is an early political, allegorical play by the poet John Skelton called *Magnificence* (c. 1515) in which Magnificence stands, not for Mankind, but

121

"a prynce of great myght." The play is not so much a mirror for man as a mirror for princes, a lesson in the art of good government. It is also possible to see the movement to a political emphasis rather than a religious one in the allegorical *Respublica* (1553) in which Respublica ("good Englande") comes to ruin when ruled by Avarice, Insolence, Oppression, and Adulation until the People ("the poore Commontie") and Nemesis correct what is amiss.

The earliest employment of outright secular historical material in the English drama comes earlier than *Respublica* in the play *King John* (1538) by John Bale. Essentially this is a morality play with historical personages. King John is assailed by the abstractions Sedition, Dissimulation, and Usurped Power; but these abstractions are also given historical names.

Academic playwrights also introduced English historical subject matter to audiences. Thomas Legge's *Richardus tertius,* acted in 1579, is a trilogy in Latin based on the chronicle history of Richard III. It is divided into three "actiones," each of which is a full length play in five acts.

A combination of patriotic fervor and moral instruction made the history plays extraordinarily popular. From the defeat of the Spanish Armada in 1588 to the death of Elizabeth in 1603, over two hundred plays with historical subject matter were performed; this was more than a fifth of the total plays on the stage. The playwrights, defending the theater against Puritan complaints, vigorously evoked the nature of the history play as an example of the drama's civil benefits. Heywood's claims in *An Apology for Actors* are typical: "playes have made the ignorant more apprehensive, taught the unlearned the knowledge of many famous histories, instructed such as cannot reade in the discovery of all our English chronicles . . . because playes are writ with this ayme, and carryed with this methode, to teach their subjects obedience to their king, to shew the people the untimely ends of such as have moved tummults, commotions, and insurrections, to present them with the flourishing estate of such as live in obedience, exhorting them to allegeance, dehorting them from all trayterous and fellonious strategems." The chronicle play did not long outlast the reign of Elizabeth. It flourished until her death and survived into the Jacobean years, but after the civil wars of the seventeeth century virtually disappeared from the English stage.

Bibliography

Felix E. Schelling, *The English Chronicle Play* (1902); E. M. W. Tillyard, *Shakespeare's History Plays* (1944); Lily B. Campbell, *Shakespeare's "Histories": Mirrors of Elizabethan Policy* (1947); Allardyce Nicoll, " ' Tragical-Comical-Historical-Pastoral': Elizabethan Dramatic Nomenclature," *BJRL,* 43 (1961), 70–87; M. M. Reese, *The Cease of Majesty: A Study of*

Shakespeare's History Plays (1961); Ernest W. Talbert, *The Problem of Order* (1962); Ernest W. Talbert, *Elizabethan Drama and Shakespeare's Early Plays: An Essay in Historical Criticism* (1963); Irving Ribner, *The English History Play in the Age of Shakespeare* (rev. ed., 1965); David Bevington, "Satire and the State," *Tudor Drama and Politics: A Critical Approach to Topical Meaning* (1968), pp. 260–88; Wilbur Sanders, *The Dramatist and the Received Idea* (1968); Alvin Kernan, *"The Henriad:* Shakespeare's Major History Plays," *YR,* 59 (1969), 3–32; F. P. Wilson, "The English History Play," *Shakespearian and Other Studies,* ed. Helen Gardner (1969), pp. 1–53; Henry Ansgar Kelly, *Divine Providence in the England of Shakespeare's Histories* (1970); David Riggs, *Shakespeare's Heroical Histories: "Henry VI" and Its Literary Tradition* (1971); Eugene M. Waith, *Ideas of Greatness: Heroic Drama in England* (1971); Robert Ornstein, *A Kingdom for a Stage: The Achievement of Shakespeare's History Plays* (1972); Moody E. Prior, *The Drama of Power: Studies in Shakespearean History Plays* (1973); Martha Hester Fleischer, *The Iconography of the English History Play* (1974); Stanley J. Kahrl, *Traditions of Medieval English Drama* (1974); Herbert Lindenberger, *Historical Drama: The Relation of Literature and Reality* (1975); Anne Barton, "He that plays the king: Ford's *Perkin Warbeck* and the Stuart History Play," *English Drama: Forms and Development,* eds. Marie Axton and Raymond Williams (1977), pp. 69–93; George J. Becker, *Shakespeare's Histories* (1977); Peter Saccio, *Shakespeare's English Kings: History, Chronicle, and Drama* (1977); Edna Zwick Boris, *Shakespeare's English Kings, the People, and the Law: A Study in the Relationship between the Tudor Constitution and the English History Plays* (1978); John Wilders, *The Lost Garden: A View of Shakespeare's English and Roman History Plays* (1978).

Hymn:

"A song to praise God" (John Bullokar, *An English Expositor,* 1616); as a literary form, a lyric (q.v.) poem written in praise of a religious subject, usually a praise of God (*see* Epideictic rhetoric). English Renaissance critics and poets alike ranked the hymn as the highest kind of poetry, placing it in the hierarchy of literary forms above both tragedy and heroic poetry. Whereas the epic and tragedy imitated actions of the high born, the hymn lauded the perfection and excellence of God. The high style was considered essential for these three kinds of poetry.

The respect for hymns reflects not only an admiration for the formal beauty of classical songs and poems in praise of deities but also the sanction that Christian tradition placed upon the divine subject matter itself. George Puttenham is typical when he writes, "The matters . . . that concerne the Gods and divine things are highest of all other to be couched in writing, next to them the noble gests and great fortunes of Princes, and the notable accidents of time . . . these be all high subjectes, and therefore are delivered over to the Poets *Hymnick* & historicall who be occupied either in divine laudes, or in *heroicall* reports" (*The Art of English Poesy,* 1589). Moreover, he adds, the classical hymns sung in praise of "the gods of the Gentiles" were "the first forme of Poesie and the highest & the stateliest." Similarly, Sir Philip Sidney, in distinguishing the "severall kindes" of poetry, writes, "The Chiefe both in antiquitie and excellencie were they that did imitate the inconceivable excellencies of GOD. Such were *David* in his Psalmes, *Salomon* in his song of Songs, in his Ecclesiastes and Proverbs, *Moses* and *Debora* in theyr Hymnes, and the writer of *Job*" (*An Apology for Poetry,* 1595). "In this kinde," he remarks, "though in full wrong divinitie, were *Orpheus, Amphion,* Homer in his hymnes, and many other, both Greekes and Romaines." Such poets Sidney says "may justly bee termed *Vates*" or "a Diviner, Fore-seer, or Prophet."

In part, the writing of hymns in the vernacular (*see* Vulgar language) was given direction by a neo-Latin revival of the Greco-Roman literary hymn in the fifteenth and sixteenth centuries in Italy by such poets as Marullo, Vida, and Scaliger. Although the hymns of Marullo retained pagan subject matter, those by Vida and Scaliger adapted Christian subjects to the classical form. Besides celebrating the members of the Trinity, some of these hymns praise saints. In form these neo-Latin hymns imitated the classical literary hymn which, roughly, consists of an exordium, main body, and peroration. After an opening invocation of the muse and a catalogue of attributes of the god or goddess to be praised (exordium), the main body of the classical literary hymn treats in detail a major characteristic suggested by the catalogue. The peroration consists of an apostrophe or prayer.

Among English poets composing hymns in the vernacular are Edmund Spenser, John Milton, and Richard Crashaw. Spenser's work entitled *Four Hymns* (1596) explores the relationships between earthly and heavenly beauty and love. In like manner, Milton finds the word *hymn* appropriate to describe the "humble ode" which the poet-speaker of the prefatory stanzas of *On the Morning of Christ's Nativity* (1645) wishes to present to the Christ-child. His contemporary Crashaw uses *hymn* to designate his poem of praise of Saint Teresa in *A Hymn to the Name and Honor of the Admirable Saint Teresa* (1652).

In a somewhat special category among the hymns of praise to God were the Psalms, "the holy *Davids* Psalmes," as Sidney calls them. On occasion David was said to be an imitator of classical poets; other times, however, he was considered superior to them, even their model, and his Psalms were cited as evidence of the biblical origins of poetry. The popularity of these divine songs of praise is reflected in the great number of metrical paraphrases of them from the mid-sixteenth to mid-seventeenth century in England. Often the purpose of these paraphrases was to adapt the Psalms for congregational singing. These "sacred *Hymns* of the *Holy Ghost*" were adapted, as George Wither says, so that "the common people . . . might present him [God] with the living streams of his owne pure fountain" (*The Scholar's Purgatory,* c. 1625). Earlier, Sidney had remarked that such divine "Poesie must be used, by whosoever will follow *S. James* his counsell, in singing Psalmes when they are merry: and I knowe is used with the fruite of comfort by some, when, in sorrowfull pangs of their death-bringing sinnes, they find the consolation of the never-leaving goodnesse."

Bibliography

Frederick John Gillman, *The Evolution of the English Hymn* (1927); Israel Baroway, "The Bible as Poetry in the English Renaissance: An Introduction," *JEGP,* 32 (1933), 447–80; Philipp von Rohr-Sauer, *English Metrical Psalms from 1600 to 1660* in *Dissertations: Literature and Art,* 19 (n.d.)

[1938]; Israel Baroway, "The Lyre of David," *ELH,* 8 (1941), 119–42; Hallett Smith, "English Metrical Psalms in the Sixteenth Century and their Literary Significance," *HLQ,* 9, (1946), 249–71; Lily B. Campbell, "The Psalms as English Poetry under Edward VI" and "The Psalms as English Poetry under Elizabeth I," *Divine Poetry and Drama in Sixteenth-Century England* (1959), pp. 34–54; Philip B. Rollinson, "The Renaissance of the Literary Hymn," *Southeastern Renaissance Conference: Renaissance Papers,* (1968), 11–20; Philip B. Rollinson, "A Generic View of Spenser's *Four Hymns,*" *SP,* 68 (1971), 292–304; Coburn Freer, "Herbert and the Psalter: Method and Experience" and "Some Metrical Psalm Styles," *Music for a King: George Herbert's Style and the Metrical Psalms* (1972), pp. 1–115; Philip B. Rollinson, "Milton's Nativity Poem and the Decorum of Genre," *MiltonS,* 7 (1975), 165–88; Edward Gosselin, *The King's Progress to Jerusalem: Some Interpretations of David During the Reformation Period and Their Patristic and Medieval Background* (1976); Anne Lake Prescott, "Marot," *French Poets and the English Renaissance* (1978), pp. 1–36; Barbara K. Lewalski, *Protestant Poetics and the Seventeenth-Century Religious Lyric* (1979).

Imitation:

In literary theory of the sixteenth and early seventeenth centuries, a term referring both to the practice of copying other writers and to the process of rendering nature in art. Roger Ascham points to this dual concept of imitation when he advises writers to "folow . . . the best authors," but with the further knowledge that "all the workes of nature, in a maner be examples for arte to folow" (*The Schoolmaster,* 1570).

When Ascham urges writers to "folow . . . the best authors" and to "expresse lievelie and perfitelie that example which ye go about to folow," he is recommending a thorough and imaginative comparison of literary models before a writer refashions them. He is not encouraging an indiscriminate borrowing of incidents and phrases or the mechanical parroting of verbal and structural detail. He makes a distinction between works that imitate an inherited theme or context but use new words and works that rehearse a particular verbal formula or quotation in an original context. To Ascham the purpose of literary imitation is to capture the spirit and the principles of a literary model.

But copying in its narrowest sense was imitation, and many writers achieved subtle and complex effects by putting old words in new contexts. So a writer of the 1560s can say,"It is the custome of all writers almost, to enterlace other mens doings into their own. . . . And as *Flauius Albinus* sayth, this is one kind of fruit gotten by readings, that a man may imitate that which he lyketh and alloweth in others: and such speciall poyntes and sayinges as hee is especially delighted & in loue withall, by apt and fitte derivation maye wrest to serue his owne turne and purpose" (Franciscus Patricius, *A Moral Method of Civil Policy,* trans. Robinson, quoted in Dent). Sometimes verbal formulae were not only quoted, but also translated from one language to another. In *The Faerie Queene* (1590) Edmund Spenser stitches bits of translation from Ariosto and Tasso (who themselves were sometimes translating from Virgil, Ovid, or Catullus) into the fabric of his work. One of the most famous speeches in Shakespeare's *Antony and Cleopatra* (c. 1607) is a restatement into blank verse of North's English translation of Amyot's French version of Plutarch's *Life of Antony*.

The concept of imitation also covered the translation of an entire text from one language into another. Although distinctions between translation and imitation date back to classical times, translation was rarely defined with certainty. The line between translation and imitation was wavering and ambiguous. In the Middle Ages and early Renaissance, translation was closely connected to a tradition of textual interpretation and commentary with an overriding didactic purpose. As national states began to mature in the sixteenth century, a second strain of translation sprang up, the primary function of which was to enrich from foreign stores a developing vernacular literature. The resulting translations were often identified as such with a bow to the original writer, but just as often they were not. Sir Thomas Wyatt's translations of Petrarch's sonnets are not identified with Petrarch in *Tottel's Miscellany* (1557). The notion of translation into the vernacular (*see* Vulgar language) as an art in itself did not begin in England until George Chapman addressed the issues in works prefixed to his translations of the *Iliad* (1611).

The traditional metaphors for imitation, however, stressed imitation as a refashioning of more than one model. Seneca and countless other writers following him liken the poet to a bee who makes honey. As the bee transforms the nectars of the most varied flowers into honey, so the writer should blend whatever he has gathered from a varied course of reading into one delicious compound, which, even though it betrays its origins, is, nevertheless, different from them. Another favorite figure for imitation was digestion. Undigested material, merely memorized or copied material, can no more be transformed into an original work than undigested food can build up the body. Ben Jonson says that the true poet should be able "to convert the substance, or Riches of an other Poet, to his owne use. . . . Not, as a Creature, that swallowes, what it takes in, crude, raw, or indigested; but that feedes with an Appetite, and hath a Stomacke to concoct, divide, and turne all into nourishment. Not, to imitate servilely, as Horace saith, and catch at vices, for vertue: but, to draw forth out of the best, and choisest flowers, with the Bee, and turne all into Honey, worke it into one relish, and savour" (*Timber, or Discoveries,* 1641). Other figures used to describe imitation were the blending of diverse voices in a choir, the instruments of an orchestra, or essences of perfume.

Such literary imitation suggests a strong emphasis upon emulation and discipleship, but imitation also came to carry with it bold efforts to surpass previous masters. Italian commentators of the sixteenth century thus begin to speak of imitation as "removing the iron and making all gold and silver" or "making of the perfect the most perfect by uniting in one the perfections of many." A poet's greatest honor depended upon his models being known and surpassed.

An emphasis upon literary models was not itself new in the Renaissance. In antiquity it had become generally recognized in both theory and practice. Virgil was indebted to Homer; and Seneca, to Euripides. For medieval and Renaissance theorists, Horace's *Ars poetica* was the *locus classicus* for the doctrine of literary imitation with the Roman poet's injunction to "consider well Greek models" and his assumption that literary art is an art of studying exemplars. Rhetorical masters like Cicero and Quintilian also assumed that literary imitation was central to literary art.

Imitation in its second sense—as the process of rendering nature in art— relates in some ways to the meaning discussed above. To many writers, copying an ancient poet was copying "nature" because the earlier poet was nearer to the wellsprings of excellence; his rendering of nature was necessarily stronger and more accurate than that of a Renaissance contemporary, because the Roman poet lived in a superior civilization. Thus to copy the Roman writer was to copy nature, too.

A more profound conception of imitation also received attention in the sixteenth century, initiated by the rediscovery of Aristotle's *Poetics* and his use of the term $\mu\iota\mu\eta\sigma\iota\varsigma$ (Latin: *mimesis*). After being unnoticed in Europe for hundreds of years, the *Poetics* was newly examined by Italian critics late in the fifteenth century. Aristotle's statement that all the fine arts in their general conception are modes of imitation (I, 2) and that one art differs from another in its mode of imitation (I, 3) raised important issues which critics were quick to recognize. Many understood Aristotle's statement that art was mimetic to mean that any writer using words should render nature accurately, should compose a picture of people and actions that would provide a concrete equivalent of the external world. He seemed to be calling for realistic poetry, an art of verisimilitude. But other readers noticed that the *Poetics* also stresses the need for the marvelous in poetry and found in this a sanction for supernaturalism and fantasy or at least a heightening of everyday life.

English theorists tended to follow the second response. Imitation was an imitation of God's method of creation, rather than a faithful copying of creation itself (*see* Apology). A poet creates a second nature with his imaginative powers. Either a perfected world or an entirely imagined world could be called marvelous. The perfected world came to be equated with quasi-Platonic notions that stressed the poet's power to deal with universals. The result was an emphasis upon a static conception of objects, even though Aristotle put his own emphasis on the action of a plot. A thing was thought of as accurately represented if it was represented in the fullest development of its potentiality. Characters, for example, will behave, not as they do in history, the world of the particular event, but according to preconceived ideas of how their archetypes would act. To Sir Philip Sidney, for example, photographic verisimilitude is not imitation. He distinguishes between painters of the "meaner sort" who "counterfet onely such faces as are sette before them" and "the more excellent, who, having no law but wit" create that "which is fittest [most appropriate] for the eye to see" (*An Apology for Poetry,* 1595). The Aristotelian concept of imitation was adjusted and synthesized into a broad network of inherited ideas about the relation of image and idea as it conditioned allegory (q.v.), personification, dramatic types (*see* Decorum), mythological exemplars, and homiletic models.

Bibliography

Harold Ogden White, *Plagiarism and Imitation during the English Renaissance* (1935); Marvin T. Herrick, *The Fusion of Horatian and Aristotelian Literary Criticism,* 1531–1555 (1946); Rosemond Tuve, *Elizabethan and Metaphysical Imagery* (1947); J. A. K. Thomson, *The Classical Background of English Literature* (1948); R. R. Bolgar, *The Classical Heritage and Its Beneficiaries* (1954); R. W. Dent, *John Webster's Borrowing* (1960); Rosemond Tuve, "Sacred 'Parody' of Love Poetry, and Herbert," *Studies in the Renaissance, 8* (1961), 249–90; A. J. Smith, "Theory and Practice in Renaissance Poetry: Two Kinds of Imitation," *BJRL,* 47 (1964), 212–43; John Hazel Smith, ed., "The 'Imitation' of Source," *A Humanist's "Trew Imitation": Thomas Watson's "Absalom"* (1964), pp. 41–81; Maren-Sofie Røstvig, "Ars Aeterna: Renaissance Poetics and Theories of Divine Creation," *Mosaic,* 3 (1970), 40–61; Thomas R. Steiner, "Precursors to Dryden: English and French Theories of Translation in the Seventeenth Century," *CLS,* 7 (1970), 50–81; Robert M. Adams, "Imitations," *Proteus, His Lies, His Truth: Discussions of Literary Translation* (1973), pp. 101–14; Howard C. Cole, "Wading Farther," *A Quest of Inquirie: Some Contexts of Tudor Literature* (1973), pp. 207–324; John Steadman, *The Lamb and the Elephant: Ideal Imitation and the Context of Renaissance Allegory* (1974); William Keach, "Verbal Borrowing in Elizabethan Poetry: Plagiarism or Parody?" *Centrum,* 4 (1976), 21–31; Marion Trousdale, "Recurrence and Renaissance: Rhetorical Imitation in Ascham and Sturm," *ELR,* 6 (1976), 156–79; Gordon Braden, *The Classics & English Renaissance Poetry: Three Case Studies* (1978).

Invocation:

"A calling upon any thing with trust in the same" (Robert Cawdrey, *A Table Alphabetical of English Words,* 1604). As a literary convention, the poetic formula of *invocatio* was an address to a deity, muse, or patron spirit for aid in poetic creation.

Such appeals by poets for inspiration and knowledge are common in classical lyric and narrative poetry, especially heroic poetry. In classical literature nine goddess muses, the daughters of Zeus and Mnemosyne (memory), preside over the arts and learning, and it is to them that classical poets often make their appeals. The muses, whose names and domains of intellectual interest were familiar to English poets, are: Calliope (epic poetry), Clio (history), Erato (lyrics, especially love poetry), Euterpe (music), Melpomene (tragedy), Polyhymnia (sacred poetry), Terpsichore (choral dance and song), Thalia (comedy), and Urania (astronomy).

English poets did not confine themselves to the nine muses in their invocations. Edmund Spenser, for example, in the prefatory stanzas of *The Faerie Queene* (1590), invokes aid not only from muses and deities of classical origin but also from his reigning monarch, Elizabeth. And John Milton in *Paradise Lost* (1667) appeals to a Christian source that he variously associates with divine Light and the Holy Spirit. Among lyric poets, writers of sonnet sequences often consider the beloved their inspiring spirit; her beauty and virtue, gifts from heaven to her, guide the poet's heart and pen.

Behind this literary formula lies the suggestion that an important part of the creative process comes from a source of inspiration that is outside the poet, and the poet's essential talent or genius requires an outside force to set it in motion and to sustain it. Thomas Lodge, for example, says, "Poetrye commeth from above, from a heavenly seate of a glorious God, unto an excellent creature man" (*Defense of Poetry,* 1579). And as Ben Jonson says in *Timber, or Discoveries* (1641), "A Rymer and a *Poet* are two things"; he claims that only the latter experiences the divine madness that is "*Poeticall Rapture.*" Many other Renaissance critical treatises echo Cicero's famous statement, "No man was ever great without divine inspiration."

Jest:

A humorous anecdote written in prose; often referred to by late sixteenth and early seventeenth-century writers as "merry tales." Published in collections known as jestbooks, these anecdotes were popular reading matter throughout the English Renaissance. In their clever exploitation of incident and in their use of details from everyday life, jests contributed to the development of realistic prose narrative fictions of the late sixteenth century.

Although sometimes given a moral twist, jests for the most part are simply meant for a reader's amusement. The complete title of the 1626 edition of *The Jests of Scoggin* claims that such anecdotes are "a preservative against melancholy." In the prologue of this edition the publisher writes: "There is nothing beside the goodnesse of God, that preserves health so much, as honest mirth, especially mirth used at dinner and supper, and mirth toward bed. . . . Therefore considering this matter, that mirth is so necessary a thing for man, I published this Booke . . . to make men merrie."

With the invention of printing many of the anecdotes told around the fireside and tavern table passed into their written form as jests. Jests, however, also have some literary cousins. At a great distance are the short pithy anecdotes about historical or living people that classical orators used to enliven their speeches. Rhetorical masters like Cicero and Quintilian emphasized the power of laughter with audiences and recommended witty little tales to their students. Closer at hand are the moral *exemplum* and *fabliau* of the medieval period. Like *fabliaux,* jests are humorous, often ribald and satiric, and built on realistic detail; but unlike *fabliaux,* jests are written in prose. Like *exempla,* which are anecdotes of moral instruction used by medieval clergy in their sermons, jests sometimes conclude with a moral tag. When they do, jests with their "By this tale ye may see . . . " conclusion merely point to some general truth about human frailty or folly.

Other times, a jest will parody the moral tag, turning it into the punch line of jokes today.

The anecdotes of English jestbooks range from very simple ones to more complicated types that approach the nature of a *novella* (q.v.). In most of them the high point is a witty reply. Errant women and the clergy frequently find themselves the object of satire, but almost no one is exempt from being the butt of wit or the victim of a practical joke in jestbook tales. The everyday world created within the jests bears no resemblance to that of romantic and heroic narrative; but it is close to the middle-class and roguish worlds of the prose fiction of such contemporary writers as Thomas Deloney and Thomas Nashe.

Some jestbooks are collections of what modern scholars call detached jests; the anecdotes are independent of each other, such as those in *A Hundred Merry Tales* (1526), the earliest of the Tudor jestbooks. Other jestbooks center their anecdotes around one figure, giving them a semblance of biography. Actually most of these "jest biographies" are as unconnected structurally as the detached jests, as in, for example, *Merry Tales made by Master Skelton* (1567). The tales of still other jestbooks, such as *Westward for Smelts* (1620), are much longer and border on being *novelle*. The greater length allows more room for dialogue, description, and the author's commentary. A new concern for artistic form, with plot, setting, and a more developed characterization all contributing to the humorous effect, moves the emphasis of the "merry tale" away from the punch line of most jestbook anecdotes.

Bibliography

F. P. Wilson, "English Jestbooks of the Sixteenth and Seventeenth Centuries," *HLQ*, 2 (1939), 121–58; Merritt E. Lawlis, ed., "Introduction," *The Novels of Thomas Deloney* (1961), pp. xi—xxxii; Margaret Schlauch, *Antecedents of the English Novel, 1400–1600* (1963); P. M. Zall, ed., "The Natural History of Jestbooks: An Introduction," *A Hundred Merry Tales and Other English JestBooks of the Fifteenth and Sixteenth Centuries* (1963), pp. 1–10; Stanley J. Kahrl, "The Medieval Origins of the Sixteenth-Century English Jest-books," *Studies in the Renaissance*, 13 (1966), 166–83; P. M. Zall, ed., "The Blending of Wit and Jest: An Introduction," *A Nest of Ninnies and Other English Jestbooks of the Seventeenth Century* (1970), pp. ix–xviii; Kurt-Michael Pätzold, "Thomas Deloney and the English Jest-Book Tradition," *ES*, 53 (1972), 313–28; Raymond A. Anselment, *'Betwixt Jest and Earnest'* (1979), pp. 8–32.

Lyric:

A term used during the late sixteenth and early seventeenth centuries to distinguish one of the major kinds of poetry. Whether a song (q.v.) or a written poem and whether religious or secular in content, lyrics were mainly thought of as expressions of praise and persuasion. In exclaiming against detractors of all kinds of poetry, Sir Philip Sidney asks, "Is it the *Lyricke* that moste displeaseth, who with his tuned *Lyre* and well accorded voice, giveth praise, the reward of vertue, to vertuous acts? who giveth morall preceptes and naturall Problemes, who sometime raiseth up his voyce to the height of the heavens, in singing the laudes of the immortall God?" (*An Apology for Poetry,* 1595). Sidney's belief that a major rhetorical intention of a lyric is to praise was a common-place in English theory (*see* Epideictic rhetoric); and he and other English poets were in agreement with such sixteenth-century Italian critics as Sebastian Minturno who held that a lyric was an imitation of all those things worthy of praise (*L'arte poetica,* 1564).

In the tradition of classical poetics, many English writers associated lyric with music, and defined a lyric as a song sung by a single voice with musical accompaniment. Thus, for example, when Roger Ascham (*The Schoolmaster,* 1570) classifies poets as comic, tragic, epic, and melic (or lyric), he is pointing to distinctions between poets whose work is dramatic or narrative in the mode of presentation, and those whose work is intended to be sung. And George Puttenham, explaining the classical manner of identifying the various kinds of poets, says, "Others who more delighted to write songs or ballads of pleasure, to be song with the voice, and to the harpe, lute, or citheron, & such other musical instruments, they were called melodious Poets . . . or, by a more common name, *Lirique* Poets" (*The Art of English Poesy,* 1589).

Many English Renaissance lyrics were intended to be sung; but, as more and more poets found an audience through the printed page, they were, in effect, changing the lyric from a song to a short written poem in which a speaker expresses the thoughts and emotions appropriate for a particular situation. Francis Meres would seem to be aware of the changing view of the lyric when he compares classical poets traditionally associated with music and contemporary poets: "As Pindarus, Anacreon, and Callimachus among the Greekes, and Horace and Catullus among the Latines are the best Lyrick poets: so in this faculty the best among our poets are Spencer [sic] (who excelleth in all kinds), Daniel, Drayton, Shakespeare, Bretton" (*Palladis Tamia,* 1598). In 1606 one of these poets, Michael Drayton, called a revised and collected edition of nearly all his previous work *Poems Lyric and Pastoral.* In the collection are Drayton's odes, poems he addresses to readers although his classical models were originally songs.

Although critical discussions in English treatises about lyric poetry as a generic form are slight in comparison to those about such other kinds of poetry as epic or tragedy, there are many comments on such specific lyric conventions as the sonnet, ode, hymn, elegy, or epithalamion (qq.v.). In all of these comments there is general agreement that a major concept in lyric theory concerns function. Renaissance lyrics were thought of as "praises or dispraises of some person, attitude, condition, idea, affection, outcome of events; or they plead for or against something" (Tuve). For example, advising poets to choose rhetorical figures carefully for their love lyrics, George Gascoigne writes: "If I should undertake to wryte in prayse of a gentlewoman, I would neither praise hir christal eye, nor hir cherrie lippe, etc. For these things are *trita et obvia.* But I would either find some supernaturall cause wherby my penne might walke in the superlative degree, or els I would undertake to aunswere for any imperfection that shee hath, and therupon rayse the prayse of hir commendacion. Likewise, if I should disclose my pretence in love, I would eyther make a strange discourse of some intollerable passion, or finde occasion to pleade [to persuade] by the example of some historie, or discover my disquiet in shadowes *per Allegoriam,* or use the covertest meane that I could to avoyde the uncomely customes of common writers" (*Certain Notes of Instruction,* 1575). Similarly, Sidney, criticizing the representation of love in lyric poetry, says, "Other sort of *Poetrie,* almost have we none, but that *Lyricall* kind of Songs and Sonets; which Lord, if he gave us so good mindes, how well it might be employed, and with how heavenly fruites, both private and publike, in singing the praises of the immortall bewtie, and the immortall goodnes of that God, who giveth us hands to write, and wits to conceive . . . But truly many of such writings as come under the banner of unresistable love, if I were a mistresse, would never perswade mee they were in love: so coldly they applie firie speeches." This emphasis on praise and persuasion is a reflection of the influence of rhetorical theory upon lyric poetry.

The subject matter of English lyrics is both religious and secular, "sacred and profane." Like Italian poets who distinguished between "noble" lyrics praising gods and heroes and "ignoble" lyrics treating of human love and the good life, English poets drew similar distinctions among lyric forms. Puttenham, for example, says that "the matters . . . that concern the Gods and divine things are highest of all other to be couched in writing . . . and therefore are delivered over to the Poets *Hymnick*." "All hymnes," he adds, are to be written in the "high stile." Similarly John Milton reserves the highest positions in the lyric hierarchy for classical odes and the biblical Psalms which, he says, "of all the kinds of lyric poesy to be incomparable" (*The Reason of Church Government,* 1642). For models of lyric excellence, then, English poets turned to the poetry of such classical poets as Pindar and Horace and to the Psalms of David. Sometimes David was even considered an imitator of the classical poets; for example, Thomas Lodge says, "David was a poet, and . . . his vayne was in imitating (as S. Jerom witnesseth) Horace . . . and Pindarus" (*Defense of Poetry,* 1579). More often David was thought superior and previous to the classical poets and their model for imitation; and the many metrical paraphrases of the Psalms during the late sixteenth and early seventeenth centuries indicate the high regard for that form of religious lyric poetry.

The largest number of English lyrics were secular love poems, ones that William Webbe calls "ditties of lighter matters" (*A Discourse of English Poetry,* 1586) and Puttenham the "common Poesies of loves." Since these love poems, Puttenham says, concern "meane [average] matters," they are to be written in the "meane [middle] stile." In these love lyrics, he writes, "joyes were to be uttered in one sorte, the sorrowes in an other, and by the many formes of Poesie, the many moodes and pangs of lovers, throughly to be discovered: the poore soules sometimes praying, beseeching, sometime honouring, avancing, praising: an other while railing, reviling, and cursing: then sorrowing, weeping, lamenting: in the ende laughing, rejoysing & solacing the beloved againe, with a thousand delicate devises, odes, songs, elegies, ballads, sonets and other ditties, mooving one way and another to great compassion." Puttenham's description summarizes well the content of countless English love lyrics from Sir Thomas Wyatt to Andrew Marvell.

Despite their first-person voice, lyrics are not confessions of a particular poet's emotions. The created speakers of lyrics do, of course, reveal feelings and emotional attitudes; but they are those significant and essential to a given situation (*i.e.,* a person in prayer praising the nature of God's mercy, a lover pleading for the favor of his beloved). In a sense, lyrics are aimed more at moving a listener's emotions than in revealing the poet's. John Donne, for example, in what amounts to a warning against an autobiographical interpretation of his lyrics, says, "I did best when I had least truth for my subjects" (quoted in *Poems,* ed. H. J. C. Grierson [1912], I, 288). Another lyric poet, Ben Jonson, expresses a typical attitude when he remarks that a poet deserves that appellation not because he "writeth in measure [metrical versification] only, but that [he] fayneth and formeth a fable, and writes things like the Truth. For the Fable and Fiction is, as it were, the forme and Soule of any Poeticall worke or *Poeme*" (*Timber, or Discoveries,* 1641). As Puttenham had said, the thought and emotion appropriate to his subject were "thoroughly to be discovered" by the lyric poet.

Except for scattered attempts at "bare numbers" or English adaptations of classical quantitative verse (*see* Versifying), all the lyrics were in rhyme or, in the words of Samuel Daniel, that "number and harmonie of words, consisting of an agreeing sound in the last sillables of severall verses, giving both to the Eare an Echo of a delightful report, and to the Memorie a deeper impression of what is delivered therein" (*A Defense of Rhyme,* 1603). During the Elizabethan period lyric poets generally tended to choose regular or established stanzaic forms, such as the fourteen-line sonnet (q.v.). Many poets of the first half of the seventeenth century, however, deserted regular stanza patterns for those they invented for a particular lyric.

Bibliography

John Erskine, *The Elizabethan Lyric* (1903); John Smith Harrison, *Platonism in English Poetry of the Sixteenth and Seventeenth Centuries* (1903); Sidney Lee, "French Influence in the Elizabethan Lyric," *The French Renaissance in England* (1910), pp. 183–281; John M. Berdan, *Early Tudor Poetry, 1485-1547* (1920); George Williamson, *The Donne Tradition* (1930); F. R. Leavis, *Revaluation: Tradition & Development in English Poetry* (1936); Yvor Winters, "The 16th Century Lyric in England: A Critical and Historical Reinterpretation," *Poetry,* 53 (1938-1939), 258-72, 320-35, and 54 (1939), 35-51; Robert Lathrop Sharp, *From Donne to Dryden: The Revolt against Metaphysical Poetry* (1940); Silvio Policardi, *Lyrical Poetry in Renaissance England* (1943); Rosemond Tuve, *Elizabethan and Methaphysical Imagery* (1947); Bruce Pattison, *Music and Poetry of the English Renaissance* (1948); Ruth Wallerstein, *Studies in Seventeenth-Century Poetic* (1950); C. V. Wedgwood, *Seventeenth-Century English Literature* (1950); Catherine Ing, *Elizabethan Lyrics: A Study in the Development of English Metres and Their Relation to Poetic Effect* (1951); Sears Jayne, "Ficino and the Platonism of the English Renaissance," *CL,* 4 (1952), 214-38; Hallett Smith, "Poetry for Music," *Elizabethan Poetry* (1952), pp. 257-89; Odette de Mourgues, *Metaphysical, Baroque & Précieux Poetry* (1953); Patrick Cruttwell, *The Shakespearean Moment And Its Place in the Poetry of the 17th Century* (1954); Malcolm Mackenzie Ross, *Poetry and Dogma: The Transfiguration of Eucharistic Symbols in Seventeenth-Century English Po-*

etry (1954); Wilfrid Mellers, "Words and Music in Elizabethan England," *The Age of Shakespeare,* ed. Boris Ford (vol. 2 of *The Pelican Guide to English Literature,* 1955), pp. 386-415; Maurice Valency, *In Praise of Love* (1958); C. V. Wedgwood, *Poetry and Politics under the Stuarts* (1960); A. Alvarez, *The School of Donne* (1961); Gretchen Ludke Finney, *Musical Backgrounds for English Literature: 1580-1650* (1961); John Hollander, *The Untuning of the Sky: Ideas of Music in English Poetry, 1500-1700* (1961); Lowry Nelson, Jr., *Baroque Lyric Poetry* (1961); John Stevens, *Music & Poetry in the Early Tudor Court* (1961); Louis L. Martz, *The Poetry of Meditation* (rev. ed., 1962); O. B. Hardison, Jr., "Lyric," *The Enduring Monument: A Study of the Idea of Praise in Renaissance Literary Theory and Practice* (1962), pp. 95–106; Maren-Sofie Røstvig, *The Happy Man: Studies in the Metamorphoses of a Classical Ideal,* vol. 1, (rev. ed., 1962); Wesley Trimpi, *Ben Jonson's Poems: A Study of the Plain Style* (1962); J. M. Cohen, *The Baroque Lyric* (1963); J. B. Broadbent, *Poetic Love* (1964); H. M. Richmond, *The School of Love: The Evolution of the Stuart Love Lyric* (1964); Stanley Stewart, *The Enclosed Garden: The Tradition and the Image in Seventeenth-Century Poetry* (1966); Douglas L. Peterson, *The English Lyric from Wyatt to Donne: A History of the Plain and Eloquent Styles* (1967); Leonard Forster, *The Icy Fire: Five Studies in European Petrarchism* (1969); Fred Inglis, *The Elizabethan Poets* (1969); Earl Miner, *The Metaphysical Mode from Donne to Cowley* (1969); William H. Halewood, *The Poetry of Grace* (1970); Jerome Mazzaro, *Transformations in the Renaissance English Lyric* (1970); Joseph H. Summers, *The Heirs of Donne and Jonson* (1970); Earl Miner, *The Cavalier Mode from Jonson to Cotton* (1971); Frank J. Warnke, *Versions of Baroque: European Literature in the Seventeenth Century* (1972); Rosalie L. Colie, "Small Forms: *Multo in Parvo,*" *The Resources of Kind: Genre-Theory in the Renaissance,* ed. Barbara K. Lewalski (1973), pp. 32-75; Elizabeth W. Pomeroy, *The Elizabethan Miscellanies: Their Development and Conventions* (1973); Harold B. Segel, "Part One," *The Baroque Poem: A Comparative Survey* (1974), pp. 3-143; John T. Shawcross, "The Poet as Orator: One Phase of His Judicial Pose," *The Rhetoric of Renaissance Poetry from Wyatt to Milton,* eds. Thomas O. Sloan and Raymond B. Waddington (1974), pp. 5-36; Michael McCanles, "The Dialectical Structure of the Metaphysical Lyric," *Dialectical Criticism and Renaissance Literature* (1975), pp. 54-117; Anthony Low, *Love's Architecture: Devotional Modes in Seventeenth-Century English Poetry* (1978); Anne Lake Prescott, *French Poets and the English Renaissance* (1978); Barbara K. Lewalski, *Protestant Poetics and the Seventeenth-Century Religious Lyric* (1979).

Masque:

"Noble solemnities" (Ben Jonson, preface to his wedding masque known as *The Haddington Masque*, 1608); an elaborate court entertainment of the late sixteenth and early seventeenth centuries that integrated the arts of poetry, song, music, and dance as a sophisticated celebration of both social and divine order.

During most of the sixteenth century the word *masque* simply implied any entertainment, from simple masquerades to ornate allegorical spectacles, which involved the wearing of masks or other disguisings. In the late years of Elizabeth's reign and especially the early years of the seventeenth century when practicing poets were invited to compose court masques, these entertainments developed into a distinct literary genre of a quasi-dramatic nature, although they were the joint effort of designer, choreographer, composer, and poet. The poet who gave the court masque its literary emphasis was Ben Jonson.

Behind court masques lie various traditions, such as courtly dance; mummings (a procession of masked folk who silently went from house to house on holidays to dice and dance); and pageants (staged scenes with symbolic figures) that greeted royalty on visits to country estates or during street processions in a civic celebration. When professional poets and playwrights were charged with creating court masques, they began to acquire literary unity and design, and passed from entertainments into an art form.

Though still a social entertainment, the court masque attained a structural unity in which a slight story delicately harmonizes the various elements and also functions to compliment a noble or royal person or to honor a ceremonial occasion. The fable gives the masque unity and provides symbolic meaning to all its elements—poetry, song, music, dance, and spectacle. The story is sometimes derived from classical mythology; more often, the masque writer invents a fable to suit the occasion, the particular theme to be developed, and the compliment to be paid. Generally figures appearing in such fables are from classical or pastoral sources or are personified abstractions, such as Joy, Virtue, and Friendship.

The general form of the masque was that of an elaborated procession, the point of which was to get the complimenters or masked dancers before a complimented person and the waiting audience. Preceding the entry of the masked dancers came introductory set speeches, songs, and dialogue performed by professional actors and singers from the public theaters. Their poetry and song began the story and announced the fictive action in which the masquers would move as symbolic embodiments of virtuous qualities. Another feature before the entry of the masquers was the antimasque. Here paid professionals disguised themselves in grotesque costumes, such as those of satyrs, baboons, witches, wild men or giants, performed antic dances, and generally engaged in humorous and often ribald talk and action. The speeches of the antimasquers were frequently in prose. Their merriment and disorderly behavior served as a foil to the solemnity of the later formal dances and thematically presented the unruly qualities that harmony and order hold in check. The performers in the antimasque were banished with poetry announcing the aristocratic masquers. The entry of the masquers was colorful. For example, they emerged from opening mountains or descended from clouds. The spectacle at this point was itself expressive of the thematic transformation occurring between the antimasque and the formal dances of the "main masque." The richly costumed masquers, generally eight to sixteen in number and either noblemen or ladies, took no speaking parts. Their patterned dances were visual symbols of order and formal design, interspersed with explanatory songs and lyric poetry. After these dances and after the poetry that presented the masquers, now unmasked, to the complimented person, the masquers invited members of the audience to dance. The revels had begun. When the hours of social dancing were concluded, final songs and dialogues recalled the masquers to the scene from which they had emerged, and the masque was over.

Sir Francis Bacon, who under James I was often professionally involved in organizing masque occasions, left in his *Essays* (1625) this advice for anyone who would serve as a "chief contriver." He writes, "since Princes will have such Things, it is better, they should be Graced with Elegancy then Daubed with Cost. *Dancing to Song,* is a Thing of great State and Pleasure. . . . *Acting in Song,* especially in *Dialogues,* hath an extreme Good Grace. . . . the *Alterations of Scenes,* so it be quietly, and without Noise, are Things of great Beauty and Pleasure: For they feed and relieve the Eye, before it be full of the same Object. Let the *Scenes* abound with *Light,* specially *Coloured* and *Varied:* And let the Masquers, or any other, that are to come down from the *Scene,* have some Motions, upon the *Scene* itself, before their Comming down. . . . Let the *Songs* be *Loud* and *Cheerefull,* and not *Chirpings,* or *Pulings.* Let the Musicke likewise, be *Sharpe,* and *Loud,* and *Well Placed.* The *Colours,* that shew best by candlelight, are; White, Carnation, and a Kinde of Sea-Water Greene; and *Oes,* or *Spangs* [spangles], as they are no great Cost, so they are of most Glory. . . . Let the *Sutes* of the Masquers be Gracefull, and such as become the Person, when the Vizars are off. . . . Let *Antimasques* not be long. . . . But chiefly, let the *Musicke* of them, be Recreative . . . Some *Sweet Odours* suddenly comming forth, without any drops falling, are, in such a Company, as [because] there is Steame and Heate, Things of Great Pleasure; and Refreshment. *Double Masques,* one of Men, another of Ladies, addeth State and Variety. But All is Nothing except the Roome be kept Cleare and Neat." Bacon's remarks combine a concern for an entertainment of aesthetic beauty with a concern for its cost. Such cautions were not always heeded, however, as the enormous expense of many Jacobean and Caroline court masques indicates.

As a literary form, the masque is a symbolic representation of a single great theme, social and divine harmony and order; the masque celebrates the permanence of virtuous forces that hold in check those of disorder and mutability. In its way, the masque, like the ode or the epithalamion (qq. v.), is a poem of praise. It expresses artistically the values that, at least ideally, already existed in the very room where the masque was presented and that were felt to be embodied in a monarchy. For spectator and participant alike the masque was a mime of majesty and virtue clearly present in a banqueting hall, and a graceful formal extension of actuality through a fiction. The presentation was felt to be no illusion, but rather a mimetic celebration of the actual world and values of the court. Fiction became reality as the masquers revealed themselves to be actual members of the court, and they joined with the audience for social dancing. "The end toward which the masque moved was to destroy any sense of theater and to include the whole court in the mimesis—in a sense, what the spectator watched he ultimately became" (Orgel, *The Jonsonian Masque*). It is this lack of distinction between the courtly masquers, often members of the royal family, and their courtly audience that most sets off the court masque from plays at a public playhouse.

For English writers, like Ben Jonson, who took the masque seriously as a literary form, at least two things threatened the delicate unity supplied by the poetic fable and controlling theme. They were the antimasque and, even more, the spectacle. Rather than serve as a "foil, or false masque," as Jonson felt it should (preface, *The Masque of Queens,* 1609), the antimasque could turn into what was merely a light diversion instead of a supportive thematic device. Spectacle, too, threatened the poetic fabric of the masque, despite Jonson's claim (preface, *Hymenaei,* 1606) that poetry was the "soul" of the masque and spectacle the "body." During the reign of James

I, Jonson and Inigo Jones, the court architect, often collaborated fruitfully so that Jones's masterful scenery and mechanical devices were both expressive of the poetic idea and spectacular. During the Caroline period, however, when Jonson's influence was much less pronounced and Jones's more, the masque as a literary form began to disintegrate.

Writing in that time when spectacle tended to dominate the typical court masque, one major poet, John Milton, treated the masque primarily as a literary form. His work, *Comus* (1634), originally entitled simply *A Mask,* emphasizes spoken poetry more than it does song and dance. Still, *Comus* follows the basic pattern of a procession working towards the compliment of a nobleman, and its fictive fable became reality when the three children who took the major speaking parts of the masque were presented to their waiting parents at the end of the performance.

Bibliography

E. K. Chambers, "The Mask," *The Elizabethan Stage,* vol. 1 (1923), pp. 149–212; Mary Susan Steele, *Plays & Masques at Court During the Reigns of Elizabeth, James and Charles* (1926); Enid Welsford, *The Court Masque: A Study in the Relationship Between Poetry & the Revels* (1927); Allardyce Nicoll, *Stuart Masques and the Renaissance Stage* (1938); D. J. Gordon, "The Imagery of Ben Jonson's *The Masque of Blacknesse* and *The Masque of Beautie,*" *JWCI,* 6 (1943), 122–41; D. J. Gordon, "*Hymenaei:* Ben Jonson's Masque of Union," *JWCI,* 8 (1945), 107–45; D. J. Gordon, "Ben Jonson's 'Haddington Masque': The Story and the Fable," *MLR,* 42 (1947), 180–87; D. J. Gordon, "Poet and Architect: The Intellectual Setting of the Quarrel between Ben Jonson and Inigo Jones," *JWCI,* 12 (1949), 152–78; C. H. Herford and Percy and Evelyn Simpson, eds., "The Masques," *Ben Jonson: Works,* vol. 10 (1950), pp. 404–45; Dolora Cunningham, "The Jonsonian Masque as a Literary Form," *ELH,* 22 (1955), 108–24; W. Todd Furniss, "Ben Jonson's Masques," *Three Studies in the Renaissance* (1958), pp. 89–179; Andrew J. Sabol, ed., *Songs and Dances for the Stuart Masque* (1959); Jonas A. Barish, "Painting, Carpentry, and Prose," *Ben Jonson and the Language of Prose Comedy* (1960), pp. 240–72; John C. Meagher, "The Dance and the Masques of Ben Jonson," *JWCI* 25 (1962), 258–77; Stephen Orgel, *The Jonsonian Masque* (1965); John C. Meagher, *Method and Meaning in Jonson's Masques* (1966); Inga-Stina Ewbank, " 'These pretty devices': A Study of Masques in Plays," *A Book of Masques* (1967), pp. 407–48; Sydney Anglo, "The Evolution of the Early Tudor Disguising, Pageant, and Mask," *RenD,* 1 (1968), 3–44; John G. Demaray, *Milton and the Masque Tradition* (1968); Stanley Wells, "The intent and the event," *Literature and Drama* (1970), pp. 56–84; David M. Bergeron, *English Civic Pageantry 1558–1642* (1971), Angus Fletcher, *The Transcendental Masque* (1971); M.

R. Golding, "Variations in the Use of the Masque in English Revenge Tragedy," *YES,* 3 (1973), 44–54; Stephen Orgel and Roy Strong, *Inigo Jones: The Theatre of the Stuart Court,* 2 vols. (1973); Roy Strong, *Splendor at Court: Renaissance Spectacle and the Theater of Power* (1973); Stephen Orgel, *The Illusion of Power: Political Theater in the English Renaissance* (1975); Stephen Orgel, ed., "Roles and Mysteries," *The Renaissance Imagination: Essays and Lectures by D. J. Gordon* (1975), pp. 3–23; Muriel C. Bradbrook, "Social Change and the Evolution of Ben Jonson's Court Masques" and "Masque and Pastoral," *The Living Monument* (1976), pp. 50–83, 245–57; Marie Axton, "The Tudor mask and Elizabethan court drama," *English Drama: Forms and Development: Essays in Honour of Muriel Clara Bradbrook,* eds. Marie Axton and Raymond Williams (1977), pp. 24–47; Leah Sinanoglou Marcus, " 'Present Occasions' and the Shaping of Ben Jonson's Masques," *ELH,* 45 (1978), 201–25.

Morall:

A dramatic genre of the early seventeenth century extending the tradition of earlier popular, didactic plays called "morall interludes" or "morall plays." The term *morall* appears in a number of lists of dramatic genres of the early seventeenth century. For example, in the induction to John Marston's *What You Will* (1601) Doricus asks if the play is a "Commedy, Tragedy, Pastorall, Morall, Nocturnal or Historie." In the induction to the second edition of Marston's *The Malcontent* (c. 1604) "Harry" Condell is represented as saying that the play is "neither Satyre nor Morall." In Thomas Dekker's *The Gull's Hornbook* (1609) a gull is advised to call attention to himself by leaving in the middle of a play "be it pastorall or comedy, morall or tragedie." Licenses for acting companies included the morall in lists of permitted dramatic kinds as late as 1625.

Except for its didactic intent, the characteristics of the morall are not absolutely clear. One surviving such play, the anonymous *Two Wise Men and All the Rest Fools* (1619), defines itself as "severall discourses" of "many vices vailed over with froth and florish of words, but the same againe unmasked with substantiall matter, and laid naked to disgrace." It is "A Comicall Morall, censuring the follies of this age." The didactic nature of the morall is stressed by Thomas Heywood who in *An Apology for Actors* (1612) says, "If a morall, it is to perswade men to humanity and good life, to instruct them in civility and good manners, shewing them the fruits of honesty, and the end of villany."

The morall is a late form of a heterogenous group of popular plays now referred to as "late morality plays" or "hybrid moralities." Some of these plays were actually called "morall plays" or even "moralls" in Elizabethan times, but many were simply called "commodies" or "interludes"; the use of *morall* as an adjective referring to a play is comparatively rare.

Whatever their designation, the large class of plays now referred to as late morality plays typically have a linear, sequential plot structure combined with a markedly didactic purpose that relates them to the seventeenth-century morall. The late morality plays were the vehicles through which the main conventions of the native English drama entered the professional, popular theater of the late sixteenth century. They are distinguished by the presence of personified attributes or concepts (often mingled with type or even historical characters), satirical invective, and the presence of a Vice figure or figures. Their structure was often controlled by the requirements of a small number of players ("four men and a boy"), each of whom could act more than one role in the play. Late moralities tended to alternate comic and serious episodes with a symmetrical organization of opposing forces (e.g. good and evil counselors); and to compress the large number of personified attributes of older drama (e.g. the Seven Deadly Sins) into a single character such as Folly. They make a systematic use of soliloquy and the extended dramatic monologue.

The late morality plays descend from the popular religious and political allegorical dramas of the fifteenth and early sixteenth centuries. These plays are now referred to simply as "morality plays," although the term *morality* was not in general use in England as a designation for such plays until the eighteenth century and was not used at all in the fifteenth century. The term *moralité* was then used to refer to a form of French drama; the prologue to the famous *Everyman* (c. 1495) simply refers to it as a "morall play."

Where the older allegorical drama, like *Everyman,* had featured a single, central figure, late morality plays began to multiply and differentiate their main characters. *Humanum Genus* became less abstract and divided into types of political man, religious man, and social man. Thus when some late morality plays addressed current economic problems such as usury, their playwrights divided the central character into figures representing certain classes or "estates." At the same time, the configurations of the late morality plays began to be differentiated, with movements toward the generic distinctions of comedy, history, and tragedy. One play with a "comic" structure is close to the organization of the morall described above, *The Two Wise Men. All for Money* by Thomas Lupton (c. 1577), described as "A Moral and Piteful Comedy," begins with a lengthy prologue followed by a series of tableau-like debates between personified figures (e.g., Learning and Affluence) with Sin successfully driven back to hell. In other late morality plays, which are political-historical in nature, the central figure is a prince surrounded by good and bad advisors. The fate of the commonwealth is the issue. One such play is *Cambises* (c. 1561), although its Persian setting is at a safe distance from the intrigues of the English court. *Cambises* shows the temptations and responsibilities of royal power, with the snares of bad advice demonstrated by a Vice figure, Ambidexter. Still other late morality plays are both homilectic and "tragic," sometimes, like *Cambises,* adapted to the biography of a historical or legendary character. With the increasing individualization of the old, central figure representing Mankind, dramatists began to place such central figures in situations in which the logical possibility of damnation rather than salvation might occur: "Everyman must be saved, but a Faustus will be damned" (Potter). Types of men are given destinies particular to their own situation; in W. Wager's *Enough is as good as a Feast* (c. 1560) Worldly Man's unrepentant exploitation of a rustic tenant is punished when Satan bears him off to hell.

The Vice figure of the late morality plays is the chief comic character of English drama in the sixteenth century. Typically he carries a wooden dagger, wears a fur hood, and rides away from the action on the back of the devil. The devil is the Vice's "dad," and the Vice is on such terms with him as to call him "crook nose" and "snottie nose." As a noun used to identify a particular dramatic character, the word *Vice* first appears in John Heywood's *The Play of the Weather* (c. 1528) and *A Play of Love* (1533) where Merry Report and No-love-nor-loved are each described as "the Vyse." Slightly later, Revels documents of 1551–52 also refer to a "vyse" and strongly suggest his association with the fool or jester of social tradition. He almost certainly descends from the comic personifications of the vices who appear in the religious, allegorical plays of the fifteenth century.

Among the late morality plays there are some twenty plays in which a character is referred to as "the Vice." His names shift from play to play. In *Appius and Virginia* (c. 1564) he is Haphazard; in *King Darius* (1565) he is Iniquity; in *Like Will To Like* (c. 1568) he is Newfangle. The Vice becomes not the tempter of all mankind but a dramatic symbol for that attitude or force within the kingdom that the dramatist wishes to single out as the basic cause of contemporary evils. He variously acts as a master of ceremonies, sings, dances, scuffles, and plays the nimble buffoon. He is also the central vehicle for an oral and dramatic tradition of wordplay, slang, quibbling, and antic verbal "sporte" that colors the language of English drama well into the seventeenth century.

Neither the presence of a Vice figure nor of other allegorical personifications seems to be essential features of the seventeenth-century morall. It was an attenuated form of what had once been a flourishing tradition. What remains to make it a morall is an emphasis upon the correction of manners or civil conduct. As a practicing playwright and critic, Ben Jonson suggests that the Vice figure had been sophisticated out of existence, and is now "attir'd like men and women o' the time"; he is no longer in a "juglers jerkin, with false skirts, like the Knave of Clubs" or snapping his "wooden dagger" (*The Staple of News,* 1626). Similarly, other allegorical figures or personified abstractions of the sixteenth century are generally replaced by individualized characters. Thus in Thomas Middleton's *The*

Phoenix (1604), a prince, the Phoenix, seems to replace a principle, Honesty, of an earlier and similar play, *A Knack to Know a Knave* (1592). (It is, of course, the experience of every playgoer that however "abstract" a personification may seem in a printed text, a player's actions give that personification a vitality on stage that is individual.) But personifications did not completely disappear in the theater of the seventeenth century. In Jonson's *Staple of News,* referred to above, Mirth, Expectation, Mortgage, and Statute all make their appearance.

Bibliography

E. N. S. Thompson, "The English Moral Plays," *Transactions of the Connecticut Academy of Arts and Sciences,* 14 (1908–1910), 291–414; Charles Read Baskervill, *English Elements in Jonson's Early Comedy* (1911); William Roy Mackenzie, *The English Moralities from the Point of View of Allegory* (1914); Ola Elizabeth Winslow, *Low Comedy as a Structural Element in English Drama from the Beginnings to 1642* (1926); Willard Farnham, *The Medieval Heritage of Elizabethan Tragedy* (1936); A. P. Rossiter, ed., "Preface," *Woodstock: A Moral History* (1946), pp. 1–76; A. P. Rossiter, *English Drama from Early Times to the Elizabethans* (1950); Francis Mares, "The Origin of the Figure Called 'the Vice' in Tudor Drama," *HLQ,* 22 (1958), 11-29; Bernard Spivak, *Shakespeare and the Allegory of Evil* (1958); Lily B. Campbell, *Divine Poetry and Drama in Sixteenth-Century England* (1959); Glynne Wickham, "Morals and Interludes," *Early English Stages, 1300 to 1660,* vol. 1 (1959), pp. 229–53; W. T. H. Jackson, *The Literature of the Middle Ages* (1960); G. R. Owst, "Sermon and Drama," *Literature and Pulpit in Medieval England* (2nd rev. ed., 1961), pp. 471–547; David M. Bevington, *From "Mankind" to Marlowe: Growth of Structure in the Popular Drama of Tudor England* (1962); T. W. Craik, *The Tudor Interlude* (1962); Alan C. Dessen, "The 'Estates' Morality Play," *SP,* 62 (1965), 121–36; O. B. Hardison, Jr., *Christian Rites and Christian Drama in the Middle Ages* (1965); Thomas B. Stroup, *Microcosmos: The Shape of the Elizabethan Play* (1965); David Bevington, *Tudor Drama and Politics: A Critical Approach to Topical Meaning* (1968); A. M. Kinghorn, *Mediaeval Drama* (1968); Glynne Wickham, "The Mediaeval Heritage of Shakespearean Drama," *Shakespeare's Dramatic Heritage: Collected Studies in Mediaeval, Tudor and Shakespearean Drama* (1969), pp. 3–63; F. P. Wilson, *The English Drama 1485-1585,* ed. G. K. Hunter (1969), pp. 1–77; Sylvia D. Feldman, *The Morality-Patterned Comedy of the Renaissance* (1970); Ruth H. Blackburn, *Biblical Drama under the Tudors* (1971); Alan C. Dessen, *Jonson's Moral Comedy* (1971); Alan C. Dessen, "The Morall as an Elizabethan Dramatic Kind: An Exploratory Essay," *CompD,* 5 (1971), 138–59; Richard Levin, *The Multiple Plot in English Renaissance Drama*

(1971); Peter J. Houle, *The English Morality and Related Drama: A Bibliographical Survey* (1972); Stanley J. Kahrl, *Traditions of Medieval English Drama* (1974); Joanne Spencer Kantrowitz, *Dramatic Allegory* (1975); Robert Potter, *The English Morality Play: Origins, History and Influence of a Dramatic Tradition* (1975); John Weld, *Meaning in Comedy: Studies in Elizabethan Romantic Comedy* (1975), pp. 21–97; Edmund Creeth, *Mankynde in Shakespeare* (1976); Alan C. Dessen, "Homilies and Anomalies: The Legacy of the Morality Play in the Age of Shakespeare," *ShakS,* 11 (1978), 243–58; Robert Weimann, *Shakespeare and the Popular Tradition in the Theater: Studies in the Social Dimension of Dramatic Form and Function,* ed. Robert Schwartz (1978); Charlotte Spivack, *The Comedy of Evil on Shakespeare's Stage* (1979); Lewis Walker, "*Timon of Athens* and the Morality Tradition," *ShakS,* 12 (1979), 159–77; John Wasson, "The Morality Play: Ancestor of Elizabethan Drama?" *CompD,* 13 (1979), 210–21.

Novella:

"A novel, a new discourse, a tale, a fable, a parable. Also a tiding or newes" (John Florio, *Queen Anna's New World of Words,* 1611); an Italian term for a short prose tale. During the late Elizabethan period *novelle,* translated or freely adapted from earlier collections, introduced a wide variety of stories to English readers and provided an arsenal of plots for dramatists.

Some prose tales were imported directly from such famous Italian writers as Giovanni Boccaccio, Matteo Bandello, and Giraldi Cinthio; others passed into English through Spanish and French versions, especially the collection by Marguerite de Navarre. English translations and adaptations of these *novelle* go by several names, such as *tales, histories,* and *discourses,* as in Sir Geoffrey Fenton's *Certain Tragical Discourses* (1567). In calling a *novella* a "history," English writers mean a story, but they also point to the fact that many *novelle* are narrative accounts of events in the lives of real people. William Painter calls the stories in his *The Palace of Pleasure* (1566) "novells." Cutting off the last syllable of the word *novella,* Painter merely anglicized an Italian word.

The principal model for *novelle* was Boccaccio's collection of tales *The Decameron;* and with this model the single *novella* is integrated into a collection of tales unified by a cornice or narrative framework. The single tales are clustered into thematically related groups. In the cornice a group of characters, purportedly real people who find themselves brought together by chance or design, agree to tell stories for their pastime. Usually their storytelling is to last for a designated number of days (hence such titles as *Il decameron* and *Il pentamerone*); and specific themes (for example, peril averted by wit, patience rewarded) are selected for the tales of a particular day. A *novella* collection thus assumes two storytellers and two audiences: the author of the printed collection and his readers, and the fictive storytellers and their audience in the cornice. Because of this recitation of tales in a frame of a localized time and place, *novella* collections make a claim of verisimilitude. Moreover, the cornice allows for great freedom in the subject matter, tone, and style of the tales. There is room, for example, for the marvelous and the realistic, the tragic and the comic, the courtly and the bawdy, the high style and the low. Typically, a *novella* is strong in plot, humor, and satire, and weaker in psychological depth, character delineation, and background development.

For the most part, writers of *novelle* drew upon old tales. Like the orator who "invented" or discovered his material in existing topics, the writers of *novelle* favored existing stories; and the collections sought to preserve the familiar through an artful reworking (*see* Imitation). This emphasis on the reworking of existing stories also helps to account for the variety of the *novelle* within a collection—beast fable, folk tale, fairy story, chivalric romance, saint's life as well as narratives about contemporary, historical, biblical, and Greco-Roman characters.

Aware of this tremendous variety of *novella* in collections, Painter says in his prefatory remarks to the 1566 edition of *The Palace of Pleasure* that his stories present "a Theatre of the World." He writes, "in these histories (which by another terme I call Novelles) be described the lives, gestes, conquestes, and highe enterprises of great Princes, wherein also be not forgotten the cruell actes and tiranny of some. In these be set forth the great valiance of noble Gentlemen, the terrible combates of couragious personages, the vertuous mindes of noble Dames, the chaste hartes of constant Ladyes, the wonderful patience of puissaunt Princes, the mild sufferaunce of well disposed gentlewomen, and in divers, the quiet bearing of advers Fortune. In these Histories be depainted in livelye colours, the uglye shapes of insolencye and pride, the deforme figures of incontinencie and rape, the cruell aspectes of spoyle, breach of order, treason, ill lucke and overthrow of States and other persons. Wherein also be intermixed, pleasaunte discourses, merie talke, sportinge practises, deceitfull devises and nipping tauntes." As Painter's description indicates, the sensational was quite at home in *novelle*. Often plots, with a contemporary setting, rehearse well-known scandals and violent intrigues, using actual dates, names, and places. In such tales, erotic complexities and lurid and violent deaths are favorite subjects.

When translating or adapting *novelle*, English writers felt free to select their stories from among the various earlier collections. Hence, many of the Elizabethan collections are really compilations or anthologies of tales taken from many sources. The first English translation of a complete Italian *novella* collection, that of an anonymous rendering of the *Decameron*, did not appear until 1620. But many earlier English collections, though taken from several sources, did enclose their tales in a cornice. In Edmund Tilney's *A Brief and Pleasant Discourse of Duties in Marriage, Called the Flower of Friendship* (1568), for example, a group of men and women agree to tell tales of marriage; and in the anonymous *Cobbler of Canterbury* (1590) the rivalries and disputes of the storytellers, all members of the lower social classes on a barge on the Thames, often result in tales told at the expense of someone else. This device of a cornice was also familiar to English writers through Chaucer's *Canterbury Tales,* a work which contains poetic versions of some of the stories that appear in Italian prose collections.

Like writers of *novelle,* English adapters offered their tales for a reader's instruction and pleasure. But although Italian writers did point out the profit to be derived from their *novelle,* they tended to emphasize that the tales were light entertainment. In order to throw off the censor and to claim that their often licentious tales were not worth the serious consideration of the scholarly, Boccaccio and others had addressed their *novelle* to women; and they further justified the naughty and lurid tales by pointing out that the purportedly real recitation of the tales by characters in the cornice required their inclusion. Similarly, the printer of George Pettie's *A Petite Palace of Pettie His Pleasure* (1576) announces that he would "by my will . . . have onely Gentlewomen" as his readers, and that he offers Pettie's tales for their "common profit & pleasure." But more than the Italian writers, English adapters stressed the moral value of their stories, not only in their prefatory remarks to collections but also in the amount of moralization added within the adaptations. Painter, for example, claims that the tales of his 1566 edition "maye render good examples, the best to be followed, and the worst to be avoyded." And Fenton believes his tales to be models "for imytaction of the good, destestynge the wycked, avoydynge a present mischiefe, and preventynge any evil afore yt fall." Within his tales lusty scenes are often counterbalanced with moral statements so that the "frail youth" of England may see how "the heavy hand of God . . . blesseth the good" and "punisheth the wicked," even though the actual fates of some of his characters do not always support such a system of reward and retribution.

Whether accepted for their profit or their pleasure, English adaptations of *novelle* found a warm welcome during the late sixteenth century and the early decades of the seventeenth century. Although the many editions of the collections indicate a quick response from general readers, it was the dramatists, not the translators and adapters, who breathed new life into the well-worn plots of *novelle.* Playwrights were quick to plunder *novelle* for their plots, characters, and Italian settings; and as early as 1582 Stephen Gosson had good reason to include Painter's *Palace of Pleasure* among those works that "have been thoroughly ransackt, to furnish the Playe houses in London" (*Plays Confuted in Five Actions*). Some of the best-known plays of the English Renaissance, including Shakespeare's, take their violence, lurid and sensational events, and amorous intrigues from *novelle* (*see* Tragedy).

Critical discussion of the *novella* as a literary type was negligible. In Italy literary critics largely ignored prose fiction because the ancients had not mentioned it. When those few theorists, like Francesco Bonciani in a lecture in 1574, did consider it, they attempted to measure it by Aristotelian standards. English critics paid even less attention, except that certain of the learned reacted quite differently to *novelle* than did general readers. Roger Ascham, for example, in *The Schoolmaster* (1570) is one of the most articulate and vehement critics of almost all "bookes, of late translated out of *Italian* into English." Fearing that readers of *novelle* would come to place more value on "a tale in *Bocace* [Boccaccio], than a storie of the Bible," he argues that "suffer these bookes to be read, and they shall soone displace all bookes of godly learning." Since Italian ways of behaving are to be distrusted, Ascham feels that *novelle* are among "the inchantements of *Circes*, brought out of *Italie* to marre mens manners in England."

Bibliography

René Pruvost, *Matteo Bandello and Elizabethan Fiction* (1937); Charles Sears Baldwin, "Prose Narrative: Tales," *Renaissance Literary Theory and Practice* (1939), pp. 190–201; Maurice Valency, "Introduction," *The Palace of Pleasure*, eds. Maurice Valency and Harry Levtow (1960), pp. 1–28; Dale B. J. Randall, "Delight in Severall Shapes: The Novelas," *The Golden Tapestry: A Critical Survey of Non-chivalric Spanish Fiction in English Translation, 1543–1657* (1963), pp. 126–63; Margaret Schlauch, *Antecedents of the English Novel 1400–1600* (1963); Yvonne Rodax, *The Real and the Ideal in the Novella of Italy, France and England: Four Centuries of Change in the Boccaccian Tale* (1968); Robert J. Clements, "Anatomy of the Novella," *CLS*, 9 (1972), 3–16; Max Bluestone, *From Story to Stage: The Dramatic Adaptation of Prose Fiction in the Period of Shakespeare and His Contemporaries*, (1974); Robert J. Clements and Joseph Gibaldi, *Anatomy of the Novella: The European Tale Collection from Boccaccio and Chaucer to Cervantes* (1977).

Ode:

"An Ode is knowne to have been properly a Song, moduled to the ancient Harpe, and neither too short-breathed, as hasting to the end, nor composed of the longest Verses, as unfit for the sudden Turnes and Loftie Tricks with which Apollo used to manage it." So writes Michael Drayton in prefatory comments upon those poems in his *Odes, with Other Lyric Poesies* (1619), which he believes have not "wrongfully usurped" a designation as odes.

As Drayton goes on to say, odes are "divers," and he points to the several Greco-Roman poets, Pindar, Anacreon, and Horace, whose odes were to most influence English poets. Although not the first English poet to call certain of his poems "odes," Drayton is often regarded as the first to recognize that classical odes had been distinctive in substance and form. During the late sixteenth century the term *ode* had been used loosely to refer to almost any sort of lyric poem. The disguised Rosalind in *As You Like It* (c. 1599), for example, teases the love-sick Orlando for hanging "Oades" on the hawthorns of Arden. Such slight poems were not what seventeenth-century poets considered odes, however; and in practice they termed *odes* only those lyric poems that were weightier and longer and that extended the tradition of any of their classical models. For these poets, an ode was a lyric poem of medium length, formal and ceremonious, public in its address, social not personal in nature, noble and elevated in style and tone, and composed in an intricate metrical and stanzaic pattern. When an ode was an exalted sacred song, it was often called a *hymn* (q.v.).

A few English poets of the late sixteenth century looked to French imitations of classical odes for their models, principally those of the Pléiade poet Pierre de Ronsard; but seventeenth-century poets turned to the originals, especially the odes of Pindar and Horace, and to a lesser extent those of Anacreon. It was not so much the specific subject matter of classical odes that attracted poets; for their subjects they drew upon their own experiences and attitudes. Rather they admired that heightened spirit and tone of classical odes that was achieved through careful attention to language, metrical rhythms, and stanzaic patterns, and which invested a subject with wide, even universal, significance.

Originally the Greek word for ode was practically synonymous with lyric or song (qq.v.); and odes were distinguished as either choral (the "greater" odes), that is, sung and danced by a group; or monodic (the "lesser" odes), that is, sung by a single voice with instrumental accompaniment, usually a lyre. Pindar's triumphal songs are choral odes, composed to honor the victors in public athletic games. Employing a complex metrical structure, these songs praise an individual victor and even more his ancestors, and his city and its heroic past. This praise is further heightened by moral maxims and religious reflections. Drayton describes the odes of "the inimitable Pindarus" as "transcendently loftie, and farre more high then the Epick (commonly called the Heroique Poeme)." It was this deeply religious spirit of Pindar's odes that attracted English poets.

The simpler songs of Anacreon and his followers are monodic odes; they are celebrations of love and wine. Drayton describes these odes as "amorous, soft, and made for Chambers" and further compliments them by calling them "the very Delicacies of the Grecian Erato, which Muse seemed to have beene the Minion of that Teian old Man, which composed them." Among seventeenth-century English poets, Robert Herrick was especially influenced by Anacreon's odes.

In Roman times, principally in the work of Horace, the ode became a literary form, a poem not a song. Horace's odes are sometimes light-hearted poems, praising good food and drink, and sometimes more serious poems commenting on current events or eulogizing famous persons. Much simpler in form than Pindar's songs, Horace's poems are also more restrained in tone. Whether genial and familiar or grave and formal, they are marked by a cool equanimity. They are, in Drayton's words, odes of a "mixed kinde." The odes of Horace were especially admired in the Renaissance because of their craftsmanship; the rightness of their diction and of their formal characteristics elevated even the most commonplace thoughts and emotions.

Although there is little extended discussion of the ode in contemporary literary criticism, poets such as Sir Philip Sidney and John Milton speak of the ode as one of the highest kinds of lyric poetry. Sidney calls the ode, especially that of the "unimitable Pindar," that "kinde most capable and most fit to awake the thoughts from the sleep of idlenes to imbrace honorable enterprises" (*An Apology for Poetry,* 1595). Later, Milton ranks the "magnific odes and hymns wherein Pindarus and Callimachus are in most things worthy" only a little below the divine songs of the Psalms, which "appear over all the kinds of lyric poesy to be incomparable" (*The Reason of Church Government,* 1641). In its rapturous tone and sweeping scope of subject matter, Milton's own *On the Morning of Christ's Nativity* (1645) captures the Pindaric spirit he praises.

Renaissance odes celebrate a variety of subjects. But, whether on an important event in Christian history, as in Richard Crashaw's *A Hymn of the Nativity* (1646); on a contemporary political subject, as in Andrew Marvell's *An Horatian Ode upon Cromwell's Return from Ireland* (1681); or on the value of an evening of good food and poetry, as in Ben Jonson's *Inviting a Friend to Supper* (1616), the poet speaks in a public or social voice, expressing the sentiments of society, not just of an individual. And as odes differ from other lyric poems in their public address and social nature, so also are they generally more complicated in form. Unlike classical odes, which were always in unrhymed quantitative verse, English odes always rhyme, and they frequently employ stanzas of complex rhyme patterns with verses of varying length. Such stanza forms are suggestive of the Italian *canzone* (q.v.).

For seventeenth-century poets three forms were important—the Pindaric, Horatian, and Cowleian or irregular Pindaric ode. Of these, the English adaptation of the Pindaric form is the most elaborate. It is a fixed form which consists always of three stanzas: the strophe, antistrophe, and epode. But it is also flexible in that in the strophe the number and length of lines, the metrical patterns, and the rhyme scheme are left to the poet's invention. Once determined, this pattern, except for the rhyme sounds, is repeated in the antistrophe. The epode again allows flexibility, for it must be different from the other two stanzas. This triad is then repeated throughout the ode. In his adaptation of the Pindaric form for *Ode to Sir Lucius Cary and Sir H. Morison* (1640), Ben Jonson labels the parts of the triad as *turne, counterturne,* and *stand.*

A Horatian ode is homostrophic, that is, composed in a single stanza pattern of the poet's choice, which is repeated throughout the poem. Since this form resembles any other lyric poem in a regular stanzaic pattern, a Horatian ode must distinguish itself by its dignified mood, its direct address, and the nobility of its thought and emotion. The favorite stanza of Horace is the quatrain, with the first two lines longer by one or two feet than the last two. Most English odes before 1656 are homostrophic, although not necessarily Horatian in tone. Milton's ode on Christ's birth, for example, is Pindaric in its rapturous tone and its treatment of subject, yet the hymn regularly employs a single eight-line intricate stanza of Milton's invention. Milton's use of this stanza for all twenty-seven stanzas of the hymn reflects the freedom that he felt in drawing upon the entirety of the tradition of the classical ode.

The Cowleian or irregular Pindaric ode gives the poet the greatest degree of freedom in his composition. This ode takes as its starting point the flexibility of structure in the strophe of the regular Pindaric ode, but it then allows this same freedom for every subsequent stanza of the poem. Each stanza makes its own law. The number of lines varies from stanza to stanza; and for each stanza the poet determines new rhyme schemes, line lengths, and metrical patterns to suit the particular thoughts and emotions of that stanza. Although such irregular verse was not the invention of Abraham Cowley, it was his *Pindarique Odes* (1656) that popularized the form to such an extent that every aspiring poet felt the obligation to write an ode.

Bibliography

Robert Shafer, *The English Ode to 1660: An Essay in Literary History* (1918); George N. Shuster, *The English Ode from Milton to Keats* (1940); Carol Maddison, *Apollo and the Nine: A History of the Ode* (1960); Anthony LaBranche, "The 'Twofold Vitality' of Drayton's *Odes*," *CL,* 15 (1963), 116–29; D. S. J. Parsons, "The Odes of Drayton and Jonson," *QQ,* 75 (1968), 675–84; John Heath-Stubbs, *The Ode* (1969); Annabel M. Patterson, " 'High Talk': Canzone and Ode," *Hermogenes and the Renaissance: Seven Ideas of Style* (1970), pp. 69–96; John D. Jump, *The Ode* (1974); Mary I. Oates, "Jonson's 'Ode Pindarick' and the Doctrine of Imitation," *PLL,* 11 (1975), 126–48; Anne Lake Prescott, "Ronsard," *French Poets and the English Renaissance* (1978), pp. 76–131.

Ottava rima:

A "staffe of eight verses" that many English writers of the late sixteenth and early seventeenth centuries thought of as "English heroical verse" (title-page of Sir John Harington's 1591 translation of *Orlando Furioso*); a stanza of eight iambic pentameter lines, rhyming *abababcc*. Like the sonnet, *ottava rima* was a verse form imported into English poetry from Italy. In England, *ottava rima* competed with native rhyme royal (q.v.) as the stanza for serious narrative poetry.

English poets who chose *ottava rima* for narrative poetry had the weight of the practice of Italian Renaissance poets on their side. *Ottava rima* was an established form for the Italian heroic poem (q.v.), including the two famous poems *Orlando furioso* (1516) by Lodovico Ariosto and *Gerusalemme liberata* (finished in 1575) by Torquato Tasso. Much admired, both works influenced English poets who aspired to create heroic poems in the vernacular.

Two impressive English poems in *ottava rima* are historical narratives by Samuel Daniel and Michael Drayton. Daniel's poem, *The Civil Wars* (1609), records in eight books of *ottava rima* stanzas a portion of the long internecine strife between the Houses of York and Lancaster. Drayton's historical poem in *ottava rima* is *The Barons' Wars* (1603); its subject matter is drawn from the period of struggle (1321–30) between Edward II and rebellious noblemen, principally Mortimer. Actually *The Barons' Wars* is a major revision of Drayton's earlier poem *Mortimeriados* (1596), which he had written in rhyme royal.

In a prefatory epistle to the 1605 edition of *The Barons' Wars,* Drayton explains that, although he does not repent of his choice of subject, "matter for Trumpet or Tragedie," he regrets his choice of stanza form. He had been guilty of "insufficient handling" of that "multitude of horrid accidents." His complaint against the rhyme royal stanza *(ababbcc)* in *Mortimeriados* is that its double couplets "softned the verse more than the Majestie of the subject would permit." His preference for *ottava rima* is

157

that this stanza "of eight both holds the tune cleane thorow to the base of the columne (which is the couplet, the foote or bottome) and closeth not but with a full satisfaction to the eare, for so long detention." In other words, Drayton defends his change in stanza form on the basis of decorum (q.v.), finding the right form and language for the subject matter at hand. Elaborating further, Drayton praises the *ottava rima* stanza because "Briefly, this sort of stanza hath in it, majestie, perfection, and solidity, resembling the pillar which in Architecture is called the Tuscan, whose shaft is of six Diameters, and bases of two."

Parody:

"A turning of a verse into another signification by altering of some few words" (gloss for the Latin *parodia* in Francis Holyoke's 1640 edition of *Rider's Dictionary*). Often this "turning of a verse" (Italian *parodia,* John Florio's *A World of Words,* 1598) was associated with mockery; and as a literary device much late sixteenth- and early seventeenth-century parody criticized another literary work or a literary form, mode, or style. It gained its denigrating effects through exaggeration, distortion, or deflation, or an incongruity between subject matter and form.

One of the earliest appearances of the word *parody* in English literature comes in Ben Jonson's *Every Man in His Humour* (1598). There, in the last act, the would-be poet Matthew has been brought before a justice, and his pockets searched for a "taste of his vein." The lines produced by the search read: "Unto the boundless ocean of thy face, / Runs this poor river, charged with streams of eyes." Recognizing Matthew's unacknowledged imitation of another poet, the justice exclaims, "How? This is stol'n!" And young Knowell, who knows that a parody both imitates and distorts, further assaults the bad verse with "A parody! A parody! With a kind of miraculous gift, to make it absurder than it was." Although not so identified in the play, Matthew's lines are a parody of lines from the first sonnet of Samuel Daniel's sequence *Delia* (1592): "Unto the boundless ocean of thy beauty / Runs this poor river, charg'd with streams of zeal." (*See* Imitation.)

The mocking spirit of parody was so strong an incidental part in Renaissance plays that the drama has been called "the nursery of English parody" (Kitchen). At times some of this parody is a rough-and-tumble affair in the form of invective by one writer against a rival. More often the targets are literary fashions, the situations and characters of earlier drama, the style and devices of other contemporary dramatists, and the taste of the audience. Among prominent literary crazes parodied by dramatists are Petrarchan love poetry, the pastoral mode, and mythological-erotic narra-

159

tives, as well as the affected use of foreign and newly coined words. In one play in which parody is a sustained element, *The Knight of the Burning Pestle* (c. 1607), the dramatists Francis Beaumont and John Fletcher mock the tradition of knight errantry, the tastes of playhouse audiences for sentimental and adventurous tales of romance, and dramatic conventions like the appearance of ghosts.

Although Renaissance practice generally associated parody with mockery, at least one major poet does not limit his meaning of the word in such a way. One of the poems in George Herbert's *The Temple* (1633) carries the title *A Parodie*. In this religious lyric Herbert follows almost exactly the verse form of a secular love poem, *Soul's joy, now I am gone*. In phrasing, despite some verbal echoes, and in subject the two poems are quite different, although both treat the general notion of grief and absence. *A Parodie* is not in a mocking vein, and editors of Herbert's work describe the relation between his religious poem and the original secular love poem as a "neutral" one. Herbert's use of parody has a basis in musical tradition, where the term is sometimes used to refer to the practice of framing new words to an existing melody (*see* Song).

Bibliography

Rosemond Tuve, "Sacred 'Parody' of Love Poetry, and Herbert," *Studies in the Renaissance,* 8 (1961), 249–90; Rosemary Freeman, "Parody as a Literary Form: George Herbert and Wilfred Owen," *EIC,* 13 (1963), 307–22; Lewis Lockwood, "On 'Parody' as Term and Concept in 16th-Century Music," *Aspects of Medieval and Renaissance Music,* ed. Jan LaRue (1966), pp. 560–75.

Pastoral:

A play or "representation of shepheards and shephearddesses, with their actions and passions" (John Fletcher, preface, *The Faithful Shepherdess*, c. 1609); a designation for an assortment of plays all of which to some extent draw upon the established conventions of the pastoral mode. A few such plays, all tragicomedies (q.v.) and all indebted to Italian pastoral plays by writers such as Torquato Tasso and Giovanni Baptista Guarini, are generically pastoral in subject matter, setting, and characters. Others, the far larger number, make only incidental use of pastoral conventions and were called "pastorals" mainly because of a rustic setting. Since not all English playwrights thought of a pastoral play as one modeled after the formal Italian pastoral play, they freely attached the term *pastoral* to a wide variety of plays. Shakespeare's Polonius indicates that broad sweep of English practice when he includes in his list of dramatic kinds the "pastoral, pastoral-comical, historical-pastoral, [and] . . . tragical-comical-historical-pastoral" (*Hamlet*, c. 1601).

In England plays controlled by pastoral conventions form a distinct though small genre. Such dramas are what John Fletcher refers to when he says that a pastoral play is properly "a representation of shepheards and shephearddesses, with their actions and passions . . . such as all the ancient Poets, and moderne of understanding, have receaved them" (*The Faithful Shepherdess*). Formal pastoral plays are set in the Arcadian golden world with traditional shepherds and shepherdesses as the characters. Love and honor (or love vs. honor) are principal motifs. All are tragicomedies (though, of course, not all English tragicomedies are pastoral plays), and contributed to the development of that larger dramatic kind.

The few English plays that are generically pastoral are indebted in varying degrees to the formal pastoral drama that entertained aristocratic circles in late sixteenth-century Italy. In an Arcadian setting peopled with shepherds, nymphs, satyrs, and mythological deities, this pastoral drama treats complicated love intrigues in a standard five-act plot. It often

161

develops the conflict between two traditional pastoral topics about love: "that's lawful which does please," and its converse, "only if it's lawful, does love please." Love affairs, often of three pairs of shepherds and shepherdesses or nymphs, crisscross, with a satyr as the villain of the plot. Action is often reported rather than represented dramatically on stage, leaving much time for lyric expression of sentiment. Despite serious threats and mishaps, the plays end happily. Italian writers of pastoral plays thought of their plays as tragicomedies. Although Italian theorists and writers of pastoral plays believed that the origins of such plays lay in the classical eclogue (q.v.), they generally called the genre "modern," since they found no examples of the form in Greek and Latin literature.

The chief examples of Italian pastoral drama are Tasso's *Aminta* (an "Ecloga" or a "Comedia Pastorale," published 1581) and Guarini's *Il pastor fido* (published 1590). Both Italian models were known through translations to English writers by the turn of the century. Ben Jonson alludes to the new Italian influence upon English pastoral drama in general when, in *Volpone* (c. 1606), his Lady Wouldbe remarks: "Here's PASTOR FIDO ... All our *English* writers / I meane such, as are happy to th' *Italian,* / Will deigne to steale out of this author, mainly" (III, iv).

Despite a recognition of formal Italian pastoral plays during the early years of the seventeenth century, most English playwrights and publishers called plays *pastoral* that made only incidental use of pastoral elements. For example, in 1584 the publisher of George Peele's *The Arraignment of Paris,* whose leading characters are gods and goddesses, called that mythological play a *pastorall* on the title page; in 1640 the publisher of James Shirley's *Arcadia* still found *pastoral* an appropriate designation for that play. Shirley's play is only one of at least seven plays that dramatized matters from Sir Philip Sidney's pastoral-chivalric romance, the *Arcadia* (1590). While the setting is the countryside, the major characters are courtly persons in disguise as shepherds, not native shepherds. In other words, throughout the English Renaissance most writers of pastoral plays were indebted to traditions and sources other than the Italian pastoral drama. Chief among these sources were pastoral poems or eclogues and especially the prose romance (q.v.). Many of the pastoral plays, such as *As You Like It* (c. 1599), are what Polonius would probably classify as "pastoral-comical."

The large difference between most English plays with pastoral elements and the few formal pastoral plays is that in the former, as in the prose romance, the pastoral countryside is a temporary retreat for courtly characters, whose adventures and loves are the center of attention. The plays are "characterized by a more or less prevalent court atmosphere, disguisings and adventures in shepherd's garb forming the mainstay of the plot, while the genuine pastoral elements supply little beyond the background of the action" (Greg). The court is never far away from the countryside or woods; and much of the dramatic tension comes from a confrontation between courtly and pastoral values. The "green world" can supply a needed period of refreshment or a haven of refuge, but it can also hinder the nobly born from the heroic achievements of a valued active life. It is to the court that the main characters return, once the rural setting has provided a place for lovers to find themselves and each other, for families to be reunited, and for misunderstandings and mishaps to be corrected. In most "pastoral" plays of the English Renaissance, courtly figures enjoy but a sunshine holiday before they return to the main business of life.

Bibliography

Josephine Laidler, "A History of Pastoral Drama in England until 1700," *Englishe Studien,* 35 (1905), 194–259; Edwin Greenlaw, "Shakespeare's Pastorals," *SP,* 13 (1916), 122–54; Ernest Grillo, ed., "Renaissance Pastoral Drama," *Torquato Tasso: "Aminta," A Pastoral Drama* (1924), pp. 3–45; Violet M. Jeffery, "Italian and English Pastoral Drama of the Renaissance," *MLR,* 19 (1924), 435–44; Violet M. Jeffery, "Lyly's Pastoral Plays," *John Lyly and the Italian Renaissance* (1928), pp. 73–94; Marvin T. Herrick, "Pastoral Tragicomedy," *Tragicomedy: Its Origin and Development in Italy, France, and England* (1955), pp. 125–71; Richard Cody, *The Landscape of the Mind: Pastoralism and Platonic Theory in Tasso's "Aminta" and Shakespeare's Early Comedies* (1969); David Orr, "Pastoral and Tragi-Comedy," *Italian Renaissance Drama in England before 1625: The Influence of "Erudita" Tragedy, Comedy, and Pastoral on Elizabethan and Jacobean Drama* (1970), pp. 73–103; Thomas McFarland, "Comedy and Its Pastoral Extension," *Shakespeare's Pastoral Comedy* (1972), pp. 3–48; David Young, "A Singular Gift in Defining," *The Heart's Forest: A Study of Shakespeare's Pastoral Plays* (1972), pp. 1–37.

Poulter's measure:

"The long verse of twelve and fourtene sillables" (George Gascoigne, *Certain Notes of Instruction,* 1575); a rhymed couplet (q.v.) composed of a first line of iambic hexameter and a second line of iambic heptameter (*see* Fourteener). Gascoigne calls this couplet "the comonest sort of verse which we use now adayes." Then he adds, "I know not certainly howe to name it, unlesse I should say that it doth consist of Poulters measure, which giveth xii. for one doze[n] and xiiii for another." Also calling attention to the poultryman's alleged practice of giving his customer a dozen eggs in his first purchase and fourteen in his second, other writers simply refer to this couplet as poulter's measure.

Englishmen became familiar with poulter's measure as early as Tottel's *Miscellany* (1557), where it appeared in the work of Sir Thomas Wyatt and Henry Howard, Earl of Surrey. It then attracted a large number of poets and almost completely dominated English poetry during the next two decades. Poets selected poulter's measure for a wide range of subject matter in both the lyric and narrative mode. Gascoigne rightly points out that "the long verse of twelve and fouretene sillables" is "now adayes used in all Theames."

Within its two lines poulter's measure contains a feature as essential to the form as the line lengths themselves. This is the pause or caesura after the third foot of the first line and again after the fourth foot of the second line. As Gascoigne observes, "in verses of twelve, in the firste and fouretene in the seconde, wee place the pause commonly in the midst of the first, and at the ende of the first eight sillables in the second." The metrical structure of poulter's measure thus consists of units of three feet, three feet, four feet, three feet in ruthless repetition. After the prosodic confusion of the late medieval period and early Renaissance, poulter's measure helped to point the way to scansion by foot and syllable; but, that lesson once learned, poets abandoned poulter's measure in favor of meters of less infinite monotony. (*See* Versifying.)

Proportion of figure:

"Your last proportion [harmonious relationship] is that of figure, so called for that it yelds an ocular representation, your meeters being by good symmetrie reduced into certaine Geometricall figures, whereby the maker is restrained to keepe him within his bounds" (George Puttenham, *The Art of English Poesy,* 1589); a poem in which the words are arranged to represent a specific object or form. By varying the length of the lines, a writer can shape his poem into whatever design he chooses. Puttenham says that the poet's restraint to "keepe him within his bounds. . . sheweth not onely more art, but serveth also much better for briefnesse and subtiltie of device." These "ocular representation[s]," Puttenham continues, "are . . . fittest for the pretie amourets in Court to entertain their servants and the time withall, their delicate wits requiring some commendable exercise to keepe them from idlenesse."

Such poems, today called pattern poems, had their origins in Greek poetry, principally that of the *Greek Anthology,* and very likely in even earlier Oriental writings. The most notable of the poets whose pattern poems appeared in the *Greek Anthology,* a tenth-century compilation of surviving poems of earlier writers, is Simias of Rhodes (300 B.C.); his poems take the forms of an egg, ax, or wings. Shapes used by other Greek bucolic poets include the shepherd's pipe and the altar. Sanctioned by classical precedent, all of these shapes, along with many more, appeared in English Renaissance pattern poetry.

Probably under the influence of French adaptations of pattern poems deriving from the *Greek Anthology,* the first English poet to create a pattern poem was Stephen Hawes during the first decade of the sixteenth century. Hawes was only the forerunner of hundreds of poets who were attracted to the practice, especially during the later part of the century and the early decades of the seventeenth century.

English poets were exploring the still new possibilities for calling attention to the appearance of a poem as printed matter. In this sense pattern poems are experiments into the relations between typography and the critical formula that the poem is a "speaking picture" (*see* Ut pictura poesis). In their appeal to the eye as well as the ear, pattern poems are akin to other poetic forms, such as acrostics, anagrams, and emblems (qq.v.).

Drawing upon examples he has heard about in Oriental literature, Puttenham cites some fifteen figures for possible pattern poems. These, he admits, will "at the beginning . . . seeme nothing pleasant to an English eare, but time and usage will make them acceptable inough, as it doth all other new guises." Among figures that he considers important are the "lozange" or "a quadrangle reverst" and the "Piller" or "Pillaster," a figure "among all the rest of the Geometricall most beawtifull." The "Round," however, is the "most excellent," since it "doth resemble the world or univers," and, "having no speciall place of beginning nor end, beareth a similitude with God and eternitie."

Not all English critics were so generous in their attitude to pattern poems. Gabriel Harvey, for example, calls "Simmias Rhodius . . . a folishe idle phantasticall poett" for having "first devised this odd riminge with many other triflinge and childishe toyes to make verses, that shoulde in proportion represent the form and figure of an egg, an ape, a winge, and sutche ridiculous and madd gugawes and crockchettes"; and he regrets that the practice has been "late foolishely revivid by sum, otherwise not unlernid" (*Letter-Book,* letters written 1573-80, ed. E. J. L. Scott, 1884). And in 1596 the satiric pamphleteer Thomas Nashe (*Have with you to Saffron-Walden*) ridicules the extreme variety of objects into which lines of poetry were forced. These include, Nashe tells us, "a paire of gloves, a dozen of points, a Colossus, a Pyradmide, a Painters eazill, a market-crosse, a trumpet, an anchor, a paire of pothookes."

Bibliography

Margaret Church, "The First English Pattern Poems," *PMLA,* 61 (1946), 636-50; A. L. Korn, "Puttenham and the Oriental Pattern-Poem," *CL,* 6 (1954), 289-303; Dick Higgins, *George Herbert's Pattern Poems: In Their Tradition* (1977).

Quatrain:

A stanza or "staffe of foure verses" (George Puttenham, *The Art of English Poesy,* 1589). Always rhymed during the English Renaissance, the quatrain was one of the most popular stanza patterns for lyric poetry. The quatrain often contained "in it selfe matter sufficient to make a full periode or complement of sence" (Puttenham), as it did in much epigrammatic poetry; or it served as a structural unit in a longer poem. It was rarely used for extended narrative poems. Two of the most common rhyme patterns in the quatrain were *abab* and *abba.* Another, *abcb,* was known as the ballad stanza. (*See* Versifying.)

Rhetoric:

A discipline that teaches the art of discourse for a popular audience. A Renaissance rhetoric book defines its subject as "the art to set furthe by utterance of wordes, matter at large, or (as Cicero doeth saie) it is a learned, or . . . an artificiall declaration of the mynde, in the handelying of any cause . . . that maie through reason largely be expounded for mannes behove" (Thomas Wilson, *The Art of Rhetoric,* 1553).

Rhetoric had been for over two thousand years the most important discipline to anyone interested in poetry; in the sixteenth century theories of rhetoric and theories of poetry were virtually indistinguishable. "Nearly all our older poetry was written and read by men to whom the distinction between poetry and rhetoric, in its modern form, would have been meaningless" (C. S. Lewis, *English Literature in the Sixteenth Century,* 1954). Originating in the significant role of public oratory in Greco-Roman culture, rhetoric became in the course of time "a science, an art, an ideal of life, and indeed a pillar of antique culture" (Ernst Curtius, *European Literature and the Latin Middle Ages,* trans. Willard Trask, 1953). It was supported by a highly intellectual and carefully defined set of principles, which dominated all forms of verbal discourse, spoken or written, well into the eighteenth century.

As the English Renaissance received it, rhetoric was primarily embodied in the works of Cicero and Quintilian and in a work attributed to Cicero, *Rhetorica ad Herennium.* Ben Jonson, educated towards the close of the sixteenth century, remarks to his friend William Drummond that a thorough knowledge of Quintilian was all a poet needed. Quintilian's *Institutio oratoria* (which includes a reworking of material from Cicero's more speculative discussions on the nature of oratory) was the foundation for most English sixteenth-century rhetorics in the vernacular. Rhetoric was the keystone of Renaissance education and the central discipline for literary criticism and creation.

The equation between the poet and the orator, between poetry and

168

oratory, was traditional. Dante's formula was much quoted: "poetry is a rhetorical fiction [invention] set to music" ("una fintione retorica posta in musica," *De vulgari eloquentia*). While the logician uses induction and the syllogism as his forms of argument, the orator uses the enthymeme and the example; and these are the same forms employed by the poet. Both poetry and rhetoric are arts of *sententiae* (q.v.) and elocution. Poetry differs from oratory in that its argument is concealed and thus is more persuasive. "The Poet is the neerest Borderer upon the Orator, and expresseth all his vertues, though he be tyed more to numbers; is his equall in ornament, and above him in his strengths" (Ben Jonson, *Timber, or Discoveries,* 1641).

Literary concepts of decorum (q.v.), of propriety and appropriateness to levels of subject, form, and language, derived directly or indirectly from rhetoric. As early as the time of Cicero, decorum was defined in its application not only to oratory but also to poetry. The idea of hierarchical classes of poetry, of degrees of "weight" or significance among poetic genres, came from the tendencies of rhetoricians to categorize discourse in this way. So to Sir Philip Sidney the "heroicall" poem is "the best and most accomplished kinde of Poetry," and a pastoral poem is "lowest" (*An Apology for Poetry,* 1595).

With a hierarchy of genres, rhetoric also assumed a hierarchy of style. Theorists of Ciceronian rhetoric distinguished three levels of language or diction: grand, middle, and simple or low. A rhetoric book much used in the schools explains: "The grand style consists of a smooth and ornate arrangement of impressive words. The middle style consists of words of a lower, yet not the lowest and colloquial class, of words. The simple style is brought down even to the most current idiom of standard speech" (*Rhetorica ad Herennium,* trans. Harry Caplan). Each of these levels of language was linked, in poetic theory, to certain genres, the simple assigned to satire, for example, and the grand to the heroic poem.

Just as rhetoric contributed a theory of language stressing the correlation between genre and diction, rhetorical assumptions that every kind of discourse serves a particular function were paralleled by a poetic theory that assigned special purposes to the various genres. Poetry and rhetoric had the same general ends; poetry like oratory was to teach, to delight, and to persuade. More specifically, orations were divided into three kinds, each with its own particular purpose; and the particular functions of the oratorical kinds were transferred to poetic theory. One kind is the "Oration deliberative" whereby "we do perswade, or disswade, entreate, or rebuke, exhorte, or dehorte." This is the oration of public assembly and councils "whereby we advise our neighbour to that thyng, which we thynke most nedeful for hym or els to cal him backe from that folie, which hindereth much his estimacion." The second kind of oratory is the judicial oration, "an earnest debatyng . . . of some weightie matter before a judge." The third kind of oration is the demonstrative or epideictic (q.v.) kind in which an orator "standeth either in praise or dispraise of some one man, or of some one thyng, or of some one deede doen." In the deliberative oration the matter consists of what is profitable or unprofitable; in the judicial oration the matter consists of what is right or wrong; in the epideictic oration the matter consists of praise or dispraise (all quotations above from Wilson).

The vocabulary associated with the oratorical kinds permeates contemporary discussion of poetry. Generally it is the epideictic's purposes of praise and blame that find their way into English discussions of poetry, but the ancient rhetoricians had noted that the instructive function of deliberative oratory often intermingles with the ceremonial function of epideictic rhetoric. Aristotle in his *Rhetoric* reminds readers that what one might suggest in counseling becomes encomium (q.v.) by a change of phrase (I.9). Quintilian notes too that encomium is often advisory (*Institutio oratoria,* III.4). Italian critics of the sixteenth century were inclined to extend and systematize these remarks. Tommaso Correa, for example, finds that there are judicial epigrams, deliberative epigrams, and epideictic epigrams (*De toto eo poematis genere,* 1569). Pietro Pagano claims that the sonnet belongs to the judicial kind of discourse (*Discorso sopra il secondo sonnetto del Petrarca,* 1570?).

More loosely, the stance of the judicial debater and that of the argumentative counselor color fictions of every kind. The long set speech of the drama is an extension of school training in oratory, while well-developed arguments are part of the structure of narratives of every kind. The orator's profession is to master every question, whether infinite ("as thus, whether it is best to marie, or to live single; which is better, a courtier's life, or a scholar's life") or definite ("as thus, whether it be best here in England, for a Prieste to mari, or to live single") (Wilson).

The study of rhetoric also addresses the relations of a speaker to his audience with attention to the speaker's power to establish his "voice" or character (*ethos*) for a specific purpose and to the creation of a desired state of feeling (*pathos*) in an audience that is congruent with a speaker's purpose. The student of rhetoric was in the continual situation of creating appropriate "characters" for presentation to an audience and of creating a discourse that would affect an audience in a desired manner. As applied to poetics, a studied interplay between speaker and audience suggested the possibility of a fictive speaker apart from an author and a fictive audience different than an actual reader. Renaissance genres often assume conventional relations between speaker and audience. Thus the *ethos* of the Petrarchan sonnet requires a split addresser whose voice as a speaker differs from that of the author, and a fictive audience, usually the speaker's beloved, different than the actual reader.

Equally far-reaching was the transfer to poetics of rhetorical theories about style (*see* Elocutio). Traditionally rhetoric consisted of five closely related operations designated as *inventio, dispositio, elocutio, pronunciato,* and *memoria:* that is, invention, "finding" one's material, usually with the corollary that one found it in the various "places" where one had stored it, such as the "places" of one's common-place book (*see* Common-place); disposition or arrangement of one's material; elocution or style; delivery; and memory. The last two stages of composition, delivery and memory, were important to an orator memorizing his speech and delivering it with an appropriate set of gestures. But the emphasis in rhetorical training was on style, and style as a departure from common speech.

Rhetoricians assumed that the most expressive discourse was a heightened and shaped discourse, removed from the careless flow of ordinary speech. "Figure" was thus the central study of rhetoric; for, as Henry Peacham puts it, "a figure is a fashion of words, Oration of sentence, made new by Arte, tourning from the common manner and custome of wryting or speaking" (*The Garden of Eloquence,* 1577). While rhetoricians had always stressed figure as essential to fullness and variety of expression, there is a noticeable increase in this emphasis throughout the sixteenth century. It is suggestive that the inherited rhetoric book *Ad Herennium* lists only 65 figures of speech and that the revised *Garden of Eloquence* of 1593 discusses in detail 175 figures. The impact of rhetorical theories of figure permeates Renaissance fictions in their every form, as writers, trained in *elocutio* by grammar school and university exercises, brought to fictions the fruit of their training.

This elaborate theory of language also transferred to poetry the ethical power related to the systematic strategies of rhetoric itself and its sister art, logic. All artful discourse, regardless of audience, was assumed to have a didactic purpose. Rhetoric was the art of popular discourse; logic was the art of learned and philosophical discourse. Poetry—and here poetry is any imaginative fiction—was, like rhetoric, a form of popular discourse, but popular discourse with a "veiled" power to move men to virtue. The ancient metaphors that point up the strategies of popular versus learned discourse are those of the "open palm" and the "closed fist"; a popular audience requires amplification, copiousness, figures; a learned audience requires a tightly constructed argument. "By plaine teachyng, the Logician shewes hymselfe, by large amplification and beautifying of his cause, the Rhetorician is alwaies knowne" (Wilson). As discourse with a hidden significance, poetry has rhetoric's "open palm" but one made especially attractive by fiction. Because it uses fiction and characterization, poetry "speaks" two simultaneous languages; one in its "entertainment" and the other in its didactic power to provide images of vice and virtue.

The close adjustments between poetics and rhetoric were not immutable.

Late in the sixteenth century, the impact of a new school of rhetoric began to make itself felt in England; this was Ramist rhetoric, a system developed by the French philosopher Peter Ramus (1515–72), a school reformer and rhetorician. Ramism both expresses and reinforces great shifts in European culture and looks ahead to developments in communication theory that become profoundly "modern." Before the Ramists, logic and rhetoric, while addressed to different audiences, had gradually become conflated. The conceptual structure of logic was almost identical to that of rhetoric; both were dependent upon common methods of invention and disposition. In both disciplines one "found" one's argument in topics or common-places and "disposed" them into the form of a valid statement. In the name of pedagogical efficiency, Ramists reoriented this process with a rigor that eventually displaced the older relations between rhetoric and logic. Ramists assigned to logic alone the processes of invention and disposition, and to rhetoric alone the process of *elocutio* as the verbal expression of the thoughts found and ordered by logic. By their insistence on "methodizing" and recompartmentalizing what traditionally had been a rather loose and overlapping set of categories, Ramists eventually refocused the way men thought about the arts of discourse. It has been claimed that Ramism tended to objectify the creation process by separating the finding of an idea from its expression; *inventio* is located solely in logic and *elocutio* is located solely in rhetoric. Eventually, too, *elocutio,* in particular the use of figured language, will be considered, not an integral clarification of an "idea," but a "mere" embellishment to the processes of "logical" thought.

Bibliography

J. E. Spingarn, *A History of Literary Criticism in the Renaissance* (rev. ed., 1908); D. L. Clark, *Rhetoric and Poetry in the Renaissance: A Study of Rhetorical Terms in English Renaissance Literary Criticism* (1922); C. S. Baldwin, *Medieval Rhetoric and Poetic* (1928); William G. Crane, *Wit and Rhetoric in the Renaissance* (1937); C. S. Baldwin and D. L. Clark, *Renaissance Literary Theory and Practice,* ed. D. L. Clark (1939); Richard McKeon, "Rhetoric in the Middle Ages," *Speculum,* 17 (1942), 1–32; Karl R. Wallace, *Francis Bacon on Communication & Rhetoric* (1943); T. W. Baldwin, *William Shakspere's Small Latine & Lesse Greeke,* 2 vols. (1944); J. W. H. Atkins, *English Literary Criticism: The Renascence* (1947); Miriam Joseph, *Shakespeare's Use of the Arts of Language* (1947); Rosemond Tuve, *Elizabethan and Metaphysical Imagery* (1947); D. L. Clark, *John Milton at St. Paul's School: A Study of Ancient Rhetoric in English Renaissance Education* (1948); J. W. H. Atkins, *English Literary Criticism: 17th and 18th Centuries* (1951); Donald L. Clark, "The Rise and Fall of Progymnasmata in Sixteenth and Seventeenth Century Grammar Schools," *Speech Mono-*

graphs, 19 (1952), 259–63; Eugene M. Waith, *"Controversia* in the English Drama: Medwall and Massinger," *PMLA,* 68 (1953), 286–303; Wilbur S. Howell, *Logic and Rhetoric in England, 1500–1700* (1956); Walter J. Ong, *Ramus, Method, and the Decay of Dialogue* (1958); K. G. Hamilton, *The Two Harmonies: Poetry and Prose in the Seventeenth Century* (1963); N. G. Lawrence and J. A. Reynolds, eds., *Sweet Smoke of Rhetoric: A Collection of Renaissance Essays* (1964); Frances A. Yates, *The Art of Memory* (1966); Walter J. Ong, "Tudor Writings on Rhetoric," *Studies in the Renaissance,* 15 (1968), 39–69; Lee A. Sonnino, *A Handbook to Sixteenth-Century Rhetoric* (1968); Norman K. Farmer, Jr., "A Theory of Genre for Seventeenth-Century Poetry," *Genre,* 3 (1970), 293–317; Annabel M. Patterson, *Hermogenes and the Renaissance: Seven Ideas of Style* (1970); Brian Vickers, *Classical Rhetoric in English Poetry* (1970); Edward P. J. Corbett, *Classical Rhetoric for the Modern Student* (2nd ed., 1971); Peter Dixon, *Rhetoric* (1971); Annette Drew-Bear, *Rhetoric in Ben Jonson's Middle Plays: A Study of Ethos, Character Portrayal, and Persuasion* (1973); Lisa Jardine, *Francis Bacon: Discovery and the Art of Discourse* (1974); Thomas O. Sloan and Raymond B. Waddington, eds., *The Rhetoric of Renaissance Poetry from Wyatt to Milton* (1974); Wilbur S. Howell, *Poetics, Rhetoric, and Logic: Studies in the Basic Disciplines of Criticism* (1975); Richard A. Lanham, *The Motives of Eloquence: Literary Rhetoric in the Renaissance* (1976); Joel B. Altman, *The Tudor Play of Mind: Rhetorical Inquiry and the Development of Elizabethan Drama* (1978); Daniel Javitch, *Poetry and Courtliness in Renaissance England* (1978); William J. Kennedy, *Rhetorical Norms in Renaissance Literature* (1978).

Rhyme royal:

"A verse of tenne sillables, and seven such verses make a staffe [stanza], whereof the first and thirde lines do aunswer (acrosse) in like terminations and rime, the second, fourth, and fifth, do likewise answere eche other in terminations, and the two last do combine and shut up the Sentence" (George Gascoigne, *Certain Notes of Instruction,* 1575); a fixed stanza of seven iambic pentameter lines rhyming *ababbcc.*

Renaissance critical theory linked rhyme royal to certain kinds of subject matter. Gascoigne says that "Rhythme royall is fittest for a grave discourse." In *A Short Treatise on Verse* (1584), King James VI of Scotland prescribes rhyme royal, or as he calls it the *"Troilus* verse," for "tragicall materis, complaintis, or testamentis." George Puttenham comments that this stanza is "the chiefe of our ancient proportions used by any rimer writing any thing of historical or grave poeme, as ye may see in *Chaucer* and *Lidgate* th'one writing of the loves of *Troylus* and *Cresseida,* th'other of the fall of Princes" (*The Art of English Poesy,* 1589). Since decorum (q.v.) so clearly assigned rhyme royal to "grave discourse," it became an important stanza form for both reflective lyric verse and serious narrative poetry in the sixteenth century.

As Puttenham's remark suggests, rhyme royal was a stanza form that Renaissance poets inherited from their native literary tradition. Possibly finding his model in slightly earlier French poetry, Chaucer cast several of the *Canterbury Tales* and *The Parlement of Fowles* and *Troilus and Criseyde* in rhyme royal. His use of it set a fashion; and rhyme royal dominated English poetry in the century after his death (1400). The form is frequently said to have received its name during the fifteenth century from its use by King James I of Scotland in *The King's Quair.*

A major early Renaissance work which kept alive the native literary tradition was the gigantic and popular narrative *Mirror for Magistrates* (1559). Like John Lydgate's *Fall of Princes* (some 36,000 lines in rhyme royal written between 1430 and 1438), the *Mirror* narrates the downfall of famous persons. Most of these didactic narrative poems are in rhyme royal, the best known being the *Induction* and *Complaint of Buckingham* by Thomas Sackville in the 1563 edition.

Following the tradition of the *Mirror,* many narrative poems during the later sixteenth century are in rhyme royal; and all of them belong within Gascoigne's classification of "grave discourse." They are historical and tragic in subject matter, elevated in style, and serious in tone. Samuel Daniel, for example, chose rhyme royal for his *The Complaint of Rosamond* (1592), a poem which established the vogue for complaint (q.v.) poems in its decade. Shakespeare, too, used rhyme royal in his narrative poem *The Rape of Lucrece* (1594), also a kind of complaint poem. Michael Drayton's *Mortimeriados* of 1596 is a historical poem in rhyme royal, recording the struggles between Edward II and his nobles.

Lyric poetry in rhyme royal was typically restricted to "grave" as opposed to "light" subject matters. When Edmund Spenser wrote *Fowre Hymnes* (1596) fusing Neo-Platonic and Christian attitudes about love and beauty, he signaled his respect for his subject with the rhyme royal stanza.

The rival to rhyme royal as the appropriate vehicle for "grave discourse" was *ottava rima* (q.v.), an eight-line stanza form imported from Italy where it had been widely used for heroic poetry (*see* Heroic poem). Puttenham says that he personally prefers *ottava rima* for serious poetry because "it receaveth better band," that is, because, unlike rhyme royal, it contains only one rhyming couplet. When Drayton revised *Mortimeriados* as *The Barons' Wars* (1603), one of the important changes he made was to rewrite it entirely in *ottava rima.* It has been said that Drayton's revision sounded the death knell of rhyme royal in English poetry. As a stanza pattern, rhyme royal was used only occasionally after the turn of the sixteenth century. (*See* Versifying.)

Romance:

"Gallant Legendary, full of pleasurable accidents, and proffitable discourses" (Gabriel Harvey, *Pierce's Supererogation,* 1593); a lengthy narrative of love and adventure unfolding in a complicated plot. Such narratives were written in both poetry and prose.

During the late sixteenth century in England the prose romance was a distinct and popular genre. The fable of prose romances ends happily, uniting lost noble kindred or long separated lovers. The fable is typically interlaced with subplots, philosophical debates, and moral discourses; peopled with highly idealized characters; and set in a pastoral world or in exotic realms. English prose romances of the late Elizabethan period helped to establish the use of vernacular prose as a medium for serious narratives.

Prose romances are tales of adversity successfully endured. The title page of Robert Greene's *Menaphon: Camilla's Alarm to Sleeping Euphues* (1589) emphasizes this motif when it says that in this prose romance "are deciphered the variable effects of Fortune, the wonders of Love, the triumphes of inconstant Time." It describes the fable as "Displaying in sundrie conceipted passions (figured in a continuate Historie) the Trophees that Vertue carrieth triumphant, maugre the wrath of Envie, or the resolution of Fortune."

The use of the term *romance* is more Italian than English, and English writers often simply entitled their prose romances histories. Greene, for example, calls his *Pandosto, the Triumph of Time* (1588) "a pleasant Historie" and *Menaphon* "a pastoral historie." When English writers used the term *romance,* they tended to refer either to medieval verse romances or to heroic poems (q.v.) with multiple plots akin to the successful Italian romantic epic *Orlando furioso* (1516) by Lodovico Ariosto. George Puttenham, for example, writes that the "*Romance,* or short historicall ditty" relates the "old adventures & valiaunces of noble knights of the round table, Sir *Bevys* of *Southampton, Guy* of *Warwicke* and others like" (*The Art of English Poesy,* 1589). When John Milton refers to "lofty Fables and

Romances" (*Apology for Smectymnuus,* 1642), he is thinking about romantic epics. At least one English writer of a prose romance, Sir Philip Sidney, may well have thought of his *Arcadia* (1590), a revised version of his earlier unpublished prose romance known today as the "old" *Arcadia,* as a heroic poem in prose.

The pioneer works in the genre of English prose romance are John Lyly's *Euphues: The Anatomy of Wit* (1579) and its successor, *Euphues and his England* (1580), and Sidney's *Arcadia.* None of the later prose romances, such as those by Greene, Thomas Lodge's *Rosalind: Euphues' Golden Legacy* (1590), or Gervase Markham's *The English Arcadia* (Part I, 1607; Part 2, 1613), expands the already spacious boundaries set by Lyly and Sidney.

Gabriel Harvey, commenting on the *Arcadia,* explains the appeal of prose romances in general when he urges that Sidney's "gallant Legendary" be read "for three thinges especially very notable—for amorous Courting . . . for sage counselling . . . and for valorous fighting . . . and delightfull pastime by way of Pastorall exercises may passe for the fourth." Harvey's comment points not only to the subject matter of prose romances but also to their didactic aim. Much of the "sage counselling" comes from a tendency to anatomize—to halt the narrative movement and analyze an issue or topic—a technique that Lyly's *Euphues* made popular (*see* Anatomy). Other "profitable discourses" are found in scenes built around witty disputations of fashionable topics: the recklessness of youth and the prudence of old age, the rival claims of love and friendship, the fickleness of women, faith versus doubt in religion, and the shortcomings of a university education compared with experience in the world. The ideals for courtly behavior emerge in prose romances through the treatment of plot as a kind of exemplum showing vice or virtue in action. Long speeches elaborate in general terms the moral doctrine illustrated in an action; and *sententiae* (q.v.) often succinctly summarize a moral point to be learned from an action. One seventeenth-century reader puts the matter this way: the *Arcadia* is a "book which besides its excellent language, rare contrivances, and delectable studies, hath in it all of the strains of Poesy, comprehendeth the universal art of speaking, and to them that can discerne and will observe, notable rules for demeanour both private and publike" (Peter Heylyn, *Microcosmus: a Little Description of the Great World,* 1620).

Although each writer marks his prose romance with his own style, the "excellent language" of such fictions is usually that of the high style (*see* Decorum). While racy and colloquial language was appropriate in certain situations, a highly self-conscious and patterned eloquence was the general rule, befitting romance's high-born characters. Lyly's prose style especially recommended itself as a model; and many later prose romances were influenced by Lyly's highly balanced and rhythmic sentence structure, and

177

by his abundant use of incidents from history or poetry to illustrate a point, *sententiae* or maxims, and similes drawn from science or natural philosophy. Writing in 1632, the publisher of Lyly's *Six Court Comedies,* Edward Blount, acknowledges Lyly's impact upon English prose style: "Our Nation are in his debt for a new English which hee taught them." He adds, "*Euphues and his England* began first, that language. [He should have said *Euphues: the Anatomy of Wit*.] All our Ladies were then his Scholars; And that Beautie in Court, which could not Parley *Euphueisme,* was as litle regarded as shee which now there, speakes not French."

Actually the "new English" or Euphuism had a long rhetorical tradition behind it (*see* Elocutio). The schemes that characterize Lyly's prose are those traditionally associated in classical rhetoric books with the figures of Gorgias, a Greek teacher of rhetoric. They are figures that aim at striking symmetry and parallelism in sound and form. Chief among them are *isocolon* (succeeding phrases or clauses equal in length) and *parison* (succeeding phrases or clauses identical in structure). This syntactic parallelism is further embellished by making the corresponding words in the members begin with the same sound (*alliteratio*), or end with the same sound (*homoioteleuton*). Combined with these figures are others of repetition, antithesis, rhetorical questions, and exclamation.

Rosalynds passion, in Lodge's *Rosalind,* illustrates the Euphuistic style which Blount calls the "new English." "Infortunate ROSALYND, whose misfortunes are more than thy yeeres, and whose passions are greater than thy patience. The blossomes of thy youth, are mixt with the frostes of envie, and the hope of thy ensuring frutes, perish in the bud. Thy father is TORISMOND banisht from the crowne, & thou the unhappie daughter of a King, detained captive, living as disquieted in thy thoughts, as thy father discontented in his exile. Ah ROSALYND, what cares wait upon a crown, what griefes are incident to dignitie? what sorrowes haunt royal Pallaces!"

In the creation of prose romances English writers drew generously and at will from several literary traditions (*see* Imitation). One of Sidney's contemporaries, John Hoskins, points to two of the traditions when he writes, "For the web, as it were, of his story, he [Sidney] followed three: Heliodorous in Greek, Sannazarius' *Arcadia* in Italian, and *Diana* [by] de Montemayor in Spanish" (*Directions for Speech and Style,* written c. 1599). To Hoskins's mention of a Greek prose romance and two sixteenth-century pastoral romances may be added the chivalric prose romances of the late Middle Ages. The practice of English writers was to blend these several traditions for their own particular fictional purposes.

The Greek prose romances of the third century had been retold throughout the Middle Ages and were available to English writers mainly in Latin versions and later translations. These elaborate tales provided models for complicated stories, ending happily, of wandering high-born lovers. Among the best-known of the Greek romances to Elizabethans were the *Aethiopica* by Heliodorus, *Clitophon and Leucippe* by Achilles Tatius, and *Daphnis and Chloe* by Longus. Thomas Underdowne calls his translation of Heliodorus (*An Ethiopian History,* 1587) a "most honest . . . historie of love." Sidney ranks Heliodorus with Virgil in composing an "absolute heroical poem" and praises Heliodorus for inventing "so true a lover as Theagenes" (*An Apology for Poetry,* 1595). This emphasis on love was probably what led some English prose romancers to label their works "love pamphlets."

Equally important to English writers were the later chivalric prose romances, mainly from fifteenth-century Spain and Portugal. When not known in their original languages, these tales of extraordinary chivalric actions were available through translations. Some of the better known translations were the work of Anthony Munday: *Palmerin d'Oliva* (1588), *Palladine of England* (1588), *Amadis of Gaul* (1595), and *Palmerin of England* (1596). In these romances the claims of love and chivalry upon the hero are one claim, but daring and courageous feats of arms are the mainstay of the plots. Sidney claims that through the feats of arms recorded in the *Amadis of Gaul* many men "have found their harts mooved to the exercise of courtesie, liberalitie, and especially courage." The happy endings of chivalric romances are constantly forestalled by episode upon episode in which questing knights encounter almost every conceivable difficulty, including disguises, magic, and witchcraft. For their settings the translated chivalric romances "usually have a vaguely Arthurian colouring and a theatre of operations somehow based in England, or they are located in fabulous Eastern realms, or they shift back and forth between the two areas" (Schlauch).

A third strain in English prose romances comes from the conventions of the pastoral tradition, which lent to many of them an idealized country setting. Shepherd's apparel often provided a disguise for nobly born knights and ladies. The pastoral setting had found its way into one of the early Greek prose romances, *Daphnis and Chloe.* Later writers continued the practice of combining pastoral and romance. For example, Sannazaro's Italian romance, the *Arcadia* (1501),. consists of a dozen eclogues (q.v.), each introduced by a long prose narrative. Another influential pastoral romance was Jorge de Montemayor's *Diana* (1559), a Spanish prose fiction with interwoven and interspersed poems.

Bibliography

J. J. Jusserand, *The English Novel in the Time of Shakespeare* (1890); Samuel Lee Wolff, *The Greek Romances in Elizabethan Prose Fiction* (1912); Ronald S. Crane, *The Vogue of Medieval Chivalric Romance During the English Renaissance* (1919); Ernest A. Baker, *The History of the English*

Novel, vol. 2 (1929), pp. 11–125; R. W. Zandvoort, *Sidney's "Arcadia": A Comparison between the Two Versions* (1929); Mary Patchell, *The "Palmerin" Romances in Elizabethan Prose Fiction* (1947); E. C. Pettet, "The Romance Tradition," *Shakespeare and The Romance Tradition* (1949), pp. 11–35; David Kalstone, "The Transformation of Arcadia: Sannazaro and Sir Philip Sidney," *CL,* 15 (1963), 234–49; Margaret Schlauch, *Antecedents of the English Novel, 1400–1600* (1963): William G. Crane, "The Sentimental Novel and Romance," *Wit and Rhetoric in the Renaissance* (1964), pp. 162–78; John Danby, "Sidney's Arcadia: The Great House Romance," *Elizabethan and Jacobean Poets* (1965), pp. 46–73; Walter R. Davis and Richard A. Lanham, *Sidney's "Arcadia"* (1965); Ben Edwin Perry, *The Ancient Romances: A Literary-Historical Account of Their Origins* (1967); Walter R. Davis, *Idea and Act in Elizabethan Fiction* (1969); Carol Gesner, Chs. 1 & 2, *Shakespeare and the Greek Romance: A Study of Origins* (1970), pp. 1–46; John J. O'Connor, *"Amadis de Gaule" and Its Influence on Elizabethan Literature* (1970); Herschel Baker, ed., *Four Essays on Romance* (1971); Howard Felperin, "Background and Theory," *Shakespearean Romance* (1972), pp. 3–54; A. C. Hamilton, "Sidney's *Arcadia* as Prose Fiction: Its Relation to Its Sources," *ELR,* 2 (1972), 29–60; Stephen J. Greenblatt, "Sidney's *Arcadia* and the Mixed Mode," *SP,* 70 (1973), 269–78.

Satire:

"A tarte and carpying kynd of verse, / An instrument to pynche the prankes of men" (Thomas Drant, *A Medicinable Moral,* 1566). While a "tarte and carpying" tone infused many types of Renaissance writings (*e.g.,* prose narratives and pamphlets, plays, and popular songs and ballads), critics and writers generally reserved the word *satire,* often spelled *satyre,* to refer to a particular kind of verse: a quasi-dramatic poem, frequently a monologue, in which a carefully defined speaker, shocked by the vice or folly of the world around him, condemns or ridicules it as a deformity. As a genre, satire was classified as "humble" or "low," partly because of its informal, conversational style and partly because the satirist appeared before the reader as a "plain-dealer," one who would present the truth about society and unmask any of its deformities (*see* Decorum).

The principal intention of verse satire was dispraise (*see* Epideictic rhetoric). George Puttenham calls satirists the "spiers out of all . . . secret faults" (*The Art of English Poesy,* 1589). The satirist is no mere detached observer; instead he is driven to protest and to pass judgments, and he wishes to persuade others of the rightness of his indignation. He holds up a mirror (a favorite image of Renaissance satirists), and he anatomizes faults (*see* Anatomy). The early Tudor poet Alexander Barclay, for example, in some remarks on his *Ship of Fools* (1509) identifies satire with the "reprehencion of foulysshnes"; and Joseph Hall in the prologue to his verse satires entitled *Virgidemiae* (1598) tells his muse: "Goe daring Muse on with thy thankless taske, / And do the ugly face of vice unmaske. . . . Truth be thy speed, and Truth thy Patron bee." To use a favorite Renaissance term, satire "bites" its readers. "I cannot chuse but bite," cries the speaker in one of John Marston's verse satires in *The Scourge of Villainy* (1598); and, as John Milton in the *Apology for Smectymnuus* (1642) asks, "if it bite neither the person nor the vices, how is it a satire?" The aim of the satiric writer, then, is to shock the reader into a realization of the difference between what is and what ought to be; and he chooses his

181

rhetorical weapons accordingly: irony; paradox; exaggeration; colloquial language; frank and vivid, often obscene, expression.

Because of a misunderstanding regarding the etymology of the word *satire,* English theorists and poets alike often connected verse satire with the speeches of satyrs, grotesque creatures, half human, half beast, who served as a chorus in ancient Greek burlesque drama. The word *satire* (Latin *satura,* "a medley") seems originally to have designated only a collection of miscellaneous poems; however, by the time of the Renaissance *satire* had become confused with the Greek *satyros,* "satyr." Thomas Langley, for example, defines "A Satyre" as "a Poesy, rebukying vyces sharpelye, not regardying anye personnes" (*An Abridgement of the Notable Work of Polydore Vergil,* 1546). Then, unaware of the confusion over the etymology, he writes, "The Satyres had theyr name of uplandyshe Goddes, that were rude lassivious, and wanton of behavior." Similarly Puttenham reports that satire as a poetic form derived from speeches delivered in the Greek satyr play. He says that the Greek satyr play, along with comedy and tragedy, arose in ancient times as a corrective for human vice and folly: "And the first and most bitter invective against vice and vicious men was the *Satyre:* which to th' intent their bitternesse should breede none ill will . . . they [writers] made wise as if the gods of the woods, whom they called *Satyres* or *Silvanes,* should appear and recite those verses of rebuke." This notion of a satyr-speaker carried over into verse satires. At the beginning of one of his verse satires entitled *Vice's Executioner: or the Satyr's Self-description of Himself* (1620), George Wither says:

> Though in shape I seeme a Man,
> Yet a Satyr wilde I am;
> Bred in Woods and Desert places,
> Where men seldome shew their faces;
> Rough and hayrie like a Goate,
> Clothed with Dame Natures coate.

Often illustrations of satyrs accompanied volumes of verse satires. The idea that "poetic satire had its origin in a dramatic form distinguished for its viciousness of attack and spoken by rough satyrs was the basis for nearly all Elizabethan theories of satire" (Kernan). In 1605 the French classical scholar Isaac Casaubon exposed the error of the satire-satyr connection, but the tradition remained strong into the seventeenth century. Not only had it bedded itself in the spelling of *satire* (*satyre*), but more importantly it had shaped the conception of the poetic form as a kind of quasi-dramatic poem.

The uninhibited, brash manner of the coarse, frank language of the satyr's speeches of rebuke was thought appropriate for the language of verse satire. The result of this application of the theory of decorum is that Renaissance poets often felt obligated to strive for a harshness and roughness not only of language but also of versification. Just as the content and attitude of verse satire opposed deceptive appearance or "seeming," so was the language and versification the opposite of worldly smoothness and elegance. Satire is to be "harsh of stile," Joseph Hall claims, as well as "harsh of conceipt." Yet at times the rustic crudity of the satyr's speech seemed inadequate to convey the intensity of the satirist's attack. Something more like the lofty style of tragedy was felt to be needed. Marston, for example, invoking his muse in one of the satires in *The Scourge of Villainy*, exclaims:

> Grim-fac'd *Reproofe*, sparkle with threatening eye
> Bend thy sower browes in my tart poesie.
> Avant yee curres, houle in some cloudie mist,
> Quake to behold a sharp-fang'd Satyrist.
> O how on tiptoes proudly mounts my Muse,
> Stalking a loftier gate then Satyres use.
> Me thinkes some sacred rage warmes all my vaines,
> Making my spright mount up to higher straines.

In addition, as late Elizabethan poets also began to imitate certain Roman models of verse satire, which they found difficult in style and obscure in allusions, some English satirists felt their poetic satire should be "dark" or obscure (*see* Imitation). They interpreted the difficulties in style and allusion of some classical satire as deliberate attempts at camouflage in order to obtain greater freedom in attacking specific situations or persons. Hence, English poets occasionally emulated the Roman models with "dark enigmas" in their own poetry, despite the fact that this practice ran counter to the plain and straightforward manner of the satyr-speaker.

Behind the verse satires of the English Renaissance lie two important generic traditions—one native and the other classical. Puttenham points to these two traditions when he says, "There was yet another kind of Poet, who intended to taxe the common abuses and vice of the people in rough and bitter speaches, and their invectives were called *Satyres,* and themselves *Satyricques:* such were *Lucilius, Juvenall,* and *Persius* among the Latines, & with us he that wrote the booke called Piers plowman." Renaissance critics generally believed that their conception of verse satire, that is, a dramatic poem of moral censure, had the support of both native and Roman examples.

The native tradition had its roots in the sermons and writings of medieval monks as they rebuked sinfulness. Rhetorical techniques used in these rebukes, such as irony, allegory, anecdotes, personified abstractions, character sketches, and beast fables, were also those of medieval poetry; and by the close of the fourteenth century a native tradition of poetic satire had established itself, with Chaucer and William Langland, the *Piers Plowman* poet, its most outstanding practitioners. In addition, the medieval complaint (q.v.) poem had its influence upon the development of native verse satire. Permeated with the theme of *contemptus mundi,* complaint poems repeatedly point out the vanity of worldly existence, and they direct general attacks against the ecclesiastical and courtly ruling classes and against sinful human behavior. A homiletic quality with the preacher's stock of rhetorical techniques passed from medieval satiric poetry to Renaissance verse satires.

The important Roman verse satirists, imitated by English poets, were Horace (65–8 B.C.), Persius (34–62 A.D.), and Juvenal (c. 60–130 A.D.). The satires of Horace include character sketches, scenes of contemporary city life, philosophical reflections on life in the country, literary discussions, and even passages of autobiography. One of his favorite themes, a praise of country life and an advocacy of withdrawal from the distractions of the city and court, found special favor with English poets. Like those of later Roman verse satirists, Horace's satires are written in hexameter, the Latin meter more often associated with heroic verse. His style Horace describes as "mixed"—conversational, sometimes sad, sometimes humorous, aimed at ridicule rather than invective; and the tone of his satires is nearly always personal, intimate, and reflective rather than aggressive. English writers admired Horace particularly for the polish and care of his style and for his ironic and urbane wit. Often his satires are in the form of a dialogue with one character a *persona* for the poet himself and the other a type being criticized. Other satiric pieces are epistles (q.v.) to friends or patrons. As a critic of human foibles, Horace maintains that his satires hurt only the guilty; and such a disclaimer often accompanies English Renaissance verse satires. Hall, for example, in a postscript to *Virgidemiae* advises his readers, "Art thou guilty? Complain not, thou are not wronged. Art thou guiltless? Complain not, thou are not touched."

The milder Horatian tone contrasts with the savage and bitter voice of both Persius and Juvenal. The verse satires of Persius are dialogues between two speakers; and while conversational, their language is often obscure and difficult, a trait that English satirists of the last decade of the sixteenth century imitated. Even though as a reflective satiric poet, Persius often advises *tecum habita* ("live within yourself"), his satires against social ills are marked with a cutting wit. It was the scope and aggressive indignation of Juvenal's attack against what seems to be an almost totally corrupt and degenerate human society, however, that most attracted late Elizabethan verse satirists. The speaker in many of Marston's satires, for example, shares with Juvenal's speakers an utter disgust at human depravity, especially sexual misconduct. Hall distinguishes between his "toothless" verse satires, those modeled on the milder Horatian tone, and his "biting" satires, those more resembling Juvenal's.

In actual practice English Renaissance poets felt quite free to emulate either tone in a particular verse satire; and, in turn, the desired tone affected the poet's choice of language and syntax. But no doubt it was the thundering denunciations of English satire of a Juvenalian nature with its dramatic realism and declamatory rhetoric that caused ecclesiastical officials to take notice. In 1599 the Archbishop of Canterbury and the Bishop of London ordered a ban on the publication of satirical works; their edict, however, had little practical effect, for verse satires continued to be printed in the early decades of the seventeenth century.

The native and Latin traditions account for a difference between the personalities of speakers in Renaissance satire. Often going under the name of Piers, the plowman-speaker of native verse satire is a plain, humble, unlearned ("lewd") man, in contrast to the more sophisticated, witty, malcontent speaker in satires modeled along Roman lines. The plowman stresses his life of hard, honest work on the land as well as his literary naiveté; his moral and ethical code is thoroughly grounded in Christianity. In his rusticity and simple virtue, he is an idealized figure, always standing in sharp contrast to the sinful world around him. Hardly a satyr figure, the plowman *persona,* with his contempt for vice and his harsh, open criticism of it, fits comfortably in the general theory of verse satire. During the Renaissance this humble speaker is often a shepherd and takes the name, among others, of Colin Clout. Whether plowman or shepherd, the speaker of native verse satire contrasts with more misanthropic snarlers of the verse satires in the Juvenalian tradition. This railer, often a disenchanted young scholar or a dissatisfied courtier, almost seems infected by the very vices and depravity that he is criticizing.

Elizabethan and early seventeenth-century English poets associated no single metrical form with verse satire. Among the various verse forms chosen by satirists were *terza rima;* rhyme royal; the fourteener; the decasyllabic couplet (qq.v.), with the regularity of the iambic pentameter line broken to imitate the Latin hexameter; iambic pentameter with alternate rhyme; and even, in the hands of George Gascoigne (*The Steel Glass,* 1576), blank verse (q.v.). Still, by the middle of the seventeenth century the decasyllabic or "heroic" couplet had begun to dominate other meters.

Bibliography

Raymond MacDonald Alden, *The Rise of Formal Satire in England Under Classical Influence* (1899); Samuel Marion Tucker, *Verse Satire in England Before the Renaissance* (1908); Hugh Walker, "Elizabethan & Jacobean

Verse Satire," *English Satire and Satirists* (1925), pp. 57–90; Mary Claire Randolph, "The Medical Concept in English Renaissance Satiric Theory," *SP,* 38 (1941), 125–57; Mary Claire Randolph, "The Structural Design of the Formal Verse Satire," *PQ,* 21 (1942), 368–84; Arnold Stein, "Donne and the Satiric Spirit," *ELH,* 11 (1944), 266–82; Harold F. Brooks, "The 'Imitation' in English Poetry, especially in the Formal Satire, before the Age of Pope," *RES,* 25 (1949), 124–40; J. A. K. Thomson, "Satire," *Classical Influences on English Poetry* (1951), 196–238; Hallett Smith, "Satire," *Elizabethan Poetry* (1952), pp. 194–256; William P. Holden, *Anti-Puritan Satire 1572–1642* (1954); John Peter, *Complaint and Satire in Early English Literature* (1956); James Sutherland, *English Satire* (1958); Alvin Kernan, *The Cankered Muse: Satire of the English Renaissance* (1959); Robert C. Elliot, *The Power of Satire: Magic, Ritual, and Art* (1960); Bernard Harris, "Men Like Satyrs," *Elizabethan Poetry,* gen. eds. John Russell Brown and Bernard Harris (1960), pp. 175–201; Anthony Caputi, *John Marston, Satirist* (1961); G. R. Owst, "The Preaching of Satire and Complaint," *Literature and Pulpit in Medieval England* (2nd rev. ed., 1961), pp. 210–470; Sam H. Henderson, "Neo-Stoic Influence on Elizabethan Formal Verse Satire," *Studies in English Renaissance Literature,* ed. Waldo F. McNeir (1962), pp. 56–86; K. W. Grandsen, ed., "Introduction," *Tudor Verse Satire* (1970), pp. 1–29; Annabel M. Patterson, " 'Savage Indignation': Elizabethan Satire," *Hermogenes and the Renaissance: Seven Ideas of Style* (1970), pp. 97–121; Doris C. Powers, *English Formal Satire: Elizabethan to Augustan* (1971); R. Selden, "Roughness in Satire from Horace to Dryden," *MLR,* 66 (1971), 264–72; Ejner J. Jensen, "The Wit of Renaissance Satire," *PQ,* 51 (1972), 394–409; Peter E. Medine, "Praise and Blame in Renaissance Verse Satire," *PCP,* 7 (1972), 49–53; R. B. Gill, "A Purchase of Glory: The Persona of Late Elizabethan Satire," *SP,* 72 (1975), 408–18; Raman Selden, "The Elizabethan Satyr-Satirist," *English Verse Satire, 1590–1765* (1978), pp. 45–72; Heather Dubrow, " 'No man is an island': Donne's Satires and Satiric Traditions," *SEL,* 19 (1979), 71–84.

Senecan style:

A prose style "Not long but Pythy . . . Such as the grave, acute wise *Seneca* sings . . . Well setled, full of nerves, in breife 'tis such / That in a little hath comprized much" (Thomas Randolph, *Poems,* 1638). The Senecan manner in prose reflected a movement away from the expansive, oratorical style associated with Cicero and took as its primary source of imitation (q.v.) the conversational style of Seneca's philosophic epistles.

The Senecan movement in England was led by Sir Francis Bacon in a late sixteenth-century reaction to the excesses of the Ciceronian manner (*see* Ciceronian style). The Senecan emphasis is upon brevity, the appearance of fluency, and the "weight" of ideas. The pithy and weighty nature of Seneca's prose is a recurring theme of his imitators: Seneca is "seriously succinct, and full of Laconisme," says his translator, Thomas Lodge (*To the Reader, Works of Seneca,* 1620). In contrast, the symmetrical embellishment and the careful use of repetitions in the Ciceronian style are denounced by Senecans as "long and distended . . . tedious to the eare, and difficult for their retaining." They are "*Cart-rope* [long-reined] *speeches,* that are longer then the memorie of man can fathome" (Owen Feltham, *Of Preaching,* in *Resolves,* 1628).

The brevity of the Senecan style is achieved primarily by the omission of ordinary transitional and connective devices, so that the individual members of a period seem to stand far apart. Members tend to be short, though the complete period may be quite long. Ben Jonson, himself a master of the Senecan style, suggests that a desired brevity in prose is to be attained by "avoiding . . . superfluous circuit of figures, and digressions: In the composition by omitting Conjunctions (Not onely; But also) (both the one, and the other) (Whereby it cometh to passe) and such like idle Particles, that have no great business in a serious Letter" (*Timber, or Discoveries,* 1641). A comparatively staccato, discontinuous style controls the tone of many of Bacon's earlier essays: "A Man that is young in yeeres, may bee old in houres; if he have lost no time. But that happeneth rarely. Generally youth is like the first cogitations, not so wise as the second: For there is a youth in thoughts, aswell as in ages" (*Of Young Men and Age,* in *Essays,* 1612).

The lack of connectives between members of a period gives to each individual member an increased weight, a weight that pulls it in the direction of the "sentence" or *sententia* (q.v.). Anti-Ciceronians praised Seneca for delivering his mind "significantly," for the "native gravitie of his countenance" (*Congratulatory Letter to Thomas Lodge, The Works of Seneca,* trans. Lodge, 1620). Senecan "gravity" is partly the seriousness of the *sententia* and the profusion of moral maxims in his discourse, while the disconnectiveness of the Senecan style brings the impact of brief statements into the foreground of a reader's attention. Thus words will "leade the *minde* to something beside the naked *terme*" (Feltham).

The weight associated with the Senecan performance, an abundance of maxims, is a density of thought resulting from an emphasis upon matter rather than manner. The debate over prose style was centered on the attention to be placed on *res* or on *verba;* on the "things" in the head of the writer or on the words with which such "things" were clothed. Senecans were convinced that Ciceronian writers paid too much attention to style at the expense of thought. Bacon voices this argument when he says that "men hunt more after words than matter" (*Advancement of Learning,* 1605). Hence an emphasis upon brevity and an order that appears emergent and spontaneous rather than patterned and premeditated.

At the extreme range of the aim for brevity, some writers turned to the Latin historian Tacitus as a model for radical truncatedness and a desired, thought-provoking obscurity (*see* Strong lines). Tacitus is praised as very terse, ingenious, and clipped by his admirers. "For Tacitus I may say without partiality, that hee hath writen the most matter with best conceyt in fewest Wordes of anie," says Anthony Bacon in the preface to Sir Henry Savile's translation, *Four Books of the Histories of Tacitus* (1591). "But he is harde . . . the second reading over will please thee more then the first, and the third then the second."

Still other writers, however, emphasized fluency rather than brevity as essentially Senecan and subscribe to a meditative, "loose" manner, opening consistently forward, generating modifications of a core idea as they move along. Frequently they begin with an idea in one form that is closely followed by a series of clauses and phrases that expand, modify, and restate the original idea. While at first glance the loose style often seems similar to the Ciceronian, it shows a more organic order of thought; and its symmetry of structure is more evasive. The style of the philosophic essay is described by Seneca himself as conversational and apparently spontaneous: "I prefer that my letters should be just what my conversation would be if you and I were sitting in one another's company or taking walks together,— spontaneous and easy; for my letters have nothing strained or artificial about them. . . . One should not . . . bestow very much attention upon mere words" (*Epistulae morales,* LXXV, trans. Richard Gummere).

English writers of the first half of the seventeenth century extended the Senecan model to create a prose that if anything exaggerates their paradigm. With the extreme freedom of its internal elements, this Senecan performance lends itself especially to "the expression of quick shifts of feeling, of afterthoughts, self-corrections, unexpected interpolations or dislocations of attention" (Barish). So Robert Burton announces in the preface to the 1651 edition of *The Anatomy of Melancholy* that he has "an extemporean stile . . . writ with as small deliberation as I doe ordinarily speak." His style is "free," not "reined" in the Ciceronian manner; one idea is related to another without apparent premeditation, in contrast to the Ciceronian style, which often suggests a predefined pattern. The unlabored fluency of the loose Senecan mode appears in this quotation from Sir Thomas Browne's *Hydrotaphia* (1658): "But the iniquity of oblivion blindely scattereth her Poppy, and deals with the memory of Men without distinction to merit of perpetuity. Who can but pity the Founder of the Pyramids? Herostratus lives that burnt the Temple of Diana, he is almost lost that built it; Time hath spared the Epitaph of Adrians Horse, confounded that of himself."

Traditional models for various tones of oratory supported stylistic decisions by Senecan writers. Cicero himself distinguished three tones of oratory: the grandiloquent, the smooth, and the plain. This latter tone he terms "Attic." (The Attic emphasis is close to the style of the Senecan epistles.) The Attic orator, says Cicero, is "restrained and plain, following ordinary usage." His style is released from "the bonds of Rhythm," "loose but not rambling; so that it seems to move freely." The Attic orator will avoid "cementing his words together too smoothly," but "this freedom from periodic structure . . . will make it necessary for him to look at other requisites." The short and concise clauses must not be handled carelessly ("There is such a thing even as careful negligence"). The Attic orator will employ "an abundance of apposite maxims [*sententiae*] dug out from every conceivable hiding place." He will be sparing in figures of repetition and rhyme, avoiding elaborate symmetry, but metaphor is appropriate for the Attic speaker. "He will use both humor and wit which are the outstanding mark of the Attic style" (*Orator,* XXIII–XXVI, trans. H. M. Hubbell).

Echoing the Ciceronian distinctions, English rhetoricians also assumed that particular figures would contribute to the tone of discourse, and they defined strategies associated with contrasting styles (*see* Elocutio). Thus Henry Peacham's *The Garden of Eloquence* (1593) links the "figures of repetition" that are the staple of the grandiloquent style "rather to harmonie and pleasant proportion, then to gravitie and dignitie." Figures that condense belong to the most serious discourse. *Membrum,* a figure that in "few words endeth the construction, but not the sence" is "meet for grave causes." Similarly, the rhythmic bias of sixteenth-century Ciceronian prose is associated with a "pleasant" rather than "grave" style. The figure *compar,* which is a figure to "maketh the members of an oration to be almost of a just number of sillables" is a "harmonicall" figure, "most agreeable for pleasant matters than grave causes."

Senecan prose in English makes its most obvious appearance in the essay or meditation, the character (q.v.), and the satiric prose comedies (q.v.) of Ben Jonson, just as in classical times the plain style (*genus humile*) was associated with the epistle, the epigram, and satire (qq.v.). But although its appearance is closely linked to a studied development of certain genres, it is also significant apart from its identification with any particular literary kind. Many writers adopted the Senecan manner without restricting themselves to its Latin generic models.

Bibliography

Morris W. Croll, *Style, Rhetoric, and Rhythm: Essays by Morris W. Croll,* eds. J. Max Patrick, et al. (these essays were originally published between 1914 and 1929; they appear together in the above volume published in 1966); Richard F. Jones, "Science and English Prose Style in the Third Quarter of the Seventeenth Century," *PMLA,* 45 (1930), 977–1009; Richard F. Jones, "Science and Language in England of the Mid-Seventeenth Century," *JEGP,* 31 (1932), 315–31; W. Fraser Mitchell, *English Pulpit Oratory from Andrewes to Tillotson: A Study of Its Literary Aspects* (1932); Philip A. Smith, "Bishop Hall, 'Our English Seneca,' " *PMLA,* 63 (1948), 1191–204; George Williamson, *The Senecan Amble: A Study in Prose Form from Bacon to Collier* (1951); Jonas A. Barish, *Ben Jonson and the Language of Prose Comedy* (1960); F. P. Wilson, *Seventeenth Century Prose: Five Lectures* (1960); Wesley Trimpi, *Ben Jonson's Poems: A Study of the Plain Style* (1962); Robert Beum, "The Scientific Affinities of English Baroque Prose," *EM,* 14 (1963), 59–80; K. G. Hamilton, *The Two Harmonies: Poetry and Prose in the Seventeenth Century* (1963); Joan Webber, *Contrary Music: The Prose Style of John Donne* (1963); Ian A. Gordon, "The Seventeenth Century," *The Movement of English Prose* (1966), pp. 105–19; Robert Adolph, *The Rise of Modern Prose Style* (1968); Brian Vickers, *Francis Bacon and Renaissance Prose* (1968); Joan Webber, *The Eloquent "I": Style and Self in Seventeenth-Century Prose* (1968); Stanley E. Fish, ed., *Seventeenth-Century Prose: Modern Essays in Criticism* (1971); Stanley E. Fish, *Self-Consuming Artifacts: The Experience of Seventeenth-Century Literature* (1972); Joseph Anthony Mazzeo, "Seventeenth-Century English Prose Style: The Quest for a Natural Style," *Mosaic,* 6 (1973), 107–44; James Stephens, "The Philosopher, His Audience, and Popular Rhetoric," *Francis Bacon and the Style of Science* (1975), pp. 1–54.

Sententia:

"Gnome, otherwise called Sententia, is a saying pertaining to the manners and common practices of men, which declareth by an apt brevitie, what in this our life ought to be done, or left undone," says Henry Peacham (*The Garden of Eloquence,* 1593); a succinct and striking moralized statement, maxim, or gnome. The *sententia,* often called the *sentence* by contemporaries, was a guide to life, "an Oracion, in fewe woordes, shewyng a godlie precept of life, exhorting or diswadyng . . . whiche is asmoche to saie, a rule or square, to direct any thyng by, for by them, the life of manne is framed to all singularitie" (Richard Rainold, *The Foundation of Rhetoric,* 1563). *Sententiae* were cherished elements of Renaissance discourse of every kind: "Precious pearles," "beautifull flowers," "glorious lightes" (Peacham).

Some rhetoricians distinguished between the *sententia* and other detachable brief rules of life. Sometimes the proverb, for example, was separated from the sentence as a homely, popular, and concrete metaphor or simile ("a rolling stone gathers no moss"), while the sentence was more philosophical and abstract ("he is nowhere who is everywhere"); but in practice *maxim, gnome, adage, aphorism, precept, proverb,* and *sententia* all became interchangeable terms to identify compressed, memorable statements of the truths of human experience.

Technically *sententiae* were classed as schemes among the figures of speech (*see* Elocutio); they were carefully divided and categorized by rhetoricians as universal or specific, direct or figurative, single or double. Their use in the Renaissance was sanctioned by their traditional place in Greek and Roman rhetoric. Orators were encouraged to scatter them throughout all parts of a speech, and this oratorical habit of mind was transferred to written matter of all kinds. With the introduction of printing, the taste for *sententiae* was, if anything, magnified. Erasmus and other humanist educators taught that one should read for content; men dutifully read and noted, so that the notebook and the common-place book took on critical importance. The task of noting down easily applicable precepts was made easier for readers by signs indicating particularly choice examples of *sententiae.* Sometimes printers used a hand and pointing finger, the mark made by many readers themselves, or put inverted commas in the margin of a book to point out a sentiment particularly worthy of observation. In this sense, the *sententia* is a common-place (q.v.). Thus the manuscript of Thomas Watson's Latin tragedy *Absalom* indicates its *sententiae* with a small "c" for common-place (see *A Humanist's "Trew Imitation": Thomas Watson's Absalom,* ed. John Hazel Smith, 1964).

Rhetoric books of all kinds trained speakers to move easily and fluently from the particular case to its moral generalization or common application. Erasmus, for example, shows readers how to take the case of the death of Socrates and draw from it such common-places as: truth creates hatred; outstanding virtue wins envy; death is even desirable to those who are conscious of living a virtuous life; the sort of life a man has lived is most clearly apparent at death (*De utraque verborum ac rerum copia,* 1512, trans. Donald B. King and H. David Rix).

The "heaping up" of *sententiae* is associated with both "weight" and "vehemence" (persuasive force) in rhetoric books (*see* Copia). Peacham says the *sententia* makes the oration "not onely beautifull and comely, but also grave, puissant, and full of majesty. The school text *Rhetorica ad Herennium* says that the grand style must have "impressive thoughts" such as are used in amplification (IV, viii, trans. Harry Caplan). "We encrease our cause by heapyng of wordes and sentences together, couchyng many reasons into one corner which before were scaterde abrode, to the end that our taske might appere more vehement," says Thomas Wilson. "In praisyng, or dispraisyng, we must bee well stored ever with suche good sentences, as are often used in this our life." Closely related to the power to vary an idea while reiterating it, the heaping of sentences gives a speaker dignity and his audience valued insights into the ways of the world.

Moral generalizations were widely used by writers in fictions of all kinds and validated the poets' claim that the function of poetry is essentially ethical (*see* Apology). The poet is often identified as quite simply one who combines fictions with sentence. In this vein, Sir Philip Sidney, contrasting the poet with the historian, says the historian is limited, "wanting the precept," because he is so tied to the particular truth of things "that his example draweth no necessary consequence, and therefore a less fruitful doctrine" (*An Apology for Poetry,* 1595). The force of the sentence had particular associations with tragedy (q.v.) and the heroic poem (q.v.), genres which required the high style (*see* Decorum). Classical models like the tragedies of Seneca and the *Aeneid* of Virgil were strikingly sententious. Nicholas Udall's translation of Erasmus's *Apophthegmes* (1542) locates the assignment of *sententia* to the high-born, the natural subjects of the "high" genres, in the social habits of such subjects: "And all these universall sorte of wrytynges as doo comprehend proverbs, sage sentencies, and notable saiynges or actes, is moste fitte for Princes & noble menne, who for the urgente causes and busie maters of the commenweale have not leasure to spend any greate parte of their life in studie or in readyng of books." An influential Italian critic Julius Caesar Scaliger maintains that the grand style is a kind of poetry that comprises important persons and excellent actions, from which spring choice aphorisms. The actions of the great give rise to valuable generalizations. The dramatists' use of *sententiae* in tragedy causes one writer to compare unfavorably the power of the preacher with the power of the theater: "The waighty *lines* men finde upon the *Stage,* I am perswaded, have beene the *lures,* to draw away the *Pulpits followers*" (Owen Feltham, *Of Preaching,* in *Resolves,* 1628).

English writers were reinforced in their views of the value of *sententiae* in the high style by the response of Italian critics to Aristotle's *Poetics.* Many Italian critics translated Aristotle's requirement that a tragedy must have "thought" as one of its elements to the requirement that it must have *sententiae* (the Latin *sententia* is literally "thought"). They often seemed to seek nothing more than an occasional philosophical generalization from dramatic characters as an expression of Aristotle's requirement for "thought" in tragedy. The genres were valued according to the extent that they contained in the form of *sententiae* admonitions to virtue, guides to good living, and scornful attacks upon vice. A critic praises Torquato Tasso's *Gerusalemme liberata* on the basis that no other Latin or Italian poem is "richer in precepts, more copious in reasons, more pregnant with beautiful sententiae . . . gayer in most beautiful sayings, graver in mature arguments" (Nicolò degli Oddi, *Dialogo in difesa di Camillo Pellegrini,* 1587, trans. Bernard Weinberg).

Despite the emphasis in Ciceronian rhetoric books upon the value of *sententiae,* prose theorists of the early seventeenth century found the Ciceronian style (q.v.) itself deficient in sentence. Their Senecan models were weighty with *sententiae,* Seneca's *Epistulae morales,* like his tragedies, was traditionally associated with a profusion of maxims. More sentence in prose became part of an emphasis upon matter (thought) over manner (style) (*see* Senecan style).

Sententiae are central to late medieval epistemology. Sir Francis Bacon, for example, treats the sentence of unusual intellectual authority, the aphorism, as a special mode of communication (*The Advancement of Learning,* 1605). Because aphorisms were easily memorized, medical works in particular relied heavily on them to train beginning doctors: "Old men endure fasting most easily, then men of middle age, youths very badly, and worst of all, children." In fact, a 1604 dictionary (Robert Cawdrey, *A Table Alphabetical*) defines an aphorism very simply as a "generall rule in physick." The *Aphorisms* of Hippocrates is probably the most famous medical work ever written. In this context, aphorisms are suggestive of a presystematic science detailing the scattered conclusions of observation and diagnosis. Cawdrey's definition is incomplete, however, for aphorisms, as Bacon knew well, were also maxims used for the study of law. The "rules," ancient and medieval, of law were typically phrased for students as easily memorized aphorisms. Similarly, the maxims of politics in the extensive literature of "Advice to Princes" took the form of aphorisms. Machiavelli's *The Prince* (1532) is laced with concise empirical "rules" for governors and the governed: "He that gives the means to another to become powerful, ruins himself."

Bibliography

Bromley Smith, "Some Rhetorical Figures Historically Considered," *QJS,* 20 (1934), 16–29; Katherine Lever, "Proverbs and *Sententiae* in the Plays of Shakespere," *SAB,* 13 (July and October, 1938), 173–83, 224–39; Bartlett Jere Whiting, *Proverbs in the Earlier English Drama* (1938); Rosemond Tuve, "The Criterion of Significancy," *Elizabethan and Metaphysical Imagery* (1947), pp. 145–79; Morris P. Tilley, ed., *A Dictionary of the Proverbs in England in the Sixteenth and Seventeenth Centuries* (1950); G. K. Hunter, "The Marking of *Sententiae* in Elizabethan Printed Plays, Poems, and Romances," *Library,* 6 (1951), 171–88; Robert William Dent, *John Webster's Borrowing* (1960); Charles G. Smith, *Shakespeare's Proverb Lore: His Use of the "Sententiae" of Leonard Culman and Publilius Syrus* (1963); Margaret Mann Phillips, *The "Adages" of Erasmus: A Study with Translations* (1964); Walter J. Ong, "Oral Residue in Tudor Prose Style," *PMLA,* 80 (1965), 145–54; Brian Vickers, "The Aphorism," *Francis Bacon & Renaissance Prose* (1968), pp. 60–95; F. P. Wilson, "The Proverbial Wisdom of Shakespeare," *Shakespearian and Other Studies,* ed. Helen Gardner (1969), pp. 143–75; Charles G. Smith, *Spenser's Proverb Lore: With Special Reference to His Use of the "Sententiae" of Leonard Culman and Publilius Syrus* (1970); Lisa Jardine, *Francis Bacon: Discovery and the Art of Discourse* (1974), pp. 169–250; Elizabeth McCutcheon, *Sir Nicholas Bacon's Great House Sententiae,* English Literary Renaissance Supplements, No. 3 (1977).

Sixain:

A stanza or "staffe . . . of six verses" (George Puttenham, *The Art of English Poesy,* 1589). Among English rhymed stanza patterns, the sixain, Puttenham continues, is "not only most usual, but also very pleasant to th'eare." Contrasting the four-, five-, and six-line stanza forms, he says that the "staffe of five verses is not much used, because he that can not comprehend his periode in foure verses will drive it into six then leave it in five, for that the even number is more agreable to the eare than the odde is" and that the sixain "serveth for a greater complement [of the sense] then the inferiour staves, which maketh him more commonly to be used." Earlier George Gascoigne (*Certain Notes of Instruction,* 1575), in a brief discussion of a few established English stanza forms, had associated the sixain with "shorte Fantazies" (ingenious inventions). English poets of the late sixteenth and early seventeenth centuries selected the sixain for both narrative and lyric (q.v.) poetry, much of which treats the topic of love.

In his comments on the sixain Puttenham notes that in English verse the "staffe of six hath ten proportions [arrangements], whereof some be usuall, some not usuall, and not so sweet as another." Of these possible rhyme patterns, one is known today as the Venus and Adonis stanza. This sixain in iambic pentameter rhymes *ababcc;* it is a stanza composed of the traditional quatrain *abab* capped with a concluding couplet. It is called the Venus and Adonis stanza because Shakespeare chose it for his Ovidian narrative poem *Venus and Adonis* (1593).

Gascoigne nominates the Venus and Adonis stanza, although naturally not by that name, as one that serves best for "light matters," or "matters of love." With similar assumptions late Elizabethan and early seventeenth-century poets chose the Venus and Adonis stanza for two related kinds of narrative poetry—the Ovidian epyllion (*see* Heroic poem), clearly amatory, and the complaint (q.v.), which is often a story of unhappy love. The first of the Ovidian epyllia, Thomas Lodge's *Scylla's Metamorphosis* (1589), was written in the Venus and Adonis stanza. After Lodge, Shakespeare used it for his story of the unfortunate passion of Venus for the disdainful youth Adonis. At least five other erotic epyllia were written in this particular sixain. As a stanza form for complaint poems, the Venus and Adonis stanza was rivaled in popularity only by rhyme royal (q.v.).

"Light matter" is not the subject for all poems in the Venus and Adonis stanza, however; often religious poets exploited the amatory associations of this sixain for a parody (q.v.) of profane poetry. Robert Southwell, who encouraged the transfer of techniques associated with secular love poems to lyrics of sacred love, argues, "Passions I allow, and *loves* I *approve, only I would wishe that men would alter their *object* and better their intent" (preface, *Mary Magdelene's Funeral Tears,* 1591). He regrets that "the finest wittes loose *themselves* in the vainest follies"; and he hopes that his own attempt to parody the devices of secular love poetry on a sacred subject "may wooe some skilfuller pennes from *unworthy* labours." The best known poems by Southwell in the Venus and Adonis stanza are those in his volume *Saint Peter's Complaint* (1595). In the preface to this work Southwell again laments that the "devill" has possessed "most Poets with his idle fansies," and he hopes through his own verse to show secular love poets the errors of their ways by weaving "a new webbe in their owne loome," that loom being the Venus and Adonis sixain.

The sixain also figures prominently in another poetic form popular during the late sixteenth and early seventeenth centuries. It is the sestina, a poem composed of seven stanzas, the first six of which contain six lines each, usually in unrhymed pentameter, with an ingenious arrangement of terminal words. The seventh stanza has three lines. In *A Discourse of English Poetry* (1586) William Webbe calls the sestina one of the "sundry kindes of rare devises and pretty inventions which come from the fine poeticall vaine of manie in strange and unacustomed manner." For an example Webbe asks his readers to "looke uppon the rufull song of *Colin* sung by *Cuddie* in the *Sheepheardes Calender* [August eclogue], where you shall see a singular rare devise of a dittie framed upon these six wordes *Woe, sounde, cryes, part, sleep, augment,* which are most prettilie turned and wounde uppe mutually together, expressing wonderfully the dolefulnesse of the song."

As Webbe indicates, the sestina requires the repetition throughout each stanza of the six words that conclude the six lines of the first stanza. In the first six stanzas the six words appear in a continually changing but mathematically regular order. Representing the terminal words of the first stanza by numbers up to six, the arrangement could run as follows:

First stanza . . . . 1 – 2 – 3 – 4 – 5 – 6
Second stanza . . . . 6 – 1 – 5 – 2 – 4 – 3
Third stanza . . . . 3 – 6 – 4 – 1 – 2 – 5

Fourth stanza	5 – 3 – 2 – 6 – 1 – 4
Fifth stanza	4 – 5 – 1 – 3 – 6 – 2
Sixth stanza	2 – 4 – 6 – 5 – 3 – 1

In a three-line concluding stanza, all six words occur. Words 1 – 3 – 5 are placed at either the beginning or the middle of the three lines, and words 2 – 4 – 6 at the ends of those lines. Obviously this repetition places enormous emphasis on just six words at already emphatic positions in a stanza. The danger of the sestina, George Puttenham points out, is that "by chusing six words out of which all the whole dittie is made," the poet places upon himself a restraint which "to make the dittie sensible will try the makers cunning" (*The Art of English Poesy,* 1589).

Bibliography

Alastair Fowler, "Sestina Structure in *Ye Goatherd Gods*," *Conceitful Thought: The Interpretation of Renaissance Poems* (1975), pp. 38–58.

Song:

"Sphear-born, harmonious sisters, Voice and Vers" (John Milton, *At a Solemn Music,* 1645). Milton's phrase expresses the intimate relationship between poetry and music during the late sixteenth and early seventeenth centuries. So akin were they that the word *song* was often used to refer either to words set to music or to a literary composition (*see* Lyric).

George Puttenham also links poem and song as "harmonious sisters." Commenting on the "proportion" or harmony that derives primarily from the formal properties of an artifact and satisfies a beholder's senses and intellect, he says: "Poeticall proportion holdeth of the Musicall, because . . . Poesie is a skill to speake & write harmonically, and verses or rime be a kind of Musicall utterance, by reason of a certaine congruitie in sounds pleasing the eare" (*The Art of English Poesy,* 1589). As makers of harmonious artifacts, both the poet and composer sought to imitate the divinely created harmony that they believed existed in a perfectly ordered universe.

Renaissance critics and poets alike were aware that historically the roots of poetry lie in an oral tradition, and that many of their inheritances in literary genres were songs before they were written poems. Critical theory typically made singers like Orpheus and David the archetype of the poet. "Even," as Sir Philip Sidney says, "among the most barbarous and simple Indians where no writing is, yet have they their Poets, who make and sing songs" (*An Apology for Poetry,* 1595). With *song* as a synonym for *poem,* Edmund Spenser calls his *Epithalamion* (1595) a "Song made in lieu of many ornaments" to honor his bride; John Donne's love poems carry the 1635 subtitle *Songs and Sonets;* and John Milton to begin his heroic poem (q.v.), *Paradise Lost* (1667), invokes his "heavenly Muse" to aid him in the composing of his "advent'rous Song." For the stately marriage poem, the witty amorous poem, or the grave epic, the word *song* could equally apply.

Many lyric poems that found their way into print, principally in the poetical miscellanies, were originally written to be sung. Conversely, printed or manuscript poems were given musical settings by alert composers. Both poets and publishers of miscellanies recognized that their lyrics were fair game for composers. Sidney, for example, assumes that a poetic text will almost inevitably be set to music. He says that a poet "commeth to you with words sent in delightfull proportion, either accompanied with, or prepared for, the well inchaunting skill of Musicke." In prefatory comments to *The Paradise of Dainty Devices* (1576), one of the most frequently reprinted poetical miscellanies, a publisher, Henry Disle, even recommends his "ditties both pithy and pleasant" to readers because the poems "will yielde a farre greater delight, being as they are so aptly made to set to any song in .5 partes, or song to instrument." He knows that the printed poems will be sung as madrigals or airs. This kinship between music and poetry, between "Voice and Vers," continued through the middle years of the seventeenth century. It is not amiss to say that when music and poetry go their separate ways, the English Renaissance is over.

Although it was inferior to the divinely ordained music of the spheres and to angelic choirs of Heaven, all man-made music held a special place of honor in Renaissance thought. The *quadrivium,* the higher division of the seven liberal arts, included music along with arithmetic, geometry, and astronomy as an essential part of theoretical knowledge. In its harmony and rhythm music reflected God's creation and imitated the divine order of the cosmos; that order in turn was reflected in the desired order of the political state and in the soul and body of the individual human being. Not only delightful to the ear, music was both instructive and renewing to the listener. The "solemn and divine harmonies of music," writes Milton, "have a great power over dispositions and manners to smooth and make them gentle from rustic harshness and distempered passions" (*Of Education,* 1644).

English Renaissance music includes both instrumental and vocal compositions, but the greater interest was in vocal music. John Dowland reflects this preference when he claims: "That harmony ... which is skilfullie exprest by Instruments, albeit, by reason of the variety of number & proportion of it selfe, it easilie stirs up the minds of hearers to admiration & delight, yet for higher authoritie and power, hath been ever worthily attributed to that kind of Musicke which to the sweetness of instrument applied the live voice of man, expressing some worthy sentence or Excellent Poeme" (*The First Book of Songs or Airs,* 1597).

Two of the most popular kinds of Renaissance songs were the homophonic air and the polyphonic madrigal. An air is a song for a single voice, usually with instrumental accompaniment. Thomas Campion, one of the best-known composers of such pieces, defines an air as a song "for one voyce with the Lute, or Violl" (*Two Books of Airs,* c. 1613). The words of many airs or "lute-songs" were drawn from lyric poems that in their simple, clear expression of an emotion lent themselves to musical setting.

Music and poetry were on an equal footing, "lovingly coupled together" as one composer puts it; and because the verbal sense of the poem could be easily heard, the air was most likely to be sung to an audience. The homophonic nature of the air allowed the composer to use a single musical setting for a poem of several stanzas, and generally the stanza form of the poem was repeated to go along with the repetition of the melody.

A madrigal is a short poem set for several voices, generally without the accompaniment of a musical instrument. The number of parts for voices in English madrigals ranged from two to eight, but most often was five. Hence William Byrd's first published collection of madrigals (1588) carries a lengthy title that is worded *Psalmes, Sonets, & songs of Sadnes and pietie, made into Musicke of five parts.* His madrigals, Byrd says, are appropriate "for the recreation of all such as delight in Musicke." An Italian form, the madrigal was naturalized in England during the last decades of the sixteenth century, and some forty volumes of madrigals were published in London between 1590 and 1620. Some of the texts of the madrigals were translations from Italian, but more often English lyric poems provided words for musical composers.

In contrast to the usual part song where only one voice carries the melody, a madrigal makes all parts of equal interest and importance, and often with the same melodic material. Voices enter the singing successively, not simultaneously, treating the text of the song in phrases, each repeated several times and frequently overlapping in the different voices. Because of this repetition of the words of the song, madrigal composers usually selected a poem of single-stanza length to set to music.

Whether they wrote their own words or set another's poem to music, composers of songs tended to treat the words of their text kindly, attempting to make their music illustrate the mood and meaning of the words. Thomas Morley expresses the commonly held assumption among composers that the function of music is to reveal the meaning of the words when he writes: "dispose your musicke according to the nature of the words which you are therein to expresse, as whatsoever matter it be which you have in hand, such a kind of musicke must you frame to it" (*A Plain and Easy Introduction to Practical Music,* 1597).

Musical compositions, like purely literary works, were governed by the concepts of decorum (q.v.) and hierarchy. Airs, for example, were generally considered to be a part of what was called "light" music, the word *light* referring not only to the less complicated nature of homophonic music, but also to the predominately secular subject matter of the poetry. Many composers regarded the motet, a polyphonic choral composition for liturgical purposes, as the height of achievement for a musician. The dedication of *A Book of Airs* (1601), a collection by Thomas Campion and Philip Rosseter, states "as in Poesie we give the preheminence to the

Heroicall Poeme, so in Musicke we yeeld the chiefe place to the grave, and well invented Motet." Within the musical hierarchy the "grave" motet and the "light" air were what the serious heroic poem (q.v.) and the slighter lyric were within contemporary literary traditions. Airs, Campion further tells us, are the epigrams (q.v.) of music: "What Epigrams are in Poetrie, the same are Ayres in musicke." Airs are "in their chief perfection when they are short and well seasoned."

Bibliography

Manfred Bukofzer, *Music in the Baroque Era: from Monteverdi to Bach* (1947); Frances A. Yates, "The Measured Poetry and Music," *The French Academies of the Sixteenth Century* (1947), pp. 36–76; Manfred Bukofzer, *Studies in Medieval & Renaissance Music* (1950); Ernest Walker, chs. 2–5, *A History of Music in England* (3rd ed., rev. by J. A. Westrup, 1952), pp. 18–171; Gustave Reese, *Music in the Renaissance* (1954); Nan Cooke Carpenter, *Music in the Medieval and Renaissance Universities* (1958); John Hollander, *The Untuning of the Sky: Ideas of Music in English Poetry 1500–1700* (1961); Morrison Comegys Boyd, *Elizabethan Music and Musical Criticism* (2nd ed., 1962); Gretchen Finney, *Musical Backgrounds for English Literature, 1580–1650* (1962); Joseph Kerman, *The Elizabethan Madrigal* (1962); John Buxton, "Music," *Elizabethan Taste* (1963), pp. 171–220; Wilfred Mellers, *Harmonious Meeting: A Study of the Relationship between English Music, Poetry and Theatre, c. 1600–1900* (1965); E. H. Fellowes, *English Madrigal Verse 1588–1632* (3rd ed., rev. by Frederick W. Sternfeld and David Greer, 1967); Gerald Abraham, ed., *The Age of Humanism 1540–1630* (1968); John H. Long, ed., *Music in English Renaissance Drama* (1968); Edward Doughtie, ed., "Introduction," *Lyrics from English Airs 1596–1622* (1970), pp. 1–41; Bruce Pattison, *Music and Poetry of the English Renaissance* (2nd ed., 1970); Esther Garke, *The Use of Songs in Elizabethan Prose Fiction* (1972); Paula Johnson, *Form and Transformation in Music and Poetry of the English Renaissance* (1972); Jerome Roche, *The Madrigal* (1972); Michael Smith, "English Translations and Imitations of Italian Madrigal Verse," *JES*, 4 (1974), 164–77; Dorothy Koenigsberger, "Harmony and Naturalism in Music," *Renaissance Man and Creative Thinking: A History of Concepts of Harmony 1400–1700* (1979), pp. 173–212; John Stevens, *Music and Poetry in the Early Tudor Court* (2nd ed., 1979).

Sonnet:

"Some thinke that all Poemes (being short) may be called Sonets, as in deede it is a diminutive worde derived of *Sonare,* but yet I can beste allowe to call those Sonets which are of fouretene lynes, every line conteyning tenne syllables" (George Gascoigne, *Certain Notes of Instruction,* 1575). Gascoigne's comment indicates that English writers of the late sixteenth and early seventeenth centuries used the word *sonnet* not only to refer to any short lyric (q.v.) or "little song" but also to designate a lyric poem of fourteen iambic pentameter lines using one of several arbitrary and conventional rhyme patterns. As a fourteen-line verse form, the sonnet was also sometimes called a "quatorzain." Michael Drayton, for example, entitles his sonnet sequence *Idea's Mirror, Amours in Quatorzains* (1594). No lyric verse form is more characteristic of the late Elizabethan period than the fourteen-line sonnet, many of which appeared in the sonnet sequences (*see* Sonnets in Sequence) that abounded between 1591 and 1600.

English writers thought of the sonnet in the strict formal sense as an appropriate form for concentrated lyric expression (*see* Epigram). Samuel Daniel, for example, calls the sonnet "an Orbe of order and forme" (*A Defense of Rhyme,* 1603). "Being but onely imployed for a present passion," the sonnet, Daniel says, is "neither too long for the shortest project, nor too short for the longest." Thus, "much," is "excellently ordred in a small-roome, or little, gallantly disposed and made to fill up a space of like capacitie, in such sort, that the one would not appeare so beautifull in a larger circuite, nor the other do well in a lesse." Similarly, the speaker in John Donne's *The Canonization* (1633) claims that even if his love and that of his beloved prove "no peece of Chronicle," it will find fit home in "sonnets pretty roomes." Such a "well wrought urne," he declares, may contain the "greatest ashes, as halfe-acre tombes"; and then he boldly announces that "by these hymnes, all shall approve / Us *Canoniz'd* for Love."

As Donne's speaker suggests, English writers often associated the sonnet with the motif of secular love and the rhetorical function of praise (*see* Epideictic rhetoric). George Puttenham, for example, calls love "the first founder of all good affections," and cites the sonnet as one of those lyric forms best suited for the praise of "amorous affections and allurements" (*The Art of English Poesy*, 1589). Still because "blame," the converse of praise, was considered a function of lyric poetry, some poets used the sonnet to scorn, not laud, their subject.

The fashion for sonnet writing was a European phenomenon, given particular force by the work of the Italian poet Francis Petrarch (1304–74), whose sonnet sequence entitled *Canzoniere* or *Rime* provided the principal model for imitation (q.v.) by later poets. Only one of many English writers lauding Petrarch, Gabriel Harvey writes, "All posterity honour Petrarck, that was the harmony of heaven; the lyfe of Poetry; the grace of Arte; a precious tablet of rare conceits [q.v.], & a curious frame of exquisite workemanship; nothing but neate Witt, and refined Eloquence" (*Pierce's Supererogation*, 1593). Moreover, he adds, "Petrarckes Invention, is pure Love it selfe; and Petrarckes Elocution, pure Bewty it selfe: His *Laura* was the Daphne of Apollo, not the Thisbe of Pyramus: a delitious Sappho, not a lascivious Lais; a saving Hester, not a destroying Helena; a nimph of Diana, not a Curtisan of Venus." Harvey's claim that "All the noblest Italian, French, and Spanish Poets, have in their severall Veines Petrarchised" is not exaggeration; and he praises a contemporary as "an Inglishe Petrarck," who, like his model, "gratiously confined Love within the limits of Honour; Witt within the boundes of Discretion; Eloquence within the Termes of Civility."

Petrarch's influence on courtly lyric poetry can hardly be overstated. His major themes—the psychological and spiritual conflicts of love as well as its ennobling power—were repeated by later poets who made them their own in further analyses of human love. Conventionally the subject of such sonnets is a refined love for a distant lady, a lady considerably exalted by the neo-Platonism of Italian academies. Poets catalogue the beauties of the lady and the symptoms of the lovesickness of a speaker who laments an unrequited love, yet who is unable to stop loving. The lady's physical attributes are but outward manifestations of an inner virtue; and in praising her physical beauty the poet-lover is led to a praise of the lady's inward grace. Hence the ennobling effects of love. Even the pains suffered by the lover are often an oblique praise of the lady since somehow these agonies are pleasurable; and the paradox of pleasurable pain is a common-place (q.v.) in many of the sonnets.

Equally important is the fact that Petrarch's sonnets provided a model of excellence in style that was a source of inspiration and imitation (q.v.) long after his death. Petrarch's use of the vernacular (*see* Vulgar language) encouraged Renaissance poets of many nationalities to write in their native language; and his use of the sonnet to record his idealized love for Laura elevated that poetic form to an almost unrivaled dominance in later short lyric poetry. Speaking of two of the earliest Tudor poets to come under the influence of Italian poets like Petrarch, George Puttenham writes that in the "latter end" of the reign of Henry VIII (died 1547) there sprang up "a new company of courtly makers, of whom Sir *Thomas Wyat* th'elder and *Henry* Earle of Surrey were the two chieftaines, who having travailed into Italie, and there tasted the sweete and stately measures and stile of the Italian Poesie, as novices newly crept out of the schooles of *Dante, Arioste,* and *Petrarch,* they greatly polished our rude & homely maner of vulgar poesie from that it had bene before, and for that cause may justly be sayd the first reformers of our English meetre and stile." Figures of paradox and elaborate similitudes are special hallmarks of that Petrarchan style. The tone of such love sonnets, according to contemporary poets and critics, is that of "honey sweetness." Francis Meres, for example, praises Shakespeare's "mellifluous and honey-tongued" manner in his "sugar'd sonnets" (*Palladis Tamia,* 1598).

At the height of its vogue, the Petrarchan sonnet became vulnerable to parody (q.v.). Some poets turned away from a "honey-tongued" tone, elaborate Petrarchan conceits, and an idealization of the beloved. Their love poems not only mocked the imagery of the traditional Petrarchan vocabulary but also deflated the attributes of the lady and the ennobling effects of love. Occasionally this attitude, obviously more a dispraise than a praise of love, appeared in individual sonnets within a sequence that itself remained predominantly Petrarchan. At other times, an entire sonnet sequence, such as the "gulling sonnets" by Sir John Davies, might satirize the typical language, attitudes, and tone of the many Petrarchan cycles.

Not all Renaissance sonnets, however, whether individual poems or part of a sequence, are secular love poems. English poets were aware, for example, that the Italian poet Torquato Tasso had codified his sonnets as "Love Sonnets," "Heroical Sonnets" (usually compliments to a friend or a public figure), and "Sacred and Moral Sonnets"; and they, too, used the sonnet form for praise of a variety of subjects. Many a published work is fortified by the inclusion of individual sonnets, some dedicatory and some commendatory. The use of the sonnet for such commendation accords with the advice of James VI of Scotland, who writes, "For compendious praysing of any bukes, or the authouris thairof . . . use *Sonet* verse, of fourtene lynis, and ten fete in every lyne" (*A Short Treatise on Verse,* 1584). Other poets, such as John Donne and George Herbert, chose the sonnet form for expression of sacred subjects. The use of the sonnet for religious subjects had been recommended earlier by Sir Philip Sidney who claims that the sonnet as "a *Lyricall* kind" is especially appropriate for "singing the praises of the immortall bewtie, the immortall goodnes of that God, who giveth us hands to write, and wits to conceive" (*An Apology for Poetry*, 1595).

English sonnets generally took one of two forms, known today as the Petrarchan or Italian and the Shakespearean or English. The structure of the Petrarchan sonnet is bipartite, dividing between an octave, the first eight lines, and a sestet, the last six lines. The octave consists of two quatrains, ordinarily rhyming *abba abba* (enclosed rhyme); the sestet consists of two tercets of interlaced rhyme. The sestet allows for varied rhyme patterns, including *cde cde, cdc cdc,* and *cde dce.* An oversimplified but still useful approach to this two-part structure is to see the sonnet as presenting a problem, question, or desire in the octave, with an amplification, resolution, or answer in the sestet. English versions of the Italian sonnet, however, made a less pronounced break in thought between octave and sestet than did the sonnets of Petrarch. Starting with Sir Thomas Wyatt, who is credited with introducing the Italian sonnet into England, English poets generally modified the rhyme scheme of the Petrarchan sestet by concluding it with a couplet. This practice may have derived from a sonnet pattern of three quatrains and a concluding couplet in the work of Italian poets other than Petrarch. Usually the sestet of the English versions of the Italian sonnet rhymes *cddc ee* or *cdcd ee.*

The most frequently used sonnet form in the Elizabethan period was a marked alteration of the Italian model with its octave and sestet. English poets naturalized the sonnet with a pattern of three quatrains and a concluding couplet; the rhyme scheme is *abab cdcd efef gg.* Gascoigne describes the fourteen lines of this sonnet form by saying that the "firste twelve do ryme in staves of foure lines by crosse meetre, and the last twoo ryming togither do conclude the whole." Now known as the English or Shakespearean sonnet, this form allows the poet greater freedom through additional rhymes. Where the Italian sonnet is limited to five rhymes at the most, the English sonnet has seven. Frequently the English sonnet explores and amplifies a subject in the three quatrains and then offers a general comment on that subject in a concluding couplet.

Bibliography

L. E. Kastner, "The Elizabethan Sonneteers and the French Poets," *MLR,* 3 (1907–8), 268–77; Alfred H. Upham, "The Elizabethan Sonnet," *The French Influence in English Literature from the Accession of Elizabeth to the Restoration* (1908), pp. 91–144; Sidney Lee, "French Influence on the Elizabethan Lyric," *The French Renaissance in England* (1910), pp. 183–284; Walter L. Bullock, "The Genesis of the English Sonnet Form," *PMLA,* 38 (1923), 729–44; Lu Emily Pearson, *Elizabethan Love Conventions* (1933); Paul N. Siegel, "The Petrarchan Sonneteers and Neo-Platonic Love," *SP,*

42 (1945), 164–82; Ernest H. Wilkins, "A General Survey of Renaissance Petrarchism," *CL,* 2 (1950), 327–42; Sears Jayne, "Ficino and the Platonism of the English Renaissance," *CL,* 4 (1952), 214–38; Hallett Smith, "The Sonnets: Modes of the Search for Vitality," *Elizabethan Poetry* (1952), pp. 131–93; A. Lytton Sells, "The Sonnet-books," *The Italian Influence in English Poetry from Chaucer to Shakespeare* (1955), pp. 230–44; Mario Praz, "Petrarch in England," *The Flaming Heart* (1958), pp. 264–86; M. J. Valency, *In Praise of Love: An Introduction to Love-poetry of the Renaissance* (1958); F. T. Prince, "The Sonnet from Wyatt to Shakespeare," *Elizabethan Poetry,* eds. John Russell Brown and Bernard Harris, Stratford-upon-Avon Studies 2 (1960), 11–29; J. B. Leishman, *Themes and Variations in Shakespeare's Sonnets* (1961); David Kalstone, "The Petrarchan Vision," *Sidney's Poetry: Contexts and Interpretations* (1965), pp. 105–32; Robert M. Burgess, "The sonnet—a cosmopolitan literary form—in the Renaissance," *Proceedings of the IVth Congress of the International Comparative Literature Association,* ed. Francois Jost (1966), pp. 169–84; Patrick Cruttwell, *The English Sonnet* (1966); Douglas L. Peterson, *The English Lyric from Wyatt to Donne: A History of the Plain and Eloquent Styles* (1967); Barbara Herrnstein Smith, "Closure and Formal Conventions: The English Sonnet," *Poetic Closure: A Study of How Poems End* (1968), pp. 50–56; Stephen Booth, *An Essay on Shakespeare's Sonnets* (1969); Leonard Forster, "The Petrarchan Manner: An Introduction" and "European Petrarchism as Training in Poetic Diction," *The Icy Fire: Five Studies in European Petrarchism* (1969), pp. 1–83; Annabel M. Patterson, " 'True Nakedness': Elizabethan Sonnets," *Hermogenes and the Renaissance: Seven Ideas of Style* (1970), pp. 122–52; John Fuller, *The Sonnet* (1972); Rosalie L. Colie, "*Mel* and *Sal:* Some Problems in Sonnet-Theory," *Shakespeare's Living Art* (1974), pp. 68–134; J. W. Lever, *The Elizabethan Love Sonnet* (2nd ed., 1974); Anne Lake Prescott, *French Poets and the English Renaissance: Studies in Fame and Transformation* (1978); Richard Waswo, "The Petrarchan Tradition As A Dialectic of Limits," *SLitI,* 11 (1978), 1–16.

Sonnets in sequence:

An Elizabethan expression for the modern *sonnet sequence,* but both referring to a series of sonnets by a given poet. Although each sonnet (q.v.) retains its integrity as an individual poem, taken together the sonnets amplify and vary the ideas that unify the sequence.

The use of the term *sequence* to designate a collection of sonnets is more modern than Elizabethan. Almost all English collections of sonnets, if they were called anything at all, were simply referred to in a vague way; the publisher of the 1609 edition of Shakespeare's sonnets, for example, speaks only of "these insuing sonnets." But at least one poet and critic, George Gascoigne, uses the word *sequence* on several occasions to call attention to sonnets linked together by a syntactic device. For example, in a prose introduction to a group of seven sonnets (*Gascoigne's Memories* in *A Hundred Sundry Flowers,* 1573), he recalls that a friend "*Alexander Nevil* delivered him this theame [*sententia*], *Sat cito, si sat bene [No haste but good,* where wisdom makes the waye], whereupon hee compiled these seven Sonets in seqence." Here the seven sonnets amplify the "delivered . . . theame"; and, as in the Italian crown of sonnets, the sequence is linked structurally by having the last line of one sonnet serve as the first line of the next. On another occasion, in *The Adventures of Master F. J.* (1573), Gascoigne introduces three sonnets into his prose narrative with these words: "And thereuppon recompting hir [Dame Elynor's] woordes, he [F. J.] compiled these following, whiche he termed *Terza sequenza,* too [to] sweete Mistresse SHE." After the three sonnets, the story continues: "When he had well sorted this sequence, he sought oportunitie to leave it where shee might finde it before it were lost." Each of Gascoigne's sonnets contains fourteen lines; but a fifteenth line, "And then," links the first and second sonnets, and another short line, "For when," links the second and third sonnets. Gascoigne's use of the singular pronoun *it* suggests that he regarded the three sonnets as a single poem.

Although most English poets did not link their "Sonets in seqence" with devices such as those employed by Gascoigne, they did unify their collections with the motif of secular love, and they, or rather their fictive speakers, addressed their sonnets to "sweete Mistresse SHE." The remarks by "J. C.," author of *Alcilia. Philoparthens loving Folly* (1613), are a comment not only on his own sequence, but also, in effect, on the thematic unity yet variety which marks most English sonnet sequences. "J. C." writes: "The Sonnets following, were written *by the Author,* (*who giveth himselfe* this fained name of *Philoparthen,* as his accidentall attribute) at divers times and upon divers occasions, and therefore in the forme and matter they differ, and sometimes are quite contrary one to another, considering the nature and qualities of LOVE, which is a Passion full of varietie, and contrarietie in it selfe."

As "J. C." suggests, English sonnet sequences are controlled by motif, not narration. Shadows of plot and apparent references to events from the poet-speaker's own life are merely anchors to locate in a concrete world of particulars a movement of spirit and soul. While the course of the poet-speaker's love for a lady sometimes moves in a linear manner—from an admiration of the beloved's physical beauty to a worship of her spiritual virtue and its reflection of divine beauty and love—it may also just as often fluctuate in emotional and intellectual responses and never reach resolution. Thomas Nashe, for example, in the preface to the unauthorized 1591 edition of Sir Philip Sidney's *Astrophel and Stella* describes the movement of that sonnet sequence by saying: "The argument [is] cruell chastitie, the Prologue hope, the Epilogue dispaire."

Like the sonnet form itself, the sonnet sequence on secular love received its authority from a cycle, the *Canzoniere,* by Francis Petrarch. The posthumous and pirated edition of 1591 of *Astrophel and Stella* was the first of the important English sonnet sequences to be published and to take its place in an already flourishing European tradition. Others followed quickly, such as Samuel Daniel's *Delia* (1592), Henry Constable's *Diana* (1592), Michael Drayton's *Idea's Mirror, Amours in Quatorzains* (1594), and Edmund Spenser's *Amoretti* (1595).

Occasionally English sonnet sequences are religious in nature, explorations of human relationship to divine love. Such cycles include Henry Constable's *Spiritual Sonnets* (n.d.) and Henry Lok's *Sundry Christian Passions Contained in Two Hundred Sonnets* (1593). Besides his *La Corona* sequence, John Donne probably conceived of twelve of his Holy Sonnets as a kind of meditative sequence on death and God's love for sinful man. As they are arranged in certain of the manuscripts and as they are ordered in the first edition of Donne's poetry (1633), these sonnets form a "consecutive set of twelve, made up of two contrasted sets of six" (Gardner).

A distinctive kind of sonnet sequence is known as the corona or crown of sonnets. This sequence is composed of a varying number of interwoven stanzas, frequently seven in number, to form a single poem. Within the sequence, the sonnets are linked together by having the last line of each sonnet form the first line of the next, with the last line of the sequence repeating the line with which the sequence begins. In subject matter, the interwoven sonnets present a "corona" or "crown" of praise. The crown of sonnets was a popular form during the Italian Renaissance where it was often used to celebrate the Virgin Mary. Among English poets who found the crown of sonnets appropriate for elevated subjects are George Chapman and Donne. Chapman's *A Coronet for his Mistress Philosophy* (1595) praises a muse of the inward life and of divine inspiration for poetry, not one that sings "loves sensuall Emperie." Donne's *La Corona,* probably written about 1607, is a sequence of seven sonnets in praise of Christ as man's redeemer. The crown opens, and closes, with the line *"Deigne at my hands this crown of prayer and praise"* to indicate the major theme and petition of the poem.

Bibliography

Daniel E. Owen, *The Relations of the Elizabethan Sonnet Sequences to Earlier English Verse* (1903); Lisle Cecil John, *The Elizabethan Sonnet Sequences: Studies in Conventional Conceits* (1938); L. C. Knights, "Shakespeare's Sonnets," *Explorations: Essays in Criticism Mainly on the Literature of the Seventeenth Century* (1946), pp. 40–65; Helen Gardner, ed., "General Introduction," *John Donne: The Divine Poems* (1952), pp. xv–lv; William T. Going, "Gascoigne and the term 'Sonnet Sequence,' " *N&Q,* 199 (1954), 189–91; Lawrence A. Sasek, "Gascoigne and the Elizabethan Sonnet Sequences," *N&Q,* 201 (1956), 143–44; Richard B. Young, "English Petrarke: A Study of Sidney's *Astrophel and Stella,*" *Three Studies in the Renaissance: Sidney, Jonson, Milton* (1958), pp. 1–88; Claes Schaar *An Elizabethan Sonnet Problem* (1960); Louis L. Martz, "The *Amoretti:* Most Goodly Temperature," *Form and Convention in the Poetry of Edmund Spenser,* ed. William Nelson (1961), pp. 146–68; Hilton Landry, *Interpretations in Shakespeare's Sonnets* (1963); J. W. Lever, *The Elizabethan Sonnet* (2nd ed., 1966); C. F. Williamson, "The Design of Daniel's *Delia,*", *RES* n.s., 19 (1968), 251—60; Alexander Dunlop, "The Unity of Spenser's *Amoretti,*" *Silent Poetry: Essays in Numerological Analysis,* ed. Alastair Fowler (1970), pp. 153–69; Alastair Fowler, "Sonnet Sequences," *Triumphal Forms: Structural Patterns in Elizabethan Poetry* (1970), pp. 174-97; Thomas P. Roche, "Shakespeare and the Sonnet Sequence," *English Poetry and Prose, 1540–1674,* ed. Christopher Ricks (1970), pp. 101–17; William O. Harris, "Early Elizabethan Sonnets in Sequence," *SP,* 68 (1971), 451-69; John Fuller, "Sequences," *The Sonnet* (1972), pp. 37–49; Germaine Warkentin, " 'Love's sweetest part, variety': Petrarch and the Curious Frame of the Renaissance Sonnet Sequence," *Ren&R,* 11 (1975), 14–23; William McCarthy, "The Continuity of Milton's Sonnets," *PMLA,* 92 (1977), 96–109; Carol Thomas Neely, "The Structure of English Renaissance Sonnet Sequences," *ELH,* 45 (1978), 359–89.

Staff:

"Poeticall staffe" or stanza; "a certaine number of verses allowed to go altogether and joyne without any intermission, and doe or should finish up all the sentences of the same with a full period, unless it be in some special cases, & there to stay till another staffe follow of like sort" (George Puttenham, *The Art of English Poesy,* 1589). "The shortest staffe," he continues, "conteineth not under foure verses, nor the longest above ten, if it passe that number it is rather a whole ditty then properly a staffe." Three years earlier William Webbe had defined "staves" as "the number of verses contained with the divisions or partitions of a ditty" (*A Discourse of English Poetry,* 1586).

During the sixteenth century the Italian word *stanza,* meaning "station," entered the English literary vocabulary as a rival synonym for the native *staff.* Puttenham, for example, is aware that in Italian this basic unit of poetry was called a "*Stanza,* as if we should say a resting place." But like many other English writers, he uses the traditional word "staff," although, he says, "in our vulgare Poesie I know not why it should be called, unlesse it be for that we understand it for a bearer or supporter of a song or ballad, not unlike the old weake bodie, that is stayed up by his staffe, and were not otherwise able to walke or to stand upright." The word *stanza* gained wider acceptance in English as the tenets of Italian Renaissance criticism became more influential. Jaques, in *As You Like It,* (c. 1599), calls attention to the new term when he questions Amiens on what he calls the units of his song, "Come, more, another stanzo. Call you 'em stanzos?" (II, v). Amiens responds, "What you will."

The stanzaic forms in Renaissance poetry are invariably composed of rhymed verses, although there is great variety with reference to rhyme schemes and the number of lines and syllables. Stanza patterns range from relatively simple ones like the quatrain (q.v.) to more intricate ones like the Spenserian stanza. Many are traditional fixed stanzas and carry conventional names, like rhyme royal and *ottava rima* (qq.v.). Others are stanza patterns invented for use in a particular poem. Renaissance poets valued formal artifice, though, generally speaking, the poets of the sixteenth century preferred established stanza forms, while many of those in the seventeenth century worked in stanza forms of their own invention. In either case, print as a medium was just beginning to accustom a reader's eye to those formal divisions of a poem that had once been recognized solely by ear.

Often particular stanza forms were associated with particular genres and were felt to be appropriate for certain kinds of subject matter (*see* Decorum). The quatrain, for example, was frequently the vehicle for what Renaissance writers thought of as "light" subject matter, the pastoral or the amatory. "Weightier" matter, such as that of historical or epic narratives and of reflective lyric verse, was usually linked with such stanza patterns as *ottava rima* and rhyme royal.

Strong lines:

A seventeenth-century term referring to either prose or poetry in a style that was often rough and dissonant in cadence, close-packed and difficult in meaning, and always sinewy and concentrated. The densely textured prose and poetry of strong lines contended with established styles; and when a strong-lined style itself became a fashion, especially during the first half of the seventeenth century, it did not win unanimous approval. The term *strong lines* became mainly one of disapprobation, while admirers often praised a strong-lined style as "masculine."

In one of the earliest appearances of the term *strong lines,* Robert Burton, in the preface to the 1632 edition of *The Anatomy of Melancholy* defends his own "loose and free style" by saying that he "writ with as small deliberation as I doe ordinarily speak, without all affectation of . . . strong lines, that like *Acesta's* arrowes cought fire [i.e., ineffectively] as they flew." By the middle of the seventeenth century, Francis Osborn advises his son to "spend no time in reading, much less in writing *Strong-lines; which like tough meat, aske more paines and time in chewing, then can be recompensed by all the nourishment they bring" (Advice to a Son,* 1656).

Strong lines in prose were in large part a reaction against an established Ciceronian norm. Characterized by its fullness of expression, Ciceronian style (q.v.) was opposed by another prose style, the models for which came from Latin writers such as Seneca and Tacitus (*see* Senecan style). Achieving its concentration primarily through elliptical syntax and a staccato rhythm, such prose was especially admired for its gravity of thought. For those who admired strong-lined prose, its difficulty and obscurity were merits. Recommending Sir Henry Savile's translation of Tacitus to readers in 1591, Anthony Bacon, for example, praises Tacitus because "hee hath writen the most matter with best conceyt [thought] in fewest Wordes of anie Historiographer ancient or moderne. But he is harde. *Difficilia quae pulchra:* the second reading over will please thee more then the first, and the third then the second." And in a second edition of 1598 Richard Grenewey declared

213

in his dedication that there is in Tacitus "no woord not loaden with matter, and as himselfe speaketh of *Galba,* he useth *Imperatoria brevitate:* which although it breed difficultie, yet carrieth great gravitie."

Like its prose counterpart, strong-lined poetry was praised as "strenuous" and "masculine." Thomas Carew, for example, in his elegy upon John Donne published in the *Elegies upon the Author* in Donne's *Poems* (1633), commends strong lines when he declares that Donne had "open'd Us a Mine / Of rich and pregnant phansie, drawne a line / Of masculine expression." For the admirer of strong lines, difficulty was a virtue, not a defect. According to Thomas Fuller, it was "a *difficult plainness, difficult* at the hearing, *plain* at the *considering* thereof" which made John Cleveland an "eminent Poet" of the "masculine Stile" (*The Worthies of England,* 1662).

Strong-lined poetry was a reaction against earlier modes, a reaction mainly against "soft and smooth verses" (Izaak Walton, *The Compleat Angler,* 1653). Such "smooth" songs, Walton says, are the "old fashioned Poetrie, but choicely good, I think much better then the strong lines that are now in fashion in this criticall age." What defenders of the "old fashioned" mellifluous style disliked about strong-lined poetry were its concentrated, ingenious conceits (q.v.), its intricate stanza forms, and sometimes use of rough versification, all of which seemed to create a wilful obscurity. Francis Quarles, for example, in the preface to his *Argalus and Parthenia* (1629), says, "I have not affected to set thy understanding on the Rack, by the tyranny of *strong lines,* which (as they fabulously report of *China* dishes) are made for the third *Generation* to make use of, and are the meere itch of wit; under the colour of which, many have ventured (trusting to the *Oedipean* conceit [i.e., ability to solve puzzles] of their ingenious Reader) to write *non-sense.*" Another critic of strong lines, Dudley North, in his preface to *A Forest of Varieties* (1645), defends his own love poems as "True Turtles . . . full of simple love, and unfurnisht of all Serpentine climbing art of subtilty and knowledge." His poems are "Incense and Smoake . . . of the gentlest nature, not far fetcht Aromatiques, troublesome and intoxicating to the brain." He calls "Strong lines" the "Cromatiques" of poetry, which "of themselves may bee excellent in their Art; but long dwelt upon grow harsh and distastefull." Poetry, he continues, should be "delightfull and pleasant to the first appearance," and he disapproves of "the riding humour lately affected by many, who thinke nothing good that is easie, nor any thing becomming passion that is not exprest with an hyperbole above reason. These tormentors of their owne and their Readers braines I leave to bee admired in their high obscure flight . . . they affect to shew more wit then love, and in truth so much, that whilst they commend beyond reason, they shew either they want reason to commend, or their subject to bee commended; like ill ranging Spaniells they spring figures, and ravished with their extravagant fancies, pursue them in long excursions, neglecting their true game and pretended affection."

Bibliography

George Williamson, "Strong Lines," *ES*, 18 (1936), 152-59; Edwin Morgan, "Strong Lines and Strong Minds: Reflections on the Prose of Browne and Johnson," *Cambridge Journal*, 4 (1951), 481–91; L. A. Beaurline, "Dudley North's Criticism of Metaphysical Poetry," *HLQ*, 25 (1962), 299-313.

Terza rima:

A rhyming verse form composed of iambic tercets. The rhyme scheme progresses by making the first and third lines of each unit rhyme with the second line of the previous one (*aba, bcb, cdc,* and so on).

English Renaissance poets wrote in *terza rima* only occasionally. When they did, they seem to have been guided by an Italian preference for it in pastoral eclogues and in verse on other subjects where literary decorum (q.v.) made a "low" style appropriate. Dante had invented *terza rima* for *The Divine Comedy,* written in the fourteenth century; but despite his use of it for a serious allegorical narrative, poets of the Italian Renaissance favored *terza rima* for less elevated verse. Similarly, the practice of English poets associated *terza rima* with the "low" style. Sir Philip Sidney uses it, for example, in several of the eclogues (q.v.) interspersed in his *Arcadia* (1590), and both Sir Thomas Wyatt and Samuel Daniel chose it as an appropriate form for several of their verse epistles (q.v.).

Topographia:

"An evident and true description of a place" (Henry Peacham, 1593 edition of *The Garden of Eloquence*). Thus George Wither, in prefatory verses to the 1622 edition of Michael Drayton's *Poly-Olbion,* calls that poem a "Topo-chronographicall Poeme."

Drayton's poem takes for its subject all of Great Britain; and Wither's label "Topo-chronographicall" points to the poem's concern with the flora, fauna, and topography of Great Britain as well as with the chronology of its national history. The title of the earlier edition of *Poly-Olbion* simply calls it "A Chorographicall Description of the Tracts, Rivers, Mountains, Forests, and other Parts of this renowned Isle of Great Britaine . . . Digested in a Poem" (1613). It is this praise of an actual place, described through the use of appropriate realistic detail, that distinguishes late sixteenth and early seventeenth topographical poetry.

The figure of description, *topographia,* upon which such poems are based, was traditionally listed in Renaissance rhetorics (*see* Elocutio). Thus Peacham defines *topographia* as "an evident and true description of a place, like as Cicero describeth Syracusae a Citie in Cicilia." Through the use of this figure, he continues, a poet may describe such places as "countries, cities, townes, temples, pallaces, castles, walles, gates, mountaines, vallies, fields, orchards, gardens, fountaines, dens, and all other maner of places." For the contrasting description of fictive places Peacham assigns the figure of *topothesia,* "the fained description of a place, that is, when the Orator describeth a place, and yet no such place: As is the house of envy, in the 6 boke of Metamorphosis."

Many poems describe fictive places (e.g., the pastoral Arcadia of the eclogue); but early in the seventeenth century, stimulated by continental precedent, poets created what in effect was a new genre for English poetry. This new poetry combines realistic detail of the place with its moral signification. This new genre began to rival that of poems about fictive places. Some topographical poems, like Drayton's *Poly-Olbion,* continue a tradition established by historical chroniclers of viewing England as a particularly favored island. Other poems, often drawing their realistic details from second-hand accounts of travelers, locate the favored place in a remote region. The travelers who sing Andrew Marvell's *Bermudas* (published posthumously in 1681), for example, praise God for their safe arrival at that fertile place.

More numerous are poems describing a limited locality closer at hand or, as Peacham says, "castles, walles, gates, mountaines, vallies, fields, orchards, gardens, fountaines." An especially popular locale was the country estate of a noble family, like that of the Sidney family in Ben Jonson's *To Penshurst* (1616). Jonson's poem is modeled on an epigram (III, 58) on the villa of Faustinus by Martial. *To Penshurst* itself set a fashion for other estate poems, which include Thomas Carew's *To Saxham* (1640) and Marvell's *Upon Appleton House* (probably written between 1651–53).

A topic common to many topographical poems is a praise of the happy life of rural retirement. English poets found this theme in particular poems and passages by Latin poets like Martial, Horace, and Virgil (*see* Imitation). The notion that an inner peace could best be obtained in a country landscape was located principally in Martial's epigram *De rusticatione* (IV, 90), Horace's second epode (*Beatus ille*), and Virgil's *Georgics,* especially the second of his four books on Italian agriculture. Although these classical sources and others were available to English writers in the original Latin, John Ashmore first brought them together in his translation *Certain Selected Odes of Horace* (1621) with its appendix containing translations of other Latin poems and passages treating the topic of the happy life of the country.

Bibliography

Dwight L. Durling, *Georgic Tradition in English Poetry* (1935); Robert Arnold Aubin, Ch. 1, *Topographical Poetry in XVIII-Century England* (1936), pp. 3–32; G. R. Hibbard, "The Country House Poem of the Seventeenth Century," *JWCI,* 19 (1958), 159–74; Earl R. Wasserman, "Denham: *Cooper's Hill,*" *The Subtler Language* (1959), pp. 45–88; Maren-Sofie Røstvig, *The Happy Man: Studies in the Metamorphoses of a Classical Ideal,* vol. 1 (rev. ed., 1962); Don Cameron Allen, "Andrew Marvell: *Upon Appleton House,*" *Image and Meaning: Metaphoric Traditions in Renaissance Poetry* (rev. ed., 1968), pp. 115–53; Charles Molesworth, "Property and Virtue: The Genre of the Country-House Poem in the Seventeenth Century," *Genre,* 1 (1968), 141–57; William H. Moore, "Sources of Drayton's Conception of *Poly-Olbion,*" *SP,* 65 (1968), 783–803; John Chalker, *The English Georgic: A Study in the Development of a Form* (1969); Brendan O.

Hehir, *Expans'd Hieroglyphicks: A Critical Edition of Sir John Denham's "Cooper's Hill"* (1969); Niels Bugge Hansen, "Topographical Poetry," That pleasant place: The Representation of Ideal Landscape in English Literature from the 14th to the 17th Century (1973), pp. 128–43; H. M. Richmond, *Renaissance Landscapes: English Lyrics in a European Tradition* (1973); Raymond Williams, "Pastoral and Counter-Pastoral," *The Country and the City* (1973), pp. 13–34; William A. McClung, *The Country House in English Renaissance Poetry* (1977); J. G. Turner, "The Matter of Britain: Topographical Poetry in English 1600–1660," *N&Q* n.s., 25 (1978), 514–24; Heather Dubrow, "The Country-House Poem: A Study in Generic Development," *Genre,* 12 (1979), 153–79; Mary Ann C. McGuire, "The Cavalier Country-House Poem: Mutations on a Jonsonian Tradition," *SEL,* 19 (1979), 93–108; James Turner, *The Politics of Landscape* (1979).

Tragedy:

A "moornefull play being a loftie kind of poetrie, and representing personages of great state and matter of much trouble, a great broile or stirre: it beginneth prosperously and endeth unfortunatelie or sometimes doubtfullie, and in contrarie to a comedie" (John Florio, *A World of Words,* 1598). To practicing playwrights of the late sixteenth and early seventeenth centuries in England, tragedy was a serious drama distinguished from other kinds of plays by its basis in historical truth, its high-born characters, a heightened style, and somber conclusion. In the words of Ben Jonson it was marked by "truth of Argument, dignity of Persons, gravity and height of Elocution, fulnesse and frequencie of Sentence" (Preface to *Sejanus,* 1605). The historicity and gravity of tragedy were typically contrasted with the fabricated story and happy ending of comedy (q.v.).

There is little discussion or notice of tragedy as a separate dramatic genre in England before the establishment of the first permanent theater in London in 1576. Only eleven examples of the use of the word *tragedy* on the title pages of printed plays can be found before 1576; and of these seven appear on translations of Senecan drama. After 1576, the word *tragedy* does begin to appear with frequency on title pages of plays—and then often in combination with the adjectives *lamentable* and *true*.

If comedy is "life's looking glass," tragedy is "death's mirrour" (Thomas Tomkis, *Lingua,* c. 1607). It is firmly and almost exclusively connected with the dramatization of death, especially murder or suicide. "Thy tragedie" in *The Spanish Tragedy* (c. 1585) twice signifies death by violence. "And what are tragedies but acts of Death?" (Thomas Kyd ?, *Soliman and Perseda,* 1590). In *I Selimus* (Robert Greene ?, 1592) the Epilogue says: "If this first part gentles, do like you well, / The second part shall greater murthers tell." In the induction to *A Warning for Fair Women* (Thomas Heywood ?, 1599) the character Tragedy is "Murther's Beadle." Heywood restates a traditional view when he says: "If we present a Tragedy, we include the fatall and abortive ends of such as commit notorious murders, which is aggravated and acted with all the Art that may be, to terrifie men from the like abhorred practices" (*An Apology for Actors,* 1612).

Although most practicing dramatists contended that tragedy was to be based on historical fact, this assumption was not unchallenged. Sir Philip Sidney questions that assumption by asking playwrights to understand that "a Tragedie is tied to the lawes of Poesie" and "not of Historie" (*An Apology for Poetry,* 1595). But Shakespeare's Hamlet, in announcing a play at court, says: "This play is the image of a murder done in Vienna" and "the story is extant, and written in very choice Italian." Playwrights viewed tragedy's basis in history as a powerful element for enhancing the emotional and ethical force of tragedy. Samuel Daniel in the 1623 *Apology* to *Philotas* explains: "I thought the representing so true a History, in the ancient forme of a Tragedy, could not but have had an unreproveable passage with the time, and the better sort of men; seeing with what idle fictions and grosse follies, the Stage at this day abused mens recreations." Similarly Jonson, in the preface to the 1605 edition of *Sejanus,* offers his indebtedness to the historians Tacitus and Seutonius as evidence that he has discharged the offices of a tragic writer. He goes so far as to indicate his specific use of these writers in marginal notes throughout the printed text of the play. "But it is more agreeable with the Gravity of a Tragedy that it be grounded upon a true History, where the Greatness of a Known Person, urging Regard, doth work the more powerfully upon the Affections" (Sir William Alexander, *Anacrisis,* 1634?).

What Jonson calls "gravity and height of Elocution" and "fulnesse and frequencie of Sentence" underline the relationship of style and subject in tragedy. Not only is the action to be expressed in magniloquent amplitude (*see* Copia), but it is also to be given moral efficacy with *sententiae* (q.v.), the "wise sayings" which rhetoricians call the "jewels" or "lights" of discourse. Rhetoricians traditionally assigned serious matter a passionate, serious diction: "In weightie causes, grave wordes are thought moste nedefull, that the greatnesse of the matter, maie then rather appere in the vehemencie of their talke" (Thomas Wilson, *The Art of Rhetoric,* 1553). The convention that tragedy requires a rich and memorable style, a "stately" style, receives almost universal recognition by contemporary writers; even writers of domestic tragedy pay lip service to it by apologizing for the lack of such a style.

In the medieval tradition a tragedy was not a play but simply a story of great figures who ended unhappily. Behind such narrative tragedies are the archetypal examples of the "falls" of Lucifer and Adam. One of the most famous definitions of tragedy in late medieval times, that given by Chaucer in the prologue to *The Monk's Tale,* assumes such a fall is the action of a tragedy:

> Tragedie is to seyn a certyn storie,
> As olde bookes maken us memorie,
> Of him that stood in greet prosperitee
> And is yfallen out of heigh degree
> Into myserie, and endeth wrecchedly.

One work in the medieval tradition of tragedy as a "fall" was especially influential in the development of Renaissance conceptions of dramatic tragedy and served as source book for many plots. This was the famous and popular *Mirror for Magistrates,* a massive collection of narrative poems on the "falls" of biblical, classical, and medieval princes. The earliest (though repressed) edition of the *Mirror* (1555) was published with an earlier English poem, John Lydgate's *Fall of Princes*, which was in turn an "Englished" redaction of the French version of Boccaccio's *De casibus virorum illustrium* of the 1360s. The first widely read edition of the *Mirror* appeared in 1559; and new editions, revised, expanded, and changed by a variety of writers, appeared up to 1610 and kept alive the tradition of tragedy as the fall of a prince. It is this *de casibus* tradition that Fulke Greville assumes in discussing his own intentions for the tragic form where he will "trace out the high waies of ambitious Governours, and . . . shew in the practice, that the more audacity, advantages and good successe such Soveraignitis have, the more they hasten to their owne desolation and ruine" (*Life of Sir Philip Sidney,* 1652).

Other kinds of narrative tragedy complicated the *de casibus* pattern as playwrights brought tragedy to the stage; short prose tales, the Italian *novelle,* and stories from Italian history furnish the subjects for nearly half the stage tragedies written in the reign of Elizabeth and James I. When the *novelle* were violent and unhappy, they were called "tragedies" by their English translator-authors. Sir Geoffrey Fenton, for example, titled his collection of such tales *Certain Tragical Discourses* (1567). They are, he says, "mortal and furious tragedies" (*see* Novella).

As Englishmen noted with fascination, the plots of such Italian *novelle* are both intricate and horrific. Unlike the narratives of the *de casibus* tradition in which action is often motivated by political ambition, the Italian stories are concerned with crimes resulting from violent personal passions: malice, jealousy, and lust. So Fulke Greville says they are "contrived with variety and unexpected encounters," which "strangeness or perplexedness of witty Fictions" may give the imagination, if not the judgment, "exercise and entertainment." But the *novelle* met the requirement that tragedy be both "lamentable" and "true." They carry the stamp of authentic history since action is located in an exact place and time, and writers conventionally insist that their stories are not fictive. Some, indeed, are based on fact, as is the famous story of the Duchess of Malfi, which is the subject of John Webster's play (c. 1614) by that name.

Although English playwrights turned to Italy for plot material, there is little evidence that Italian stage tragedy was itself a direct model for English tragedies. The most important contribution of the Italian playwrights to Renaissance theater was their mastery of a complex plot with discoveries and reversals of fortune; often these were plots involving multiple lines of action, such as several love affairs and several revenges. But many such Italian tragedies of revenge and crime were themselves based on *novelle* or Roman plays, which also were available to Englishmen. And although Italians also introduced to drama a formal pattern of versification for tragedy (unrhymed verse for most of the dialogue and rhyme for choruses and some passionate speeches in the dialogue), it is difficult to find a direct influence on English theater for this practice, although Shakespeare's *Romeo and Juliet* (c. 1595) shows such a pattern of versification.

Not all English tragedies are of fallen princes or "lascivious" Italians; a small number of plays are based on the actual crimes of ordinary people, often of fairly recent murders. Domestic tragedy of this kind is an Elizabethan innovation for which there is almost no traditional or classical warrant. Departing from the magniloquence commonly assigned to tragedy, style in domestic tragedy is "plain," as would be suitable for its homely subject. Playwrights were quick to call attention to their departure from a norm. The author of *Arden of Feversham* (c. 1591) speaks of his "naked" play, and the author of *The English Traveller* (c. 1625) of his "bare lines." Domestic tragedies tend to follow a structural pattern familiar to their audiences in religious, allegorical plays of sin and punishment. Often domestic tragedies have double endings in which only the guilty die and the good are rewarded, unlike *de casibus* and Italianate tragedy in which even the innocent perish. The domestic tragedies furnish, says Thomas Heywood, "a domestike, and home-born truth" (*An Apology for Actors,* 1612).

As conceptions of tragedy crystallized in the late sixteenth century in England, the dominant classical model for imitation (q.v.) was provided by the plays of Seneca. Seneca's plays were available to readers in the original Latin throughout the Renaissance and by 1581 all were translated into English. They were closely studied in the schools and frequently imitated in the amateur plays produced in schools and universities. The success of Senecan academic drama and the importance of Seneca in the school curricula inevitably colored the popular, professional stage. Some elements from the narrative "tragedies" that were present in Senecan drama received additional sanction for their appearance on the stage and became conventional by the turn of the century: a ghost from hell, revenge as a motive for the action, and the use of *sententiae* and long declamatory speeches to heighten style.

Seneca's plays were written in unrhymed verse, however, which was in marked contrast to the traditional English use of rhyme for dramatic productions. The poet-dramatists who created tragic drama for England's professional stage also made an unrhymed verse—blank verse (q.v.)—the principal medium for their own plays. From the 1580s to the closing of the theaters, blank verse was associated with the high style of princes and the larger decorum (q.v.) of tragedy. Besides the sanction of classical unrhymed verse, English playwrights had the example of Italian playwrights who were naturalizing an unrhymed verse form in their vernacular tragedies; this eleven syllable verse, *versi sciolti,* was first employed in a substantial composition in Italian in 1515 by Giangiorgio Trisino for his tragedy *Sofonisba.*

Exalted language in a long set speech becomes a medium of special importance in Elizabethan and Jacobean tragedy. On a stage with the minimum of properties and scenery, the long, almost self-contained speech creates a verbal universe that amplifies and elaborates every idea, problem, and situation for the fullest impact upon an audience. As the plays themselves tend to be concerned with situations and circumstances that reappear from play to play (the revenger's triumph, for example), so are certain kinds of speeches recurrent in the tragedies: "report" speeches, "planning" speeches to discuss a course of action or to show decisions being framed, "conversion" speeches, and laments. One of the earliest theoretical discussions of tragedy as a drama locates its merit in its declamatory style: "*Gorboduc* . . . as it is full of stately speeches and well sounding Phrases, clymbing to the height of Seneca his style . . . [obtains] the very end of Poesie" (Sidney). The presence of set speeches in tragedy was conditioned not only by the prestige of such declamatory models in Seneca, but also by school training in rhetoric (q.v.), which made the ability both to create and to understand orations of different kinds an important aim of education. Speeches of praise and dispraise, forensic speeches to persuade in a courtroom, and "deliberative" speeches designed to impart good counsel or to change a point of view all received close attention.

Aside from the model provided by Seneca, English poets inherited a small body of purely dramatic theory that exerted varying pressures upon their practice; this theory was found primarily in the works of Aristotle and Horace as schematized by Italian critics and in immensely influential treatises on comedy (with comments on tragedy) ascribed to Donatus that were widely circulated in the more elaborate editions of Terence. Donatus makes Homer the principal source of poetic theory and claims that Homer makes the *Iliad* a model for tragedy as the *Odyssey* is a model for comedy.

Donatus also describes a doctrine accepted by all Elizabethans that comedy begins in trouble and ends in peace, while tragedy begins in calm and ends in tempest. He distinguishes social strata appropriate to comedy and tragedy: tragedy is to be concerned with courts and noble personages, and comedy with the life of ordinary citizens. He also adds that tragedy shows the kind of life that is to be shunned.

The Donatian proposition that tragedy is a negative exemplum, that it shows a life to be avoided, is one of the most widespread formulae of medieval dramatic criticism and of Renaissance theory and practice. Sidney is typical when he says that tragedy "maketh kings feare to be tyrants, and tyrants manifest their tyrannical humours." Rhetoricians, long accustomed to dividing all poetry into forms of praise and dispraise, frequently speak of tragedy as "dispraise." George Puttenham classes tragedy as "a poem reprehensive" (*The Art of English Poesy,* 1589). As reprehension, tragedy is inevitably colored by impulses close to those of satire; and tragedy, like comedy, shows actions to be avoided (*see* Epideictic rhetoric). George Chapman maintains in his dedication to *The Revenge of Bussy D'Ambois* (1610) that the "soul, limbs, and limits" of authentic tragedy are "material instruction, elegant and sententious excitation to virtue, and deflection from her contrary." The 1612 *Apology for Actors* by Thomas Heywood introduces the "tragicke Muse" who says she has "whipt Vice with a scourge of steele, / Unmaskt sterne Murther, sham'd lascivious Lust, / Pluckt off the visar from grimme Treason's face, / And made the sunne point at their ugly sinnes." Thomas Randolph makes a personification of Satire the attendant of Tragedy in his play *The Muses' Looking Glass* (1630).

Renaissance critics found little difficulty in making Donatus virtually parallel with the even more widely known and circulated formulae from Horace's *Ars poetica* that the end of poetry is "profit" and "delight." Profit was to come from moral instruction, the image of vice as reprehensible. Also from Horace comes an emphasis upon decorum, both of characterization and speech: the notion that human beings of different ages, sex, and rank have characteristic manners and appearances that should be imitated appropriately on the stage. Distinctions of this kind were also a fundamental part of the rhetorical tradition with its insistence upon levels of style and propriety in speech.

Aristotle's *Poetics* was generally known in England—when it was known at all—through commentaries by Italian critics, and his conception of tragedy as a formal structure met with little response from playwrights. Elizabethan tragedy inherited no form, as opposed to subject matter, that distinguished it from comedy or the history play. Its plot structure might be sequentially episodic or highly complex (a favorite metaphor associated with "plot" is "maze"). Comments from Aristotle made it clear that he required not only unity of action but also that the action of tragedy should be confined to one day. Commentators went on to assume that his comments also meant action should be confined to one place. Sidney repeats his version of this idea when he condemns a play for ignoring "the unities": "For where the stage should alwaies represent but one place, and the uttermost time presupposed in it, should be, both by *Aristotles* precept and common reason, but one day: there is both many dayes and many places, inartificially imagined." Such strictures, however, had little impact upon the practice of most writers of tragedy.

Similarly the Aristotelian emphasis upon unity of tone is contrary to the norms of English practice. Although writers generally assumed that tragedy is an affair of the mighty, they freely added other social levels to their plays. The tendency of clown figures in tragedies to extemporize and attract too much attention to themselves was, however, often decried, but the inclusion of comic elements in serious matters had a long sanction in dramatic practice and audience expectation that was defended by playwrights. The Chorus in Robert Greene's *James IV* (1590) says after Act III, for example: "The rest is ruthful; yet, to beguilde the time, / 'Tis interlac'd with merriment and rime." Francisco in John Webster's *The White Devil* (1612) takes a mixture of tones as necessary: "My tragedy must have some idle mirth in't, / Else it will never pass."

Playwrights were aware of several ways of "dividing" the action of a play. There were imperatives, inherited from Donatus and Horace, that certain kinds of order and divisions were appropriate to the construction of a dramatic plot. Donatus describes comedy as being divided into four parts: the *prologue* or preface; the *protasis* or proposition which includes the first act and presents the actors; the *epitasis* which is the body of the play; and the *catastrophe* or conclusion. Ben Jonson applies the same structural pattern to tragedy. But the propriety of a five-act play structure was enjoined by Horace: "Nor must the Fable, that would hope the Fate, / Once seene, to be againe call'd for, and plaid, / Have more or lesse than just five Acts" (*Horace, or the Art of Poetry,* trans. Ben Jonson, 1641); and Senecan tragedies seemed to be divided into five acts with the chorus separating one act from another. It was often assumed that the Donatian *protasis* was to be the first act of a five-act structure, the *catastrophe* the last act, and the *epitasis* acts two, three, and four. Little attempt was made to generalize about the function of each act; the end of an act was normally signified by the clearing of the stage. Early in the seventeenth century some English commentators, following the Italian critic Scaliger, added a fourth "part" to plays, the *catastasis,* "the state and full vigour of the play" as an extension of the *epitasis.* Native tradition, of course, did not emphasize act and scene divisions, and playwrights only gradually and sporadically structured their plays around such organizing principles. As the sixteenth-century drama developed, first the plays written for the schools and then the popular drama began to explore the implications of these "classical" imperatives; but the emphasis upon tragedy as a moral exemplum based on history was always of more significance to the practice of playwrights than theories of plot structure.

Bibliography

John W. Cunliffe, *The Influence of Seneca on Elizabethan Tragedy* (1893); John W. Cunliffe, ed., "Introduction," *Early English Classical Tragedies* (1912), pp. vii–c; Clarence Valentine Boyer, *The Villain as Hero in Elizabethan Tragedy* (1914); Muriel C. Bradbrook, *Themes and Conventions of Elizabethan Tragedy* (1935); Lily B. Campbell, *Tudor Conceptions of History and Tragedy in 'A Mirror for Magistrates'*(1936); Willard Farnham, *The Medieval Heritage of Elizabethan Tragedy* (1936; rev. ed., 1956); Una Ellis-Fermor, *The Jacobean Drama, an Interpretation* (1936); Theodore Spencer, *Death and Elizabethan Tragedy: A Study of Convention and Opinion in the Elizabethan Drama* (1936); Howard Baker, *Induction to Tragedy* (1939); Clarence W. Mendell, *Our Seneca* (1941); H. H. Adams, *English Domestic or, Homiletic Tragedy 1575 to 1642* (1943); Marvin T. Herrick, "Senecan Influence in *Gorboduc*," *Studies in Speech and Drama in Honor of Alexander M. Drummond* (1944), pp. 78–104; F. P. Wilson, *Elizabethan and Jacobean* (1945); W. A. Armstrong, "The Elizabethan Conception of the Tyrant," *RES,* 22 (1946), 161–81; Moody E. Prior, "The Elizabethan Tradition," *The Language of Tragedy* (1947), pp. 16–153; Mary Crapo Hyde, *Playwriting for Elizabethans, 1600–1605* (1949); Joseph A. Bryant, Jr., "The Significance of Ben Jonson's First Requirement for Tragedy: 'Truth of Argument,' " *SP,* 49 (1952), 195–213; Alfred Harbage, *Shakespeare and the Rival Traditions* (1952); Marvin T. Herrick, *Italian Tragedy in the Renaissance* (1952); Susanne K. Langer, "The Great Dramatic Forms: The Tragic Rhythm," *Feeling and Form* (1953), pp. 351–66; Madeleine Doran, *Endeavors of Art: A Study of Form in Elizabethan Drama,* (1954); Thomas Rice Henn, *The Harvest of Tragedy* (1956); Bernard Spivak, *Shakespeare and the Allegory of Evil* (1958); Fredson T. Bowers, *Elizabethan Revenge Tragedy 1587–1642* (rev. ed., 1959); Richard B. Sewall, *The Vision of Tragedy* (1959); J. V. Cunningham, "Woe or Wonder," *Tradition and Poetic Structure* (1960), pp. 135–262; Robert Ornstein, *The Moral Vision of Jacobean Tragedy* (1960); Wolfgang Clemen, *English Tragedy before Shakespeare: The Development of Dramatic Speech,* trans. T. S. Dorsch (1961); A. P. Rossiter, "Shakespearian Tragedy," *Angel with Horns,* ed. Graham Storey (1961), pp. 253–73; David Bevington, *From 'Mankind' to Marlowe* (1962); Douglas Cole, *Suffering and Evil in the Plays of Christopher Marlowe* (1962); Irving Ribner, *Jacobean Tragedy: The Quest for Moral Order* (1962); Robert Y. Turner,

"Pathos and the *Gorboduc* Tradition, 1560–1590," *HLQ,* 25 (1962), 97–120; Thomas B. Tomlinson, *A Study of Elizabethan and Jacobean Tragedy* (1964); Virgil K. Whitaker, *The Mirror up to Nature: The Technique of Shakespeare's Tragedies* (1965); Philip Edwards, *Thomas Kyd and Early Elizabethan Tragedy* (1966); Charles Osborne McDonald, *The Rhetoric of Tragedy: Form in Stuart Drama* (1966); G. K. Hunter, "Seneca and the Elizabethans: A Case-Study in 'Influence,' " *ShS,* 20 (1967), 17–26; J. M. R. Margeson, *The Origins of English Tragedy* (1967); D. J. Palmer, "Elizabethan Tragic Heroes," *Elizabethan Theatre,* eds. J. R. Brown and B. Harris, Stratford-upon-Avon Studies 9 (1967), pp. 11–35; F. P. Wilson, "Tragedy, c. 1540–c. 1584." *The English Drama 1485–1585,* ed. G. K. Hunter (1969), pp. 126–51; Glynne Wickham, "Genesis and the Tragic Hero: Marlowe to Webster," *Shakespeare's Dramatic Heritage* (1969), pp. 42–63; George C. Herndl, *The High Design: English Renaissance Tragedy and the Natural Law* (1970); Leonora L. Brodwin, *Elizabethan Love Tragedy: 1587–1625* (1971); J. W. Lever, *The Tragedy of State* (1971); G. K. Hunter, "Seneca and English Tragedy," *Seneca,* ed. C. D. N. Costa (1974), pp. 166–204; Joseph Henry Stodder, *Satire in Jacobean Tragedy* (1974); Walter Benjamin, *The Origin of German Tragic Drama,* trans. John Osborne (1977); Larry S. Champion, *Tragic Patterns in Jacobean and Caroline Drama* (1977); Howard Felperin, *Shakespearean Representation: Mimesis and Modernity in Elizabethan Tragedy* (1977); Emrys Jones, "Shakespeare and the Mystery Cycles," *The Origins of Shakespeare* (1977), pp. 31–84; Joyce E. Peterson, *Curs'd Example: "The Duchess of Malfi" and Commonweal Tragedy* (1978); Robert Weimann, *Shakespeare and the Popular Tradition in the Theater,* ed. Robert Schwartz (1978); Stephen Orgel, "Shakespeare and the Kinds of Drama," *Critical Inquiry,* 6 (1979), 107–23.

Tragicomedy:

"A tragie-comedie is not so called in respect of mirth and killing but in respect it wants deaths, which is inough to make it no tragedie, yet brings some neere it, which is inough to make it no comedie: which [comedy] must be a representation of familiar people with such kinde of trouble as no life be questiond [i.e., put in danger], so that a God is as lawfull in this as in a tragedie, and meane people as in a comedie" (John Fletcher, preface, *The Faithful Shepherdess,* c. 1608). Here Fletcher thinks of tragicomedy as a true "third kind" to be added to the traditional genres of comedy and tragedy (qq.v.). Tragicomedy avoids the restrictions of both tragedy and comedy. It does not use the grim conclusion of tragedy and is not confined to the middle-class world of comedy (though "meane" characters can appear). Its tone is not to be the vehement, passionate tone of tragedy, but neither is it to reflect the satirical bias of comedy.

Fletcher's definition of tragicomedy comes from the justifications accompanying Battista Guarini's Italian play, *Il pastor fido.* After widespread circulation in manuscript, Guarini's influential pastoral tragicomedy was first published in Italy in 1590; the next year it was published in Italian in London (*see* Pastoral). In 1602 it went into its twentieth edition in Italy and was published in an English translation (by [Edward?] Dymock) in London. Even before *Il pastor fido* appeared in print, it gave rise to a spirited controversy in which Guarini himself took a central part with two pamphlets later combined into a *Compendio della poesia tragicomica.* The *Compendio* appeared with the final revision of his play in 1602. Here Guarini appears as the first expositor of a definite critical theory in support of tragicomedy.

Guarini's essays in the *Compendio* make a theoretical case for tragicomedy that gave it a new respectability throughout Europe. He maintains that it is the best of all dramatic forms, a separate species tempering the terror of tragedy and the unrestrained effects of comedy. He assumes that the traditional end of tragedy is to reduce the strong passions, while the traditional end of comedy is to imitate the private actions of private men who through their defects move an audience to laughter and thus correct melancholy. But tempering of the passions is susceptible of gradation; if one were to moderate any one of them beyond the degree called for by the traditional genres one would approach a new genre. The mixture tragicomedy makes is entirely acceptable: "it takes from the one [tragedy] the great personages, but not the action; the verisimilar plot, but which is not true; the passions moved, but blunted; pleasure, not sadness; danger, but not death. From the other [comedy], controlled laughter, modest jests, the contrived knot, the happy reversal, and above all the comic order" (trans. Bernard Weinberg). The style of tragicomedy, says Guarini, is to be magnificent, but polished. Since its subjects are great persons, it is not proper for the characters of tragicomedy to speak in a low fashion; but because in tragicomedy the terrible is not desirable, it chooses a sweet ("dulce") middle style, which moderates the sublimity of the purely tragic form (*see* Decorum).

Guarini expands his case for tragicomedy by insisting that as a dramatic genre it serves the tastes of a contemporary audience. Comedy has decayed. Tragedy is superfluous because purgation of pity and terror has been rendered unnecessary by the precepts of Christian religion and the words of Scripture. Given the Christian religion, audiences do not need the "horrible and savage spectacles" of tragedy. The reversal of a tragicomedy, from tragic happenings to a comic ending of forgiveness and general happiness, is an imitation (q.v.) of God's providential pattern for mankind.

Although Guarini does not allude to it, a possible sanction for his emphasis upon tragicomedy as suitable for Christian audiences is provided by an international group of neo-Latin playwrights, mostly schoolmasters, who created a body of sacred drama in the sixteenth century that imposed a classical comic structure upon biblical rather than secular subject matter. Often such plays bore titles like "comoedia tragica." Nicholas Grimald calls his *Christus redivivus* (c. 1540) a "comedy or tragedy or yet both." In the dedicatory epistle to *Christus redivivus* Grimald is congratulated because in his play "great things had been interwoven with the small, joyous with sad, obscure with manifest, incredible with probable. Moreover, just as the first act yields to tragic sorrow, in order that the subject-matter may keep its title, so the fifth and last adapts itself to delight and joy; likewise, in order that variety may be opposed to satiety, in all the other intermediate acts, sad and cheerful incidents are inserted in turn" (see *PMLA*, 14 [1899], 373–83).

This body of neo-Latin plays—known collectively as the "Christian Terence"—deliberately broke down the traditional prescription that tragic characters should be high born and historical and that comic characters should be unknown. They freely mingled high characters with low, and historical characters like Christ with fictitious characters. They set comic scenes in a serious argument and more often than not had a troubled beginning with a happy ending. In contrast to Guarini's conception of tragicomedy, many had a double issue, with rewards for the virtuous and punishment for the wicked.

Although Guarini justifies his tragicomedy as suited to contemporary needs, he also defends himself against critics by finding classical harbingers of his practice. Plautus had used the term *tragicocomoedia* to refer to his play *Amphitryon,* which presents gods disguised as mortals involved in domestic intrigue. Sophocles lets servants unravel the complications of the plot in *Oedipus rex;* Euripides' play *Cyclops* mingles danger to the life of Ulysses with the Cyclops's drunkenness; Terence adds a tragic quality to one of his comedies, the *Self-Tormentor.* Aristotle recognizes in the *Poetics* (XIII) the existence of tragedies with a double plot and a happy ending for virtuous characters.

Following a traditional formula, Guarini claims that tragicomedy is a reinvention of the Greek satyr play, which was thought of as a classical "third kind," apart from comedy and tragedy. As a pastoral tragicomedy, *Il pastor fido* invokes the satyr play's setting of trees, caves, and mountains and its satyr and shepherd figures as protagonists. (English awareness of the tradition aligning tragicomedy with the satyr play is illustrated by the engraved title page to Ben Jonson's *Works* [1616]; in this design the figure Tragicomoedia appears aloft, supported on one side by Pastor and on the other by Satyr.) But the tone of pastoral tragicomedy is not rustic. As a form of tragicomedy, says Guarini, the pastoral play should have most grave and noble persons as characters (e.g. noble shepherds) with noble manners and speech.

The term *tragicomedy* and variations on it were not unknown in England before the publication of John Fletcher's preface to *The Faithful Shepherdess.* For example, *Apius and Virginia* (c. 1564), is called "*A new Tragicall Comedie,*" and the author's prologue to *Damon and Pythias* (c. 1565) calls it "a Tragicall Commedie." George Gascoigne's *The Glass of Government* (1575) is called "a tragicall Comedie so entituled, bycause therein are handled aswell the rewardes for Vertues, as also the punishment for Vices." The 1591 edition of John Lyly's *Campaspe* says it is "A tragicall Comedie of Alexander and Campaspe." John Marston's play *The Malcontent* is entered in the Stationers' Register for July 1604 as "an Enterlude called the Malecontent, *Tragiecomedia.*"

One of the aims of Fletcher's preface seems to be to formalize and regularize English dramatic practice. He is addressing not only the proposition of tragicomedy as a dramatic kind with its own integrity, but also a robust native tradition embracing dramatic mixtures of all kinds, particularly mixtures of tone. Playwrights freely mixed social classes within a play, alternated comic and serious episodes, and placed a magniloquent level of language next to a colloquial style. In statements that span the entire period from 1560 to the closing of the theaters, playwrights insisted that audiences required such mixtures. The Prologue to Thomas Garter's *Susanna* (c. 1569) claims: "nought delightes the hart of men on earth, / So much as matters grave and sad, if they be mixt with myrth." Over sixty years later the dedication to John Kirke's *Seven Champions of Christendom* (c. 1635) maintains that "Tragedy may be too dull and solid, the Comedy too sharpe and bitter; but a well mixt portion of either, doubtlesse would make the sweetest harmony." In a more philosophic vein, John Lyly in the prologue to *Midas* (1589) comments on the variety in all things that is the fashion in England, the drama being no exception: "What heretofore hath been served in severall dishes for a feaste, is now minced in a charger for a Gallimaufrey. If wee present a mingle-mangle, our fault is to be excused, because the whole worlde is become a Hodge-podge."

For the "mingle-mangle" there was even more precedent than Lyly's comments suggest. The old Tudor interludes had typically combined the seriously moral and the ludicrous; late medieval mystery plays of the saints' lives were episodic, romantic representations of high adventure and dangers overcome. Allegorical religious plays focused on serious problems brought to a happy ending in spiritual salvation.

Training in rhetoric reinforced the playwrights' impulse to vary tone. Thomas Wilson, citing Cicero as his authority, reminds his readers that the insertion of "pleasant matter" in "a weightie matter" or "hevy tale" will make an audience more attentive. "To move sporte" is "lawfull' for an orator, or "any one that shall talke, in any open assembly." "Excepte menne finde delight, thei will not long abide: delight theim, and wynne theim: werie theim, and you lose theim forever. And that is the reason, that menne commonly tary the ende of a merie plaie, and cannot abide the half hearying of a sower checkying Sermon" (all quotations from *The Art of Rhetoric,* 1553).

Denunciations of the playwrights' unclassical approach to genre is only sporadic and essentially uninfluential in the sixteenth century. Sir Philip Sidney's caustic strictures against mixtures of characters, and hence tone, on the stage go largely unheeded, though such plays are, he says, "neither right Tragedies, nor right Comedies; mingling Kinges and Clownes . . . by head and shoulders, to play a part in majesticall matters, with neither decencie nor discretion: So as neither the admiration and Commiseration, nor the right sportfulnes, is by their mungrell Tragycomedie obtained" (*An Apology for Poetry,* 1595).

It was just this "mungrell Tragycomedie" or ill-bred mixture of tones within one play that Fletcher rejected. With Francis Beaumont he created a group of plays—a new "third kind"—which, while they explore the problems of tragedy and then shift to a comic resolution, are chiefly characterized by the polished consistency of a "sweet" and effortless tone in the manner of Guarini.

Bibliography

Frank H. Ristine, *English Tragicomedy* (1910); James G. McManaway, "Philip Massinger and the Restoration Drama," *ELH,* 1 (1934), 276–304; Eugene M. Waith, *The Pattern of Tragicomedy in Beaumont and Fletcher* (1952); Madeleine Doran, "Tragi-Comedy," *Endeavors of Art* (1954), pp. 186–215; Marvin T. Herrick, *Tragicomedy: Its Origin and Development in Italy, France, and England* (1955); A. P. Rossiter, "Comic Relief," *Angel with Horns and Other Shakespeare Lectures,* ed. Graham Storey (1961), pp. 274–92; Philip Edwards, "The Danger not the Death: The Art of John Fletcher," *Jacobean Theatre,* eds. J. R. Brown and B. Harris, Stratford-upon-Avon Studies 1 (1962), 159–78; Clifford Leech, "Tragicomedy," *The John Fletcher Plays* (1962), pp. 77–107; C. G. Thayer, "Epilogue; *The Sad Shepherd,*" *Ben Jonson: Studies in the Plays* (1963), pp. 247–66; Walter F. Staton, Jr. and William E. Simeone, eds., "Introduction," *A Critical Edition of Sir Richard Fanshawe's 1647 Translation of Giovanni Battista Guarini's 'Il Pastor Fido' (1964), pp. ix–xxiv; Cyrus Hoy, "Renaissance and Restoration Dramatic Plotting,"* RenD, 9 (1966), 247–64; Peter F. Mullany, "Religion in Massinger's *The Maid of Honour,*" *RenD,* 2 (1969), 143–56; Peter F. Mullany, "Religion in Massinger and Dekker's *The Virgin Martyr,*" *Komos,* 2 (1970), 89–97; George L. Geckle, "Fortune in Marston's *The Malcontent,*" *PMLA,* 86 (1971), 202–209; Richard Levin, *The Multiple Plot in English Renaissance Drama* (1971); Ralph Berry, *The Art of John Webster* (1972); Joan Hartwig, *Shakespeare's Tragicomic Vision* (1972); Arthur C. Kirsch, *Jacobean Dramatic Perspectives* (1972); John F. McElroy, *Parody and Burlesque in the Tragicomedies of Thomas Middleton* (1972); G. K. Hunter, "Italian Tragicomedy on the English Stage," *RenD,* 6 (1973), 123–48; Carolyn Asp, *A Study of Thomas Middleton's Tragicomedies* (1974); William Babula, *"Wishes Fall Out as They're Willed":* Shakespeare and the Tragicomic Archetype* (1975); Barbara A. Mowat, *The Dramaturgy of Shakespeare's Romances* (1976); William C. Woodson, "The Casuistry of Innocence in *A King and No King* and Its Implications for Tragicomedy," *ELR,* 8 (1978), 312–28.

Type and antitype:

Prophetic figures in the Old Testament and their corresponding fulfillments in the New Testament. An elaborate system of thought located correspondences between persons and events of the New Testament and those of the Old Testament, especially in relating the life of Christ to the messages of the prophets. Christian typology originated in the belief that Christ fulfilled certain Hebraic prophecies, particularly that of a promised Messiah. Typology provided early church fathers with a means of accommodating to Christian faith the Scriptures of the Jews.

In typological exegesis, a type is an element in the Old Testament that foreshadows or prefigures its antitype in the New. Thus, Adam is the *Typos* of Christ. The antitypes of the New Testament were considered the fulfillment of types appearing in the Old Testament. A type looks forward in time, and is a historical person, event, or thing, not a mythological person or a recurrent event, such as the rising and setting of the sun. Natural objects may be types but only when they are connected with special historical circumstances. The rock that Moses struck was considered a type of Christ and the water that flowed from that rock was regarded as a type of the blood that flowed from Christ's side at the crucifixion. But this does not mean that every rock is a type of Christ.

Typology as a system of thought was one with which English Renaissance writers were thoroughly familiar. John Donne, in *Devotions upon Emergent Occasions* (1624), explains the amplitude of God's typology when he writes: "The *institution* of thy whole [God's] *worship* in the *old Law,* was a continuall *Allegory; types* & *figures* . . . flowed into *figures,* and powred themselves out into *farther figures; Circumcision* carried a *figure* of *Baptisme,* & *Baptisme* carries a *figure* of that *purity,* which we shall have in *perfection* in the *new Jerusalem.*" The typological relationship between the Old Testament and the New is also described by the angel Michael in John Milton's *Paradise Lost* (1674) as one:

234

From shadowie Types to Truth, from Flesh to Spirit,
From imposition of strict Laws, to free
Acceptance of large Grace, from servil fear
To filial, works of Law to works of Faith.   (XII, 303–306)

The basic exegetical principles, enunciated by Augustine (354–430) in *De doctrina Christiana* and constantly repeated by others, recognized a literal or historical meaning of Scripture to be found in the signification of its words and, in addition, a spiritual meaning whereby the things or events signified by the words point beyond themselves to other things or events. After Augustine, Pope Gregory the Great, (c. 540–604) promulgated in *Moralia in Job* the view that Scripture had a fourfold sense. This fourfold method of exegesis recognized three spiritual senses of Scripture beyond the literal or historical. They are: the allegorical, in which persons and events in the Old Testament prefigure Christ and various events in the New Testament; the tropological or moral, in which what Christ did is an example of what humans ought to do; and the anagogical, in which Old and New Testament events prefigure the end of time and the final communion of saints in heaven.

During the Reformation, Protestant theologians shifted slightly the emphasis of medieval typological interpretation. They revised the medieval conception of Old Testament persons and events as merely literal signs pointing to New Testament truth by asserting that such persons and events also embody, though less fully, the spiritual meaning of the New Testament antitypes. For example, rather than viewing the Old Testament manna as a literal sign prefiguring the Christian sacrament, Calvin insisted that manna was also a genuine sacrament. This shift in emphasis allowed Protestants to identify their own spiritual experiences much more closely with those of Old Testament types. Related to this shift, Protestant exegetes also modified the medieval focus upon Christ's life and death as the principal antitype fulfilling the Old Testament types; they emphasized instead the contemporary Christian as antitype, who recapitulates in himself the experiences recorded in the Old and New Testament.

Protestant modifications, giving an importance to the contemporary believer, often influenced the way in which religious poets of the early seventeenth century use references drawn from the Bible in devotional poetry. Typological symbolism became an important literary means for poets to explore the personal spiritual life with profundity and psychological complexity. The speaker in John Donne's *Hymn to God my God, in my Sickness* (1633), for example, imagines himself on his deathbed and analyzes his situation in a typological manner. He finds himself the locus of Adam's tree in the Garden of Eden (type) and of Christ's tree or cross (antitype), both of which a medieval tradition had located in the same geographical place. He experiences within himself simultaneously the agony of Adam's sin, the redemption achieved by the crucifixion of Christ, and the anticipation of heavenly glory:

> Looke Lord, and finde both *Adams* met in me;
>   As the first *Adams* sweat surrounds my face,
>   May the last *Adams* blood my soule
>   embrace.
>
> So, in his purple wrapp'd receive mee Lord,
>   By these his thornes give me his other Crowne.

Typology allows Donne in these lines to incorporate in one believer the states of sinful human nature, redemptive grace, and future glory.

As a literary device, typology is closely related to allegory (q.v.) in that one image or event is "read" as signifying or foreshadowing another; but while many allegories come from fictions, typological interpretation always assumes the historical truth of the Bible. Typology finds relations in a divinely ordered history; allegorical practice can include fictions. Typology is devoted to the discovery of God's direction of human history. The literal truth of the type is a shadow that prefigures the future; its validity depends on its phenomenal reality.

Bibliography

Erich Auerbach, "Typological Symbolism in Medieval Literature," *YFS,* 9 (1952), 3–10; Rosemond Tuve, *A Reading of George Herbert* (1952); Helen Gardner, *The Limits of Literary Criticism: Reflections on the Interpretation of Poetry and Scripture* (1956); Jean Danielou, *From Shadows to Reality: Studies in Biblical Typology of the Fathers* (1960); Victor Harris, "Allegory to Analogy in the Interpretation of Scriptures," *PQ,* 45 (1966), 1–23; Stanley Stewart, *The Enclosed Garden: The Tradition and the Image in Seventeenth-Century Poetry* (1966); William G. Madsen, *From Shadowy Types to Truth: Studies in Milton's Symbolism* (1968); John R. Mulder, "Typology: Divine Hieroglyphics," *The Temple of the Mind: Education and Literary Taste in Seventeenth-Century England* (1969), pp. 130–50; James Samuel Preus, *From Shadow to Promise: Old Testament Interpretation from Augustine to the Young Luther* (1969); David Shelley Berkeley, *Inwrought with Figures Dim* (1974); C. A. Patrides, ed., *"A Crown of Praise:* The Poetry of Herbert," *The English Poems of George Herbert* (1974), pp. 6–23; Joseph A. Galdon, *Typology and Seventeenth-Century Literature* (1975); Barbara K. Lewalski, "Typology and Poetry: A Consideration of Herbert, Vaughan, and Marvell," *Illustrious Evidence: Approaches to English Literature of the Early Seventeenth Century,* ed. Earl Miner (1975), pp. 41–69;

William J. Scheick, "Typology and Allegory: A Comparative Study of George Herbert and Edward Taylor," *Essays in Literature, ELWIU,* 2 (1975), 76–86; Barbara K. Lewalski, "Typological Symbolism and the 'Progress of the Soul' in Seventeenth-Century Literature," *Literary Uses of Typology from the Late Middle Ages to the Present,* ed. Earl Miner (1977), pp. 79–114; David S. Berkeley, "Some Misapprehensions of Christian Typology in Recent Literary Scholarship," *SEL,* 18 (1978), 3–12; Barbara K. Lewalski, "The Biblical Symbolic Mode: Typology and the Religious Lyric," *Protestant Poetics and the Seventeenth-Century Religious Lyric* (1979), pp. 111–44.

Ut pictura poesis:

A critical formula, familiar to English Renaissance theorists and poets, usually translated "as is painting, so is poetry." This ancient formula, suggesting similarity between the arts of poetry and painting, was a European common-place (q.v.) and a pronounced motif in literary theory during the late sixteenth and early seventeenth centuries in England. Roger Ascham, for example, defines the dramatic poem as "a faire livelie painted picture of the life of everie degree of man" (*The Schoolmaster,* 1570). And Sir Philip Sidney says that poetry is "an arte of imitation . . . a representing, counterfetting, or figuring foorth: to speake metaphorically, a speaking picture: with this end, to teach and delight"; and he praises the "peerelesse Poet" because his "speaking picture of Poesie" and his "notable images of vertues, vices, and what els" move men to virtuous action (*An Apology for Poetry,* 1595).

The phrase *ut pictura poesis* comes from Horace's *Ars poetica,* but English critics and poets had other classical authorities for finding a kinship between poetry and painting. One of the most frequently quoted statements about the relationship between the two arts goes back to Simonides and is repeated by Plutarch: *Poema pictura loquens, pictura poema silens* ("Poetry is a speaking picture, painting a silent poem"). This statement found its way into English in a work translated by Sir Edward Hoby (*Political Discourses,* 1586): "For as *Simonides* saide: Painting is a dumme [mute] Poesie, and a Poesie is a speaking painting: & the actions which the Painters set out with visible colours and figures, the Poets recken with wordes as though they had in deede beene perfourmed."

Ut pictura poesis suggests that painting and poetry are alike in fundamental nature, content, and purpose. Renaissance theorists thought of both painting and poetry as mimetic arts. Both were products of imitation (q.v.), and their common purpose was to instruct and to delight. The subject matter of both was nature, particularly human nature. Ben Jonson's remarks on "poetry and picture" in his commonplace book, *Timber, or Discoveries* (1641), repeat these ideas: "*Poetry* and *Picture* are Arts of a like nature, and both are busie about imitation. It was excellently said of *Plutarch, Poetry* was a speaking Picture, and *Picture* a mute Poesie. For they both invent, faine, and devise many things, and accommodate all they invent to the use, and service of nature. . . . They both behold pleasure and profit as their common Object; but should abstaine from all base pleasures, lest they should erre from their end, and, while they seeke to better mens minds, destroy their manners. . . . *Whosover* loves not *Picture* is injurious to *Truth*."

The two arts differed in their modes of imitation. The poet used language, the artist paint; and what figures of speech (*see* Elocutio) were for the poet, color was for the painter. As George Puttenham expresses the difference, "the chief prayse and cunning of our Poet is in the discreet using of his figures, as the skilfull painters is in the good conveyance of his colours and shadowing traits of his pensill, with a delectable varietie, by all measure and just proportion, and in places most aptly to be bestowed" (*The Art of English Poesy*, 1589). Renaissance rhetoricians often called figures of speech "colors."

In verbal discourse, *ut pictura poesis* was closely related to a rhetorical principle called *enargeia*, which Quintilian says "seems not so much to narrate as to exhibit" (*Institutio oratoria*, VI, ii, 32, trans. John Selby Watson). The "*Enargia*, or cleereness of representation, requird in absolute Poems is not the perspicuous delivery of a lowe invention; but high, and harty invention exprest in most significant, and unaffected phrase; it serves not a skillful Painters turne, to draw the figure of a face onely to make knowne who it represents; but hee must lymn, give luster, shaddow, and heightening; which though ignorants will esteeme spic'd, and too curious, yet such as have the judiciall perspective, will see it hath, motion, spirit, and life" (George Chapman, prefatory letter, *Ovid's Banquet of Sense*, 1595).

Following Quintilian, Henry Peacham's rhetoric book, *The Garden of Eloquence* (1593), lists the rhetorical principle of *enargeia* as *descriptio*. He writes: "Descriptio is a generall name of many and sundry kindes of descriptions, and a description is when the Orator by a diligent gathering together of circumstances, and by a fit and naturall application of them, doth expresse and set forth a thing so plainly and lively, that it seemeth rather painted in tables, then declared with words, and the mind of the hearer therby so drawen to an earnest and stedfast contemplation of the thing described, that he rather thinketh he seeth it then heareth it. By this exornation the Orator imitateth the cunning painter which doth not onely draw the true proportion of thinges, but also bestoweth naturall colours in their proper places, whereby he compoundeth as it were complexion with substance and life with countenance: for hence it is, that by true proportion and due colour, cunning and curious Images are made so like to the persons which they present, that they do not onely make a likely shew of life, but also by outward countenance of the inward spirite and affection." "So great and singuler is that science [*descriptio*]," Peacham continues, "that there is not creature under heaven, no action, no passion, no frame in art, no countenance in man, Whose true proportion and externall forme is not finely counterfaited, and wonderfully imitated."

The rhetorical figures that aid the poet in describing "to the contemplation of mans mind, any person, deede, thing, place or time, so truly by circumstances, that the hearer shall thinke that he doth plainly behold the matter" are many. Among the appropriate figures Peacham lists are: *Prosographia* ("a forme of speech by which as well the very person of a man as of a fained, is by his form, nature, maners, studies, doings, affections, and such other circumstances serving to the purpose so described, that it may appeare a plaine and lively picture painted in tables, and set before the eies of the hearer"); *Prosopopoeia* ("the faining of a person, that is, when to a thing senselesse and dumbe we faine a fit person, or attribute a person to a commonwelth or multitude"); *Pragmatographia* ("a description of things whereby the Orator by gathering together all circumstances belonging to them, doth as plainly portray their image, as if they were most lively painted out in colours, & set forth to be seene"); *Topographia* ("an evident and true description of a place, like as Cicero describeth Syracuse a Citie in Cicilia"); and *Conographia* ("when the Orator describeth anie time for delectations sake, as the morning, the evening, midnight. . . . the time of war, the time of peace, the old time").

Generally speaking, English literary critics and poets were interested in *ut pictura poesis* for comparative purposes and almost always to proclaim the greater glory of poetry. Jonson, for example, claims that "of the two [poetry and painting] the Pen is more noble, then the Pencill: For that can speake to the Understanding, the other but to the Sense." On the other hand, artists and art theorists throughout Europe valued *ut pictura poesis* because it provided a simile that gave painting a dignified position as an artistic activity. Leonardo da Vinci, for example, in his notebook jottings, known today as the *Treatise on Painting,* says: "Painting is poetry which is seen and not heard, and poetry is a painting which is heard but not seen. These two arts (you may call them both either poetry or painting) have here interchanged the senses by which they penetrate to the intellect" (cited from Sypher). Both poetry and painting needed defense or apology (q.v.), but poetry had an advantage through its connections with rhetoric (q.v.). Painting had the harder time justifying its value since it so long had been thought a mechanical art.

Bibliography

Erwin Panofsky, *Studies in Iconology: Humanistic Themes in the Art of the Renaissance* (1939); Rosemond Tuve, "*Ut pictura poesis* and Functional Sensuous Imagery," *Elizabethan and Metaphysical Imagery* (1947), pp. 50–60; E. H. Gombrich, "*Icones Symbolicae:* The Visual Image in Neo-Platonic Thought," *JWCI,* 11 (1948), 163–92; Erwin Panofsky, *Meaning in the Visual Arts* (1955); Wylie Sypher, *Four Stages of Renaissance Style* (1955); Jean H. Hagstrum, *The Sister Arts* (1958); Robert John Clements, *Picta Poesis: Literary and Humanistic Theory in Renaissance Emblem Books* (1960); Samuel C. Chew, *The Pilgrimage of Life* (1962); Frances A. Yates, *The Art of Memory* (1966); Rensselaer W. Lee, *Ut Pictura Poesis: The Humanistic Theory of Painting* (1967); Judith Dundas, "The Rhetorical Basis of Spenser's Imagery," *SEL,* 8 (1968), 59–75; Erwin Panofsky, *Idea: A Concept in Art Theory,* trans. Joseph J. S. Peake (1968); Don Cameron Allen, *Mysteriously Meant: The Rediscovery of Pagan Symbolism and Allegorical Interpretation in the Renaissance* (1970); Mario Praz, *Mnemosyne: The Parallel between Literature and the Visual Arts* (1970); Douglas Chambers, " 'A Speaking Picture': Some Ways of Proceeding in Literature and the Fine Arts in the Late-Sixteenth and Early-Seventeenth Centuries," *Encounters: Essays on Literature and the Visual Arts,* ed. J. D. Hunt (1971), pp. 28–57; John B. Bender, *Spenser and Literary Pictorialism* (1972); Forrest G. Robinson, *The Shape of Things Known: Sidney's "Apology" in Its Philosophical Tradition* (1972); John M. Steadman, chs. 5–7, *The Lamb and the Elephant: Ideal Imitation and the Context of Renaissance Allegory* (1974), pp. 106–212; José Argüelles, *The Transformative Vision* (1975); John Hollander, *Vision and Resonance* (1975); H. James Jensen, *The Muses' Concord: Literature, Music, and the Visual Arts in the Baroque Age* (1976); Roland M. Frye, *Milton's Imagery and the Visual Arts: Iconographic Tradition in the Epic Poems* (1978); Ernest Gilman, *The Curious Perspective: Literary and Pictorial Wit in the Seventeenth Century* (1978); John M. Steadman, *Nature Into Myth: Medieval and Renaissance Moral Symbols* (1979).

Versifying:

"Now, of versifying [versification: the art or theory of metered language] there are two sorts, the one Auncient, the other Moderne: the Auncient marked the quantitie of each silable, and according to that framed his verse; the Moderne, observing onely number (with some regarde of the accent), the chief life of it standeth in that lyke sounding of the words, which wee call Ryme. Whether of these be the most excellent, would beare many speeches" (Sir Philip Sidney, *An Apology for Poetry,* 1595).

Here Sidney points to the difference between (1) unrhymed classical verse in which the metrical rhythm derived from the positioning of long and short syllables determined according to duration or the time required to pronounce individual syllables and (2) native rhymed verse where metrical rhythm was determined by the number and accent of the syllables. Despite Sidney's view that English is "fit for both sorts," the general practice of late sixteenth- and early seventeenth-century poets writing in the vernacular was to choose "Moderne" versification. The distinguishing characteristics of English Renaissance "versifying" were rhyme, number of syllables, and stress or accent, which Sidney says "wee observe . . . very precisely."

Nonetheless, during the last decades of the sixteenth century a number of scholars and critics, motivated by a desire to improve the state of vernacular poetry, encouraged the use of classical quantitative meters in English. And a few Elizabethan poets, including Sidney and Edmund Spenser, experimented with them, often devising rules of their own for determining quantity in English, a task "wherein lyeth great difficultye" (William Webbe, *A Discourse of English Poetry,* 1586). In a letter written in October 1579, for example, Spenser tells his friend Gabriel Harvey that a courtly group including Sidney and Thomas Drant had proclaimed "a general surceasing and silence of balde Rymers" and had "prescribed certaine Lawes and rules of Quantities of English sillables for English Verse . . . drawne mee to their faction."

Sincere as they were in trying to polish English prosody, Elizabethan attempts to render English in the classical manner collided with strong native traditions. In the first place, English is a markedly accentual language, and the major movement of English prosody by the late sixteenth century was toward the refinement of a metrical line based on a regularized accentual pattern of unstressed and stressed syllables (*see* Vulgar language). Although long and short syllables exist in English (it takes longer, for example, to say *sprawls* than it does *hit*), English prosody does not take quantity into account, because the pattern created by syllabic stress is so much more dominant. In English accentual-syllabic verse, quantity remains only subsidiary or complementary to a basic rhythm of regularly recurring accents. Samuel Daniel, for example, speaks of the difference between quantity and accent in English prosody when, in an attack on attempts to naturalize classical measures in English poetry, he says, "All verse is but a frame of wordes confinde within certaine measure [metrical arrangement]; differing from the ordinarie speach, and introduced, the better to expresse mens conceipts [ideas], both for delight and memorie. Which frame of wordes . . . are disposed into divers fashions, according to the humour of the Composer and the set of the time. . . . For as Greeke and Latine verse consists of the number and quantitie of sillables, so doth the English verse of measure and accent. And though it doth not strictly observe long and short sillables [duration], yet it most religiously respects the accent: and as the short and the long make number, so the Acute [stressed syllable] and grave [unstressed] accent yeelde harmonie" (*A Defense of Rhyme,* 1603).

Because classical quantitative poetry was unrhymed, attempts to adapt classical quantity to the vernacular inevitably raised the issue of rhyme as well. This was partly so because Medieval Latin poetry, like that of the vernacular, had become both rhymed and accentual-syllabic. Increased attention to vernacular poetry coincided with a humanist movement to "purify" and refine Medieval Latin, to restore to poetry purely classical diction, syntax, and forms of the Latin language. Thus the rhyme and syllabic stress of Medieval Latin poetry were viewed as inseparable "barbarisms"; rhyme was associated with syllabic stress as a falling away from the "pure" practice of classical poets. Roger Ascham says, for example, that poets have to choose between "barbarous" rhyme and the "perfite" and "trew" ways of the Grecians (*The Schoolmaster,* 1570). Nevertheless, the almost exclusive practice of English poets in the late sixteenth and early seventeenth centuries, except for that of the dramatists, was to write rhymed verse.

Rhyme, or what Sidney calls the "chiefe life" of "Moderne" prosody, is what George Puttenham says makes English verse "sweetest and most solemne" (*The Art of English Poesy,* 1589). He writes, for example, "As the smoothnesse of your words and sillables running upon feete of sundrie quantities make the Greekes and Latines the body of their verses numerous or Rithmicall, so in our vulgar Poesie, and all other nations at this day, your verses answering eche other by couples, or at larger distances in good *cadence,* is it that maketh your meeter symphonicall. This cadence is the fal of a verse in every last word with a certaine tunable sound, which, being matched with another of like sound, do make a *concord.* And the whole cadence is contained in one sillable, sometime in two, or in three at the most." Similarly defending rhyme in English poetry as sanctioned by both custom and nature, Daniel says that rhyme gives "to the Eare an Eccho of a delightfull report & to the Memorie a deeper impression of what is delivered there" (*A Defense of Rhyme*). So strong in fact was the presence of rhyme in English versification that the publisher of John Milton's *Paradise Lost* says that readers of the 1667 edition "stumbled" as to "why the Poem Rimes not," and he therefore published the preface *The Verse* in the 1674 edition of that heroic poem.

The central debate over quantitative measures came at the turn of the century between Thomas Campion (*Observations in the Art of English Poetry,* 1602) and Daniel (*Defense,* 1603). Campion's book scathingly attacks rhyme which, he says, "creates as many Poets, as a hot summer flies," and then discusses eight metrical patterns which he feels are sanctioned by classical precept and hence to be appropriate for English poetry. Daniel's reply argues in favor of both rhyme and accentual rhythm, even though he says, "We could well have allowed of his [Campion's] numbers had he not disgraced our Ryme: Which both Custome and Nature doth most powerfully defend." Rhyme, he says, gives to English poetry "a Harmonie, farre happier than any proportion Antiquitie could ever shew us [and] dooth adde more grace, and hath more of delight than ever bare numbers." Since English verse "most religiously respects the accent," he says, it is that which must govern English versification, not quantity. Combined with the fact that few poets did more than experiment with quantitative meters, Daniel's *Defense* settled the matter, and the issue of quantity versus accent does not reappear in seventeenth-century critical debate.

Bibliography

R. B. McKerrow, "The Use of So-called Classical Metres in Elizabethan Verse," *MLQ,* 4 (1901), 172–80 and 5 (1902), 6–13; G. Gregory Smith, ed., "Prosody," *Elizabethan Critical Essays,* vol. 1 (1904), pp. xlvi–lv; George Saintsbury, *A History of English Prosody,* vol. 1 (1906), pp. 303–77 and vol. 2 (1908), pp. 3–356; Thomas S. Omond, *English Metrists* (1921); B. M. Hollowell, "The Elizabethan Hexametrists," *PQ,* 3 (1924), 51–57; Enid Hamer, *The Metres of English Poetry* (1930); R. C. Trevelyan, "Classical and English Verse-Structure," *Essays and Studies by Members of the English*

Association, 16 (1930), 7–25; G. D. Willcock, "Passing Pitefull Hexameters: A Study of Quantity and Accent in English Renaissance Verse," *MLR,* 29 (1934), 1–19; R. W. Short, "The Metrical Theory and Practice of Thomas Campion," *PMLA,* 59 (1944), 1003–18; G. L. Hendrickson, "Elizabethan Quantitative Hexameters," *PQ,* 28 (1949), 237–60; William A. Ringler, "Master Drant's Rules," *PQ,* 29 (1950), 70–74; Catherine Ing, *Elizabethan Lyrics: A Study in the Development of English Metres and their Relation to Poetic Effect* (1951); G. K. Hunter, "The English Hexameter and the Elizabethan Madrigal," *PQ,* 32 (1953), 340–42; Richard Foster Jones, "The Eloquent Language," *The Triumph of the English Language* (1953), pp. 168–213; John Thompson, *The Founding of English Metre* (1961); W. Sidney Allen, "On Quantity and Quantitative Verse," *In Honour of Daniel Jones,* ed. D. Abercrombie, et al. (1964), pp. 3–15; Seymour Chatman, *A Theory of Meter* (1965); Morris Halle, "On Meter and Prosody," *Progress in Linguistics,* eds. Manfred Bierwisch and Karl Erich Heidolph (1970), pp. 64–80; Joseph Malof, *A Manual of English Meters* (1970): Morris Halle and Samuel Jay Keyser, "Early Modern English Stress," *English Stress: Its Form, Its Growth, and Its Role in Verse* (1971), pp. 109–36; Howard C. Cole, "Some Theories of Poetry: Alehouse Rhyme and Roman Numbers," *A Quest of Inquirie: Some Contexts of Tudor Literature* (1973), pp. 138–61; Derek Attridge, *Well-weighed syllables: Elizabethan verse in classical metres* (1974); Sharon Schuman, "Sixteenth-Century English Quantitative Verse: Its Ends, Means, and Products," *MP,* 74 (1977), 335–49.

Vulgar language:

"The speach wherein the Poet or maker writeth . . . when it is peculiar unto a countrey . . . is called the mother speach of that people" (George Puttenham, *The Art of English Poesy,* 1589); the vernacular. The use of "Vulgar English" (Puttenham) for fictions in verse and prose is a fundamental literary convention of the late sixteenth and early seventeenth centuries. Sir Philip Sidney's praise of both the adequacy and the eloquence of English is typical of the many such claims in the last quarter of the sixteenth century. He writes, "for the uttering sweetly and properly the conceits [thoughts] of the minde, which is the end of speech," the English language "hath it equally with any other tongue in the world" (*An Apology for Poetry,* 1595).

For the first three quarters of the sixteenth century, English was generally regarded as too "rude" and "barbarous" for literary excellence. Sir Thomas Elyot, for example, says that Latin poets were able to "express them[selves] incomparably with more grace and delectation than our englische tonge may yet comprehend" (*The Governor,* 1531). And Roger Ascham claims that "the providence of God hath left unto us in no other tong, save onelie in the *Greke* and *Latin* tong, the trew preceptes and perfite examples of eloquence, therefore must we seeke in the Authors onelie of those two tonges, the Trew Paterne of Eloquence" (*The Schoolmaster,* 1570). The vernacular was often thought of as plain, serviceable, unadorned clothing as compared to the rich fabric of Latin eloquence or style as it was polished and ornamented by figures of speech. English was considered a utilitarian language most appropriate for instructional purposes so that there might be "Englishe matter in Englishe tongue for Englishe men" (Ascham, *Toxophilus,* 1545). The vernacular was for the dissemination of matter that could profit "unlettered" Englishmen and could make current the ideas available in works of other languages, especially classical languages. Henry Billingsley, for example, in the preface to his translation of Euclid's *The Elements of Geometry* (1570), says that he hopes his work can help to bring it about that "our Englishe tounge shall no lesse be enriched with good Authors, then are other strange tounges: as the Dutch, French, Italian, and Spanishe." The many translators of the period told their readers that, while English could render adequately the sense of works in other languages, it lacked eloquence, especially that of Latin works. Thus William Addington speaks of his translation of Apuleius's *Golden Ass* (1566) as "beyng now barbarously and simply framed in our Englishe tongue."

The major claims for the adequacy—even the superiority—of English for use in original literary works belong to the last quarter of the sixteenth century. After that time the question of the appropriateness of the vernacular for fictions of all kinds was settled, despite the few English writers who composed a fairly large body of literary works in Latin. Richard Mulcaster, headmaster of the Merchant Taylors' School, is but one of many writers to claim that "I do not think that anie language, be it whatsoever, is better able to utter all arguments, either with more pith, or greater planesse, than our English tung is" (*Elementarie,* 1582). And writing about 1595 Richard Carew, in *The Excellency of English,* confidently believes that he can call English the "sweetest" or most pleasant in sound of vernacular languages. The other vernaculars he dismisses by saying, "The Italyan is pleasante but without synewes, as to stillye fleeting water; the French delicate but over nice, as a woman scarce daring to open her lipps for feare of marring her countenaunce; the Spanishe majesticall, but fullsome, running to [too] much on the O, and terrible like the devill in a playe; the Dutch manlike, but withall very harshe, as one ready at every worde to picke a quarrell." About three other "pointes requisite in a Languadge," Carew is also confident that English "is macheable, if not preferable, before any other in vogue at this daye." These requisites are: *"Significancye"* ("the first and principall point sought in every Languadge is that wee maye expresse the meaning our mindes aptlye ech to other"); *"Easynes"* ("next, that we may do it readilye without great adoo"); and *"Copiousness"* ("then fullye, so as others maye thoroughlie conceive us"; [*see* Copia]).

English poets and their publishers also made the claim for the vernacular in literary works. One of the earliest of these claims appears in the preface, *The Printer to the Reader,* of *Songs and Sonnets* (1557), a poetical miscellany published by Richard Tottel. It is at once a praise of poetry and of the English language (*see* Apology and Versifying). It reads: "That to have wel written in verse, yea & in small parcells, deserveth great praise, the workes of divers Latines, Italians, and other, doe prove sufficiently. That our tong is able in that kynde to do as praiseworthely as the rest, the honorable stile of the noble earl of Surrey, and the weightinesse of the depe-witted sir Thomas Wyat the elders verse, with several graces in sondry good Englishe writers, doe show abundantly. It resteth nowe (gentle reader) that thou thinke it not evill doon, to publish, to the honor of the Englishe tong, and

247

for profit of the studious of Englishe eloquence, those workes which the ungentle horders up of such treasures have heretofore envied thee." Later, George Chapman in the preface to his translation of the first seven books of the *Iliad* (1598) declares that he intends his work to prove his "mother tongue above all others for Poesie."

In turn, English poets were often credited with refining and polishing the vernacular so that it had been "purged from faults, weeded of errours, and pollished from barbarousnes" (William Webbe, *A Discourse of English Poetry,* 1586). Puttenham calls the "courtly makers" of Tottel's miscellany, especially Sir Thomas Wyatt and Henry Howard, Earl of Surrey, "the first reformers" of the English language. Similarly, Thomas Lodge praises contemporary poets who, he says, have "brought the chaos of our tongue in frame" (*Phyllis,* 1593). And Francis Meres says that it is the eloquence of "our English poets, which makes our language so gorgeous and delectable among us." Meres cites such Elizabethan poets as Edmund Spenser, Sidney, Samuel Daniel, Michael Drayton, William Warner, Christopher Marlowe, Shakespeare, and Chapman as those by whom "the English tongue is mightily enriched and gorgeouslie invested in rare ornaments and resplendent abiliments" (*Palladis Tamia,* 1598).

The English spoken in court and by "the better brought up sort" was generally regarded as that most appropriate for the poet. Puttenham says that "This part in our maker or Poet must be heedly looked unto, that it be naturall, pure, and the most usuall of all his countrey; and for the same purpose rather that which is spoken in the kings Court, or in the good townes and Cities within the land, then in the marches and frontiers, or in port townes, where straungers haunt for traffike sake, or yet in Universities where Schoolers use much peevish affectation of words out of primative languages, or finally, in any uplandish village or corner of a Realme, where is no resort but of poore rusticall or uncivill people." Chief among the "Cities within the land" was, of course, London; and Puttenham recommends that the poet "therefore take the usuall speach of the Court, and that of London and the shires lying about London within lx. myles, and not much above" because it represents the best of "mans speach."

Nonetheless, despite the praises for English, poets and other writers believed their vernacular needed new words in its vocabulary. As Ralph Lever comments, there are "moe things, then there are words to expresse things by" (*The Art of Reason,* 1573). If English were to compete successfully with Latin, where a vocabulary already existed able to express subtle and technical thought, it had to borrow words from other languages. And while English writers generally revered the vernacular works of medieval poets, especially Chaucer, they also knew their own vernacular was not exactly that of their forefathers: "Our maker [poet] therefore at these days shall not follow *Piers plowman* nor *Lydgate* nor yet *Chaucer,* for their language is now out of use with us" (Puttenham). Finding their vocabulary inadequate, many writers felt borrowings from other languages were a necessity. George Pettie says that borrowing "is in deed the ready way to inrich our tongue, and make it copious, and it is the way which all tongues have taken to inrich them selves" (preface, *The Civil Conversation of M. Steven Guazzo,* 1581); and Mulcaster observes that English "boroweth dailie from foren tungs, either of pure necessitie in new matters, or of mere braverie, to garnish it self with all" (*Elementarie*).

Borrowing and the coining of new words did not meet unanimous approval, however, and the new words themselves were often contemptuously called "straunge ynkhorne terms" (Thomas Wilson, *The Art of Rhetoric,* 1553). The fear was that inkhorn terms would make the vernacular a hodge-podge. Sir John Cheke expresses a typical reaction against borrowing when, in a letter published in the 1561 edition of Sir Thomas Hoby's translation *The Courtier,* he says, "I am of this opinion that our own tung should be written cleane and pure, unmixt and unmangled with borowing of other tunges." By late in the sixteenth century, however, it was obvious that any battle against the borrowing of words was a futile one; the attack was then on the abuse of the practice, not the practice itself.

By the end of the sixteenth century the work of poets clearly proved "That plenteous *English* hand in hand might goe / With Greeke and Latine" (Michael Drayton, *To My Most Dearly-Loved Friend Henry Reynolds,* 1627). The vernacular did not, however, completely replace Latin. As it had been for centuries, Latin was the international language of the Renaissance, used throughout England and the continent for the dissemination of ideas of all kinds. It was the language of diplomacy, theology, and philosophy. As a matter of course Sir Francis Bacon wrote in Latin two of the works central to his grand scheme for the reconstruction of the aims and methods of human learning: *Novum organum* (1620) and the expanded version (*De augmentis scientiarum,* 1623) of *The Advancement of Learning* (1605). Moreover, Latin continued to be a language studied in English schools and universities; and writing in Latin, both verse and prose, was a standard part of students' education.

Imaginative works were also written in Latin, often in revived classical Latin in a conscious attempt to recapture the style, tone, and even the vocabulary of Roman writers. Inspired by a humanistic interest in ancient writings of all kinds, writers of this "new" poetry and prose aimed to refine what they had come to believe were the "barbarous" qualities of medieval Latin style. Generally speaking, Renaissance Latin poets attempted not only to imitate the ancients in their subject matter, attitudes, and formal techniques but also to express contemporary attitudes in the way an ancient writer—although in many instances a Christianized one—might have written. They employed a wide variety of Latin genres and meters (*see*

Imitation). Pastoral themes were especially popular, and epigrams a frequently used genre. Much neo-Latin poetry is occasional verse, having to do with births, marriages, birthdays, and deaths of public personages or with some commemorative event or public celebration.

Like neo-Latin poetry, neo-Latin drama flourished throughout Europe from the fifteenth century in Italy. It includes imitations of the classical Latin comedies of Plautus and Terence and the tragedies of Seneca, religious dramas, and plays on both classical and contemporary history. In England, neo-Latin drama was written and recited or staged almost exclusively in the schools and universities. During the last half of the sixteenth century and early decades of the seventeenth century, Cambridge especially distinguished itself with its neo-Latin comedies, a group of which paradoxically drew upon earlier Italian vernacular comedy (q.v.).

Bibliography

George H. McKnight, "Purism" and "Sixteenth-Century Rhetoric," *Modern English in the Making* (1928), pp. 110–50; R. W. Chambers, *On the Continuity of English Prose from Alfred to More and his School* (1932); Charles S. Baldwin, "Latin, Greek, and the Vernaculars," *Renaissance Literary Theory and Practice: Classicism in the Rhetoric and Poetic of Italy, France, and England 1400–1600* (1939), pp. 17–38; Rosemond Tuve, "Ancients, Moderns, and Saxons," *ELH*, 6 (1939), 165–90; Leicester Bradner, chs. 1–6, *Musae Anglicanae: A History of Anglo-Latin Poetry 1500–1925* (1940), pp. 1–200; Don Cameron Allen, "Latin Literature," *MLQ*, 2 (1941), 403–20; Vernon Hall, Jr., "England, The Fight for the Vernacular," *Renaissance Literary Criticism: A Study of Its Social Content* (1945), pp. 153–73; Richard Foster Jones, *The Triumph of the English Language* (1953); Albert C. Baugh, "The Renaissance, 1500–1650," *A History of the English Language* (2nd ed., 1957), pp. 240–305; W. Leonard Grant, *Neo-Latin Literature and the Pastoral* (1965); James E. Phillips and Don Cameron Allen, *Neo-Latin Poetry of the Sixteenth and Seventeenth Centuries* (1965); Barbara M. H. Strang, "The Chronological Sequence: 1770–1570," *A History of English* (1970), pp. 104–55; W. F. Bolton, "The Renaissance," *A Short History of Literary English* (2nd ed., 1972), pp. 38–45; F. W. Bateson, "Elizabethans, Metaphysicals, Augustans," *English Poetry and the English Language* (3rd ed., 1973), pp. 25–51; J. W. Binns, et al., chs. 1–4, *The Latin Poetry of English Poets*, ed. Binns (1974), pp. 1–120; Anne Drury Hall, "Tudor Prose Style: English Humanists and the Problem of a Standard," *ELR*, 7 (1977), 267–96.

Appendix A

Modern Literary Terms and Relevant Entries

MODERN LITERARY TERM	RELEVANT ENTRY
Attic prose style	Senecan style
Ballad	Broadside ballad
Baroque prose style	Senecan style
Bucolic poetry	Eclogue
Chronicle play	History
Didactic theory of poetry	Apology
Emblematic poetry	Emblem
Epic poetry	Heroic poem
Epyllion	Heroic poem
Figures of speech	Elocutio
History play	History
Interlude	Morall
Literary criticism	Apology
Metaphysical poetry	Strong lines; Conceit
Metrical Psalms	Hymn
Minor epic	Heroic poem
Moral play	Morall
Neo-Latin poetry	Vulgar language
Ovidian narrative poetry	Heroic poem
Pastoral elegy	Elegy
Pastoral play	Pastoral
Pastoral poetry	Eclogue; Elegy
Pattern poetry	Proportion of figure
Prose romance	Romance
Prosody	Versifying
Quantitative verse	Versifying
Sacred parody	Parody

MODERN LITERARY TERM	RELEVANT ENTRY
Sonnet sequence	Sonnets in sequence
Stanza	Staff
Topographical poetry	Topographia
Typology	Type and antitype
Vernacular	Vulgar language
Verse epistle	Epistle
Verse satire	Satire
Versification	Versifying

Appendix B

Renaissance Terms and Appropriate Categories

POETIC GENRES

Acrostic
Anagram
Aubade
Broadside ballad
Complaint
Echo poem
Eclogue
Elegy
Emblem
Epigram
Epistle
Epithalamion
Heroic poem
Hymn
Lyric
Masque
Ode
Satire
Song
Sonnet
Sonnets in sequence

DRAMATIC GENRES

Comedy
History
Morall
Pastoral
Tragedy
Tragicomedy

PROSE FORMS AND STYLES

Apology
Character
Ciceronian style
Jest
Novella
Romance
Senecan style
Strong lines

VERSIFICATION

Blank verse
Canzone
Couplet
Fourteener
Ottava rima
Poulter's measure
Proportion of figure
Quatrain
Rhyme royal
Sixain
Sonnet
Staff
Terza rima
Versifying

253

RHETORICAL TERMS

Allegory

Anatomy

Common-place

Copia

Decorum

Elocutio

Encomium

Epideictic rhetoric

Imitation

Rhetoric

Sententia

Topographia

Index

period, 188; and strong lines, 213; and
verse epistle, 100
Sententia, 58, 84, 99, 114, 174, 191–94, 207,
224; associated with vehemence, 192;
associated with "weight," 192; in Attic
oratory, 189; central to both rhetoric and
poetry, 169; and common-place, 45; and
couplets, 21; definition of, 191; in fictions,
192, 193; history of, 191; in Lyly's prose,
177; in the romance, 178; in Senecan style,
188; in tragedy, 220, 221
Seutonius, 221
Sforza-Pallavicino, Cardinal, 55
Shakespeare, William, 21, 38, 42, 248;
Anthony and Cleopatra, 55; *As You Like
It*, 75, 153, 162, 211; *The Chronicle History
of Henry the Fifth*, 119; and complaint
poetry, 48; *Cymbeline*, 18; dramatic plots
from novelle, 151; *Hamlet*, 17, 39, 161, 221;
Henry IV, Part One, 24; *King Lear*, 120;
Macbeth, 120; praise of his sonnets, 204;
The Rape of Lucrece, and rhyme royal,
175; *Richard II*, 53; *Romeo and Juliet*, 17,
223; his sonnets, 205, 207; *Venus and
Adonis*, 195; *The Winter's Tale*, 23
Shirley, James, *Arcadia*, 162
Sidney, Sir Philip, 75, 114, 115, 243, 248; *An
Apology for Poetry*, 91, 102, 192, 198, 204,
205, 221, 226, 232, 238, 242, 246; *The
Arcadia*, 35, 162, 177, 178, 216; *Astrophel
and Stella*, 208; on comedy, 40; on
decorum and subject matter, 66; definition
of poet, 5; dramatic "unities," 226;
function of poetry, 12, 90; on the heroic
poem, 108; on hierarchy of genres, 169; on
hymn, 124; on imitation, 130; on lyric
poetry, 93, 134, 135; on Pindaric ode, 154;
praise of ballad, 25; praise of *Gorboduc*,
224; praise of poetry, 12; truth in poetry, 13
Simias of Rhodes, 166; pattern poems in
Greek Anthology, 165
Simile, 240
Similitude, 84
Simonides, 44, 238
Sixain, 112, 195–97; and the broadside
ballad, 24; decorum of, 195; definition of,
195; in sestina, 196
Skelton, John, *Magnificence*, 121
Socrates, 46, 91
Song, 23, 25, 134, 154, 196, 198–201, 211, 214;
air, 199; and the broadside ballad, 24–25;

and canzone, 27; decorum of, 200; and
madrigal, 200; as ode, 28, 153; pairing of
voice and verse, 198; singers as poets, 198
Sonnet, 27, 88, 135, 137, 157, 200, 202–5,
207; anatomizing in, 10; brevity of, 202;
definition of, 202; and epigram, 96; the
ethos of, 170; form for lyrical complaints,
49; Italian, 205; as judicial discourse, 170;
as Petrarchan form, 203; Shakespearean,
205; as "song," 25; subjects of, 204;
translations of Petrarch's sonnets, 128
Sonnets in sequence, 202, 204, 207–9;
canzoni with, 28; crown of sonnets, 208;
definition of, 207
Sophocles, *Oedipus Rex*, 231
Southwell, Robert: *Preface to Mary
Magdelene's Funeral Tears*, 196; *Saint
Peter's Complaint*, 196
Spenser, Edmund, 109, 113, 242, 248;
Amoretti, 28, 208; *Astrophel*, 75; *Colin
Clout's Come Home Again*, 75; *Daphnaida*,
75; *Epithalamion*, 28, 103, 104, 198; *The
Faerie Queene*, 93, 127, 131; *Four Hymns*,
125, 175; *Letter to Raleigh*, 5, 108; *The
Shepherd's Calendar*, 8, 64, 69, 196; *The
Tears of the Muses*, 49
Staff, 211–12; decorum of, 212; definition of,
211; ottava rima, 157; quatrain, 167; rhyme
royal, 174; sixain, 195; terza rima, 216
Stockwood, John, *Progymnasma
Scholasticum*, 96
Stowe, John, *Chronicles of England*, 119
Strong lines, 188, 213–15; and character
writing, 29, 30; and conceits, 55; criticism
of, 214, 215; definition of, 213; as
"masculine," 214; in poetry, 214; in prose,
213
Stubbes, Philip, *The Anatomy of Abuses*, 9
Surrey, Henry Howard, Earl of, 19, 20, 204
Susenbrotus, Joannes, *Epitome troporum ac
schematum*, 79
Symphoresis, 83
Synchoresis, 83
Synecdoche, 79
Synonym, 59

Tacitus, 221; as model, 188; his prose style,
213
Taming of A Shrew, The, 119
Tasso, Torquato, 111, 112, 113, 115, 116, 127;
admired for canzoni, 27; *The Allegory of*

ABOUT THE AUTHORS

Marjorie Donker is Associate Professor of English at Western Washington University in Bellingham, Washington. She has contributed to *Publications of the Modern Language Association.*

George M. Muldrow is Professor of English at Western Washington University in Bellingham, Washington. He is the author of *Milton and the Drama of the Soul.*